Almost three quarters of soldiers who died in European wars between the end of the Thirty Years' War and the French Revolution succumbed to bacteria rather than bullets. Field armies doubled in size and usually endured sieges rather than battles, so this was an era of massive and protracted encampments: the Christian army that sat down before Belgrade in 1717 had more mouths than any city within 500 miles but lacked basic urban amenities like regular markets, wells, privy pits, and night soil collectors. Yet the impact of sickness on military operations has been neglected. Crucially, this study will quantify how many soldiers sickened and died and will do so by consulting the reports, registers and returns, generated by the new state-contract armies which displaced the mercenary hordes of the Thirty Years War.

As plague began to recede from Europe, this study explains what exactly were these 'fluxes and fevers' that remained to afflict European armies in wartime and argues that they formed a single seasonal continuum that peaked in late summer. The isolation and incarceration of the military hospital characterized the response of the new armies to 'disorder' and to revivified notions of contagion. However, the hospital often prolonged the late summer morbidity/mortality spike into mid-winter by generating 'hospital fever' or typhus, the lice-borne disease that erupted whenever the cold, wet, hungry, transient, and unwashed huddled together. The cure was the disease.

This scope of the study includes French army operations in Roussillon (1674), north Italy (1702 and 1734), the Rhineland (1734), and, further afield, Bohemia (1742). The study also includes case-studies involving the British Army that include Ireland (1689), Portugal (1762), Dutch Brabant (1748), and the Rhineland (1743). The outliers are studies of Habsburg operations in and around Belgrade (1717 and 1737) together with the Russian siege of Riga in 1709-10 and invasion of Crimea in 1736.

Pádraig Lenihan is a lecturer in history at the National University of Ireland Galway. He has researched and written on Irish history in the 17th century and on military history in the 17th and 18th centuries.

His books on military topics include Battle *of the Boyne 1690* (2003) and *Confederate Catholics at War 1642-49* (2003). His articles on military subjects include 'The Irish Brigade' in *Eighteenth-Century Ireland Iris An Dá Chultúr* (2016), 'Namur Citadel, 1695: A Case Study in Allied Siege Tactics' in *War In History* (2011), 'Unhappy Campers: Dundalk (1689) and After' in *Journal of Conflict Archaeology* (2007) and 'War and Population' in *Irish Economic And Social History* (1998)

He has co-edited, with Keith Sidwell, *Poema de Hibernia, a Jacobite Epic on the Williamite Wars* (2017), and, with David Edwards and Clodagh Tait, *The Age of Atrocity* (2007) and edited *Conquest and Resistance: Irish Warfare in the Seventeenth Century* (2001).

Fluxes, Fevers, and Fighting Men

War and Disease in Ancien Régime Europe
1648-1789

Pádraig Lenihan

 Helion & Company

Helion & Company Limited
Unit 8 Amherst Business Centre
Budbrooke Road
Warwick
CV34 5WE
England
Tel. 01926 499619
Email: info@helion.co.uk
Website: www.helion.co.uk
Twitter: @helionbooks
Visit our blog at http://blog.helion.co.uk/

Published by Helion & Company 2019
Designed and typeset by Mach 3 Solutions Ltd (www.mach3solutions.co.uk)
Cover designed by Paul Hewitt, Battlefield Design (www.battlefield-design.co.uk)

Text, graphs and tables © Pádraig Lenihan, 2019
Maps appearing on pages 22, 70, 82, 95, 114, 121, 123, 134, 148, 155 and 159
© Padraig Lenihan 2019
Cover: Pieter Snayers, 'Siege of Valenza' (Deutsches Historisches Museum, Berlin)

ISBN 978-1-911628-51-4

British Library Cataloguing-in-Publication Data.
A catalogue record for this book is available from the British Library.

For details of other military history titles published by Helion & Company Limited, contact the
above address, or visit our website: http://www.helion.co.uk
We always welcome receiving book proposals from prospective authors.

Contents

List of Plates

List of Abbreviations

ADPO	Archives Départementales des Pyrénées-Orientales.
AO	*Archivum Ottomanicum*
BayHStA	Bayerisches Hauptstaatsarchiv, Bavarian State Archive, Munich.
BSB	Bayerische Staatsbibliothek Digital
CSP (dom)	Calendar of State Papers, Domestic Series.
Gazette	Gazette de France.
IMC	Irish Manuscripts Commission.
JRSAI	*Journal of the Royal Society of Antiquaries of Ireland*
JSAHR	*Journal of the Society for Army Historical Research.*
JCLAHS	*Journal of the County Louth Archaeological and Historical Society.*
Loudon MS	Campbell, John 4th Earl of Loudoun, Medical Papers, Royal College of Surgeons of England.
MR	*Mercurii Relation, oder wochentliche Ordinari Zeitungen von underschidlichen Orthen* (Munich) in Bavarian State Library Bayerische StaatsBibliothek http://reader.digitale-sammlungen.de/
NLI	National Library of Ireland.
OPD	*Ordinari Postzeitung* in the digital collection of the Staats und Universitätsbibliothek Bremen. http://brema.suub.uni-bremen.de/zeitungen17/periodical/titleinfo/953068
Proc.Roy.Soc.Med.	*Proceedings of the Royal Society of Medicine*
SachsHStA	Sächsisches Hauptstaatarchiv, Saxon State Archive, Dresden
SHD.	Service historique de la défense à Vincennes
SP	State Papers, National Archives of the UK
TNA	The National Archives UK
WO	War Office, Britain

Acknowledgements

First and foremost, I want to thank my wife Caitriona Clear for her unfailing support and, well, everything. I owe so much to other family members as well. Cora compiled the bibliography while Síle served as my grammar and syntax enforcer. Donncha and Megan suggested a catchy title, Manus and Deirdre listened patiently to my table talk and made useful suggestions. I unsparingly used my brother Fionnbar, a medical doctor, as a sounding-board and he cautioned me about neglecting malaria.

Professor Gregory Hanlon of Dalhousie University, whose *Italy 1636 Cemetery of Armies* I greatly admire, wrote to me out of the blue. He had read a journal article I wrote on the 1689 epidemic associated with the Williamite camp at Dundalk (discussed in Chapter 2) and encouraged me to pursue the study of disease and early modern armies further. Michael McNally, a friend and author of many fine battlefield studies, encouraged me to publish with Helion. Andrew Bamford, Helion's Series and Commissioning Editor for the series 'From Reason to Revolution 1721-1815', has proved a consummate professional. I owe much to discussion over the years with fellow enthusiasts and experts in the Battle of Aughrim Summer School including Tomás Ó Brógain of Oireas Historical Services, Joe Kelly, Paddy Naughton, and Mike Riddle.

A research grant from the College of Arts NUI Galway assisted with securing the services of Dr Carla Lessing as an expert translator of German texts. A triennial travel grant from NUI Galway assisted me in consulting archives abroad. Sabbatical leave from the Discipline of History provided time and space for research and writing. I am grateful to my friends and colleagues in the Department of History for the environment which is supportive of research. They were always interested, never inquisitorial. I am pleased to acknowledge the help of the staff of many archives and collections including Le Service historique de la Défense (SHD) Vincennes Paris, Bibliothèque nationale de France, Archives départementales des Pyrénées-Orientales Perpignan, Royal College of Surgeons of England London, Deutsches Historisches Museum Berlin, and Bayerisches Hauptstaatsarchiv Munich.

Beannachtaí oraibh

1

Introduction

After falling seriously ill at Verdun in 1916, Corporal Louis Barthas protested that '...it didn't seem possible to us that, after all the bursting shells, machine guns, poison gas etc., one could die just from getting sick. That was just too silly'.[1] However, the Great War was almost the first in history in which death through sickness could seem aberrant. Just fifty years before Barthas scrawled these lines, two-thirds of the Union army dead in the American Civil War had been felled by sickness rather than by minié ball.

The proportion of *ancien régime* soldiers dying of disease as opposed to being killed or mortally wounded in combat is generally reckoned to be somewhat higher, between 70 and 75 percent.[2] For example, during the Irish phase (1689-91) of the Nine Years War, 71 percent of the Allied troops 'died' while the rest were 'killed' (by regular troops), or 'murdered' (by partisans or rapparees).[3] The percentage in the Catalonian *tercios* during the wartime years 1673-78 and 1693-95 who perished of sickness, as a percentage of all deaths, ran at 81 percent and the percentage of Austrian troops in the War of the Bavarian Succession (1778-79) reached an astonishing 98 percent.[4]

By some accounts, seventeenth century European armies seem to have been so ravaged by disease as to yield a mortality rate of about 20 to 25 percent per year in times of peace and war, whereas the annual death rates for civilian populations ran in the range of just 3 to 4 percent. Other authorities claim that 'the scourge of ill health and disease was probably no worse for the soldiers in his barracks and camps than for the civilian in his slum'.[5]

---

1   Edward M. Strauss (transl.), and Rémy Cazals, (ed.), *Poilu: The World War I Notebooks of Corporal Louis Barthas, Barrelmaker, 1914-1918* (New Haven CT: Yale, 2015), pp.139, 344.

2   Boris Z. Urlanis, *Bilanz der Kriege – Die Menschenverluste Europas vom 17. Jahrhundert bis zur Gegenwart* (Berlin: Deutscher Verlag der Wissenschaften, 1965) p.43; Charles Carlton, *Going to the Wars: The Experience of the British Civil Wars 1638-1651* (London: Routledge, 2002), p.146.

3   George Warter Story, *A continuation of the impartial history of the wars of Ireland* (London, 1693), p.317.

4   Antonio Espino López, 'Los Tercios Catalanes durante el reinado de Carlos II, 1665-1697' in *Brocar. Cuadernos de Investigación Histórica*, 22, (1998), p.84; Gaston Bodart, *Losses of life in modern wars, Austria-Hungary and France.* (Oxford: Clarendon Press, 1916), p.37.

5   John Childs, *Armies and Warfare in Europe, 1648-1789* (New York: Holmes and Meier, 1982), p.62.

For all its importance and its open questions, the impact of sickness is a relatively neglected subject. An excellent survey like Tallett's *War and Society in Early Modern Europe*, observes in less than two pages that deaths from illness were 'ceaseless', that military codes contained ineffectual provisions on camp hygiene, and that recruits were often poor physical specimens unable for the rigours and privations of military life.[6] Other military history surveys, with the notable exception of Luh's *Kriegskunst in Europa (1650-1800)*, are even more cursory.[7] A typical medical survey like Lindemann's *Medicine and Society in Early Modern Europe* devotes five pages to military hospitals but mentions armies only once in passing when she adverts to the possible seriousness of dysentery when speaking of 'other' diseases (other than plague, syphilis and smallpox, that is).[8] Monographs tend to concentrate on hospitals or on particular wars: examples include Monique Lucenet's *Médecine, chirurgie et armée en France* and Erica Charters, *Disease, War, and the Imperial State*. Smallman-Raynor. Cliff's *War Epidemics: An Historical Geography of Infectious Diseases in Military Conflict* pleads lack of space in passing over the period 1650-1770.[9] A fine study of army surgeons and physicians in the British army postdates the period under review.[10] Likewise, a fine-grained comparative statistical analysis of sickness by regiment and by theatre pertains to the Napoleonic Wars.[11]

The study of *ancien régime* armies and epidemics has been neglected.

An epidemic can be defined as the incidence of a disease 'clearly in excess of expectancy', and case studies of epidemics have been chosen mainly because they present relatively well-documented target groups for analysis, rather than for their military significance.[12] Poorly recorded events, be they ever so pregnant with consequence, must be ignored. The army of Charles XII of Sweden quartered in Ukraine during the inhumanly cold winter of 1708-1709 and was ravaged by 'sickness, famine, a stubborn guerrilla war, appalling weather, and doubt'. A host which numbered 49,500 in late summer would be whittled down to not much more than 30,000 fighting men, but the loss of the Swedish field chancellery records after the catastrophic defeat at Poltava (8 July 1709) makes it impossible to ascertain what exactly happened.[13]

6   Frank Tallett, *War and Society in Early Modern Europe* (London: Routledge, 1992), p.106.
7   M.S. Anderson, *War and Society in Europe of the Old Regime* (London: Fontana Press, 1988), pp.136-7; Jean Chagniot, *Guerre et société à l'époque modern* (Paris: Presses Universitaires de France, 2001), pp.42, 45; Jürgen Luh, *Kriegskunst in Europa (1650-1800)* (Köln: Böhlau Verlag, 2004), pp.59-71.
8   Mary Lindemann, *Medicine and Society in Early Modern Europe* (Cambridge: Cambridge University Press, 1999), pp.184-188.
9   M. Smallman-Raynor, and A.D. Cliff, *War Epidemics: An Historical Geography of Infectious Diseases in Military Conflict and Civil Strife, 1850–2000* (Oxford: Oxford University Press, 2004), pp.93-94.
10   Catherine Kelly, *War and the Militarization of British Army Medicine, 1793–1830: Studies for the Society for the Social History of Medicine*, (Abingdon-on-Thames: Routledge, 2011).
11   Andrew Bamford, *Sickness, Suffering and the Sword: The British Regiment on Campaign, 1805-1815* (Norman: University of Oklahoma Press, 2013).
12   Smallman-Raynor and Cliff, *War Epidemics*, p.30.
13   Peter Englund, *The Battle that Shook Europe: Poltava and the Birth of the Russian Empire* (London & New York: I.B. Tauris, 2003), pp.51, 64, 204, 246.

Methodologically, one of the most painstaking parts of this project has been the invisible process of rejecting case studies where losses through sickness cannot reliably be disentangled from overall attrition or case studies fail to yield key statistical indices of morbidity and mortality rates. Moreover, knowing how many men lay sick is meaningless unless one knows the size of the whole group (the battalion, regiment, detachment, or army) and can thereby extract a figure (such as mortality rate per month) that can be applied comparatively to other episodes.

The geographical reach will not follow European armies beyond the continent onto the high seas or to the tropics because the lethality of these encounters must be set on a different scale. In the early nineteenth century the mortality rate among British troops cantoned in Bengal (admittedly the unhealthiest of the Indian stations) was six times that of troops quartered in Britain while the death toll among sailors and ship borne troops in the tropics was frightful; of the 4,750 men who served on board the fleet sent to blockade Portobello and Cartagena in 1726-27, some 4,000 perished.[14] Moreover, shipboard epidemics possessed an unmatched claustrophobic horror. A surgeon described conditions on the ships lying idle at Cartagena in May 1741:

> The men were pent up between decks in small vessels where they had not room to sit upright: they wallowed in filth; myriads of maggots were hatched in the putrefaction of their sores, which had no other dressings than being washed in their own allowance of brandy; nothing was heard but groans and lamentations and the language of despair invoking death to deliver them from their miseries.[15]

Where the physician might dream of the perfect camp site 'in a sunny spot, open to the breeze, on firm ground across which coursed a spring-water stream' he recognised that 'necessity' usually forced a commander to choose a constricted site in the same linear order of battle as he would on the battlefield.[16] In 1674 Condé's army of 45,000 men and 10,000 horses occupied a camp near Maastricht which was about four kilometres wide and 500 metres deep, giving each man and horse about 28 square metres of space.[17] Guillaume Le Blond's plan for a battalion camp in *Essai sur la castrametation* (1748) depicts the wedge tents of the private soldiers in ordered rows and streets at the head of the camp, the kitchens in the middle, officers' tents behind them, and the victuallers or *vivandiers* at the tail of the camp. The whole was fifty *toises* wide (or about 97 metres) and thirty deep (or about 58 metres): in other

14   Mark Harrison, 'Disease and Medicine in the Armies of British India, 1750-1830' in G. Hudson (ed.), *British Military and Naval Medicine, 1600-1830* (Amsterdam and New York: Rodopi, 2007), p.90; J.R. McNeill, *Mosquito Empires: Ecology and War in the Greater Caribbean, 1620-1914* (Cambridge: Cambridge University Press, 2010), pp.1-2, 148.

15   Thomas Roscoe (ed.), *The Miscellaneous Works of Tobias Smollett ... With Memoir of the Author* (London: Henry Washbourne, 1841), p.610.

16   Johann Valentin Willie, *Tractatus Medicus de Morbis Castrensis Internis....* (Copenhagen: John Christopher Rieger: 1674), p.33.

17   Jean Philippe Cárat, 'Les Fonctions de Général Maréchal Des Logis à L'Epoque de Louis XIV, *Revue Historique Des Armées* 257 (April, 2009), p.82.

words 650-700 men crowded into an area of just 5,626 square metres, giving each solider (not to speak of officers, servants, *vivandiers*, horses, and baggage) between eight and nine square metres of living space.[18] The paper plans of numerous treatises on *castrametation* and an archaeological dig of a training camp for Louis XIV's household troops occupied in 1670 show the characteristic rectilinear tented streets laid out in imitation of the Roman *castrum*.[19] Painters like Pieter Snayers and Adam Frans Van der Meulen capture the bustle and disorder of real-life camps: horses tethered in the open, vivandiers' tents scattered untidily, and so on. In 1635, during the Thirty Years War, the little Lombard town of Valenza (population 2-3,000) situated on the Po between Genoa and Milan, held out for a month (11 September-27 October) against an encircling army of French, Parman, and Savoyard troops.[20] A detail from a Snayers painting depicts bare-bottomed French soldiers squatting just outside their works, while beside them other near-naked soldiers pluck lice out of their clothing.[21]

In actuality, camps were squalid and cramped 'instant slums'. A pop-up city of over 100,000 soldiers (not to mention servants and other camp-followers) before Belgrade in summer 1717 had more mouths than any proper city closer than Rome or Constantinople, but lacked amenities such as regular markets, paved streets, wells, houses of easement, privy pits, and night soil collectors.[22] Early modern armies, those 'ambulant and dying cities', generated epidemics: 'Whether campaigning in the field, laying siege to fortresses, or even in winter quarters it is seldom that an army is not decimated [*decimentur*] by epidemic diseases'.[23]

This is a study of *Kabinettskriege*, a style of warfare restrained by a predominance of siege warfare over battles and by limited war goals involving a slice of border territory or the succession of a favoured candidate to a disputed kingdom rather than the annihilation of the enemy. The time period, then, necessarily falls between 1648 and 1689, between the end of the Thirty Years War, the last of the Wars of Religion, and the French Revolution. The key aim of this work is to evaluate the response to the challenge of epidemic disease by using quantitative data, which generally presents a more accurate picture than the qualitative evidence. Runs of quantitative data do

---

18 Guillaume Blond, Le, *Essai sur la castrametation*, ou, (Paris, 1748) 'French Army Camp Rules and Regulations' at http://w3r-us.org/wp-content/uploads/2018/03/French-Army-Camp-Rules-and-Regulations-W3R.pdf; A. Manesson-Mallet, 1691, *Les travaux de Mars, ou l'Art de la Guerre* (Paris: 1691) Vol.III, p.229.

19 Séverine Hurard and Xavier Rochart, 'Régiments de cavalerie des troupes de Louis XIV, Les écuries du fort Saint-Sébastien de Saint-Germain-en-Laye', *Archéopages La place du cheval* no 41, January 2015.

20 Hanlon, Gregory, *The Hero of Italy: Odoardo Farnese, Duke of Parma, his soldiers and his subjects in the Thirty Years War,* (Oxford: Oxford University Press, 2014), pp.96-97, 120.

21 Peeter Snayers, 'Die Belagerung von Valenza del Po' Gm 94/2 Deutsches Historisches Museum; Humphreys, Margaret, *Marrow of Tragedy: The Health Crisis of the American Civil War* (Baltimore: The Johns Hopkins University Press, 2013), p.77.

22 Emily Cockayne, *Hubbub, Filth, Noise, & Stench in England 1600-1770* (New Haven, Conn: Yale University Press, 2007), pp.189, 197.

23 Lauro Martines, *Furies: War in Europe, 1450-1700* (New York: Bloomsbury Press, 2013), p.170; Bernardino Ramazzini, *De morbis artificum diatriba* (Venice: Joseph Corona: 1743), pp.221, 223.

1.1 Pieter Snayers, 'Siege of Valenza' c.1650. (Deutsches Historisches Museum, Berlin)

not exist before the centralization and bureaucratization of army command and administration that began in the latter decades of the seventeenth century. An *état* by a *commissaire de guerre* would typically list provisions or munitions and so cast accidental light on manpower: the *commissaire*'s account of hospital rations indirectly reveals how many men were hospitalised in Perpignan in summer 1674. By the early eighteenth century, states were giving closer attention to counting their soldiers. The *tabellen* used by many German princely armies were standardized forms enumerating in tabular format how many soldiers were sick, had deserted, been detached, died or been killed in action, and how many effectives remained at month's end. The French regimental *contrôle* instituted in 1716 is more ambitious and lists each soldier by name, nom de guerre, date of enlistment and, crucially, when and why his service terminated. Was he killed [*tué*] or was he dead [*mort*] for other reasons? Did he desert or was he *congedé*, given his ticket-of-leave?

The opening decades of *Kabinettskriege* happen to coincide with two important changes in the disease matrix. Bubonic plague slowly retreated, leaving whole regions successively plague-free, such as northern Italy after 1631, Catalonia after 1651, the Baltic region after 1713.[24] Classic camp diseases like typhus (also called *lagerpest* or the 'camp pestilence'), typhoid, and dysenteric diseases which had hitherto been overshadowed by plague now emerged more clearly.[25] The second change was that smallpox assumed a relatively new form, or mutated into a new disease.

---

24 Geoffrey Parker, *Global Crisis: War, Climate Change and Catastrophe in the Seventeenth Century* (New Haven, Conn: Yale University Press, 2013), p.630.

25 Quentin Outram, 'The socio-economic relations of warfare and the military mortality crises of the Thirty Years' War' in *Medical History*, 45: 2, (2001), p.161.

For whatever reason, smallpox grew in virulence and frequency for a century from about 1660 until the practice of variolation began to take effect among the well-to-do of north-western Europe. Nils Rosén von Rosenstein's *The Diseases of Children and Their Remedies* (1764) was a foundational text in paediatrics and it devoted one third of its attention to smallpox, concluding the disease killed 10 percent of all Swedish infants every year. The jump in frequency, among infants and adults, was not just a statistical artefact caused by better record-keeping because smallpox went on a 'regicidal rampage' amongst a privileged group that had always been well-recorded.[26] William III of England (1650-1702), for instance, lost his father, mother, uncle, and wife to smallpox between 1650 and 1692.[27]

The sudden increase in the overall size of armies in the second half of the seventeenth century remains one of the clearest markers of the so-called 'Military Revolution' but for present purposes it is not necessary to enter the fraught debate on 'revolution', 'evolution', or 'punctuated equilibrium' since we are interested only in the growth of field armies. This sharp growth andsubsequent levelling off is apparent when one compares the biggest battles fought by the French in the Netherlands or north Germany in successive wars: In round terms, 48,000 men fought at Rocroi (1643), 110,000 at Seneffe (1674), 130,000 at Neerwinden (1693), 160,000 at Malplaquet (1709) 101,000 at Fontenoy (1745) and 95,000 at Hastenbeck (1757).[28] The growing number of fighting men was only partly offset by a withering of the tail of camp-wives, servant boys, cantinières, hucksters, and sutlers.[29] The increase was associated with the fairly sudden displacement of the 'aggregate contract army' (a long-winded term for a mercenary army hired off the shelf) by the 'state-commission' army where the sovereign commissioned the officers and agreed to pay them directly. Command and administration were regularized with permanent magazines, pay, regular supply of food, uniforms and other innovations.[30]

Full-scale war was a seasonal affair, and the campaigning season did not open until the grass had begun to grow and the horses could graze. Green forage would not be available until late May or June in northern Europe, though hay, in sufficient quantities, could let the cavalry take the field a few weeks earlier.[31] While

26 Donald R. Hopkins, *The Greatest Killer:Smallpox in History* (Chicago: University of Chicago Press, 2002), p.40.

27 Alan Macfarlane, *The Savage Wars of Peace: England, Japan and the Malthusian Trap*, (Basingstoke: Palgrave Macmillan, 2003), p.286; I. and J. Glynn, *The Life and Death of Smallpox* (London: Profile Books, 2004) p.39; R. Davenport, L. Schwarz, and J. Boulton, 'The decline of adult smallpox in eighteenth-century London', *Econ Hist Rev.* Nov. 2011; 64:4, p.1290.

28 John A. Lynn, *The Wars of Louis XIV, 1667–1714* (London: Longman, 1999), pp.80-81, 125, 234, 331; D. Chandler, *The Art of Warfare in the Age of Marlborough* (Tunbridge Wells: Spellmount Books, 1990), pp.302, 304; Reed Browning, *The War of the Austrian Succession* (New York: Macmillan, 1995), pp.212-213: Daniel Marston, *The Seven Years' War* (Oxford: Osprey, 2013), pp.36-37.

29 John A. Lynn, *Women, Armies, and Warfare in Early Modern Europe* (Cambridge: Cambridge University Press, 2008), pp.125, 163, 216.

30 John A. Lynn, *The Evolution of Army Style in the Modern West, 800-2000 The International History Review*, 18:3 (Aug., 1996), pp.505-545.

31 'Proposal concerning the next year's prosecution of the war in Ireland 1690', SP 8/11 f.65.

winter raiding may have increased, the campaigning season did not lengthen across northern Europe. To take the Spanish Netherlands for example, the average number of days spent on campaign in the Netherlands was 166 in the 1640s and 167 in the 1700s.[32] However, armies in the 'warm countries of Europe' did keep the field for longer.[33] Writing from the foothills of the Pyrenees on 19 July 1674, Major General Schomberg recalled that in the 'last war' (by which he meant the war that ended in 1659), it was customary to retire into quarters during the dog-days of high summer.[34] His memory was accurate, and we see, for instance, Louis de Bourbon, Prince of Condé finding the heat of northern Spain 'excessive' and resting his troops in the hill country for all of July and August of 1647.[35] The memory of a mid-campaign break remained. In early September 1702, Louis XIV chided *Maréchal* Vendôme about his sick rolls and specifically noted that just 300 men in four cavalry regiments were fit to fight (which implies that three-quarters of the troopers were sick): the grumble throws a sidelight on what authorities considered an unacceptably high toll of sick.[36] The great king's solution was to reinstate the mid-campaign break, rest troops 'without much combat' from June right through until late September and resume campaigning only for the month of October.[37]

Finally, armies grew and kept to the field for longer during the second, and somewhat more severe, of two cold snaps that defined the worst years of the long seventeenth century's 'Little Ice Age'. This second snap was especially marked by extreme weather events, poorer harvests than usual, and more widespread famines and epidemics that culminated in the mortality peak of the 1740s, that 'outstanding fact of European demographic history'.[38] If the discourse of disease thus far has been spatial, a truly 'stereoscopic' view must include a temporal dimension.[39]

---

32 Jean de Beaurain, *Histoire militaire de Flandre, depuis l'année 1690 jusqu'en 1694* (Paris: Antoine Jombert 1755), Vol.II, pp.151, 236, 334, 383; Charles Sévin marquis de Quincy, *Histoire militaire de Louis le Grand roi de France* (Paris: Jean Baptiste Coignard et. al., 1726), Vol.I, pp.19, 21, 38, 42, 54, 55, 65, 77,81, 92, 123, 125, 197, 202, 206, 214, 219, 226, 232, 240; Vol.II, 241, 271, 343, 397, 474, 615, 645, Vol.V, pp.4, 49, 277, 287, 486, Vol. VI, pp.154, 217; Cartes des Marches & Campemens de l'Armée du Roy pendant la Campagne 1674, p.2,122; Marches & Campemens 1675, pp.1, 103, 105; Marches & Campemens 1676, pp.2,3, 41; Marches & Campemens 1677, pp.3, 114 in BNF, at http://catalogue.bnf.fr/ark:/12148/cb33281721x, Isaac De Larrey, *Histoire de France sous le regne de Louis XIV* (Rotterdam: Michel Bohm, 1718) Vol.I, p.196.
33 'A Light to the Blind', *NLI* MS 477 p.828.
34 Schomberg to Louvois, Camp at Saint-Jean de Pages, 19 July 1674, *SHD* A¹ 415, no. 70.
35 Quincy, *Histoire Militaire*, Vol.I, p.88; Lorraine White, 'Strategic Geography and the Spanish Habsburg Monarchy's Failure to Recover Portugal, 1640-1668', *The Journal of Military History*, 71:2, [2007], pp.373-374.
36 Each cavalry squadron numbered 140 men so each regiment numbered about 280: *Mercure Galant* (July, 1702) pp.194-5.
37 Louis XIV to Vendôme, 30 September 1702, *SHD* A¹ 1591, no. 320.
38 J.D. Post *Food Shortage, Climatic Variability, and Epidemic Disease in Preindustrial Europe* (Ithaca: Cornell, 1985) p.30:Geoffrey Parker, *Global Crisis: War, Climate Change and Catastrophe in the Seventeenth Century* (New Haven: Yale, 2013), pp.17-20, 22-23.
39 J.V. Pickstone, 'Dearth, dirt and fever epidemics: rewriting the history of British public health, 1780-1850' in T. Ranger and P. Slack, (eds.) *Epidemics and Ideas* (Cambridge: Cambridge University Press, 1992), p.126.

The peacetime seasonal rhythm of death among soldiers was similar to that prevalent among the civilians on whom they were billeted (by and large they did not yet live apart in purpose-built barracks), to judge by an exceptionally long run of *contrôles* for the Vivarais Regiment.[40] The general pattern was one of slight seasonal variation, albeit with mortality running a little higher in the winter months. There were regional exceptions such as garrison troops in Livonia, whose seasonal mortality peaked in May. This spike was most likely caused by 'land scurvy' due to, as we now know, a diet heavily reliant on salted meat and biscuit.[41] The garrisons of island and coastal outposts could also suffer from scurvy. Eight times as many defenders perished of 'distempers' attributed to lack of 'fresh provisions' as were killed by all other 'accidents' during the 1727 Siege of Gibraltar.[42] In contrast, during the 'Great Siege' or four month long blockade of 1779, 505 men died of sickness compared to 293 dying of wounds.[43] Pleurisy and pneumonias were the greatest killers of garrison troops at Belle-île-en-Mer, in the Gulf of Morhiban, but debilitation through scurvy 'greatly' helped the emergence of these respiratory diseases.[44] The symptoms of scurvy typically begin three months after a person stops getting enough vitamin C in their diet, though contemporary medical opinion saw diet only as a predisposing cause that caused a 'weakness of the legs' or a 'collapse', which, in turn, allowed melancholy humours to be generated in the viscera. The first symptoms include fatigue, leg pain, and later joint pain, bleeding gums and, finally, swelling caused by a build-up of fluid and heart problems.[45]

So much for peacetime rhythms: What of wartime? The Vivarais Regiment shows a pronounced spike of deaths during a December 1734 epidemic which killed 233 of an estimated 500 men.[46] Corvisier excludes this epidemic as a distortion of normal long-run trends but, given the frequency and severity of such wartime epidemics, it is difficult to discern 'normal' trends. Some authorities grouped diseases according to season: the summer/autumn diseases were bilious in that the body's bile is 'much more inclined' to putrefy until the 'night frosts' of late autumn.[47] Sir John Pringle, Physician General to George II's forces in the Low Countries and Germany during the War of the Austrian Succession, tried to capture the seasonal pattern of disease,

40   André Corvisier, *L'armée française de la fin du XVIIe siècle au ministère de Choiseul. Le soldat* (Paris: Presses Universitaires de France, 1964), Vol.II, p.684.

41   Margus Laidre, 'Förluster och sjukvård i svenska armén i Estland och Livland under senare hälften av 1600-talet' in *Karolinska förbundets årsbok* (Stockholm: Karolinska förbundet, 1989), p.45.

42   Anon. *An impartial account of the late famous siege of Gibraltar: To which are Added, Most Accurate Plans of the Town, and of the Approaches and Camp* (London: Warner, 1728), p.30.

43   Drinkwater, John, *History of the Late Siege of Gibraltar: With a Description and Account of that Garrison, from the Earliest Periods* (Dublin: Colles et al., 1786), p.334.

44   Christophe Cérino, 'L'hôpital militaire de Belle-île-en-Mer au siècle de Louis XV: les conditions sanitaires d'une garnison en milieu insulaire', *Annales de Bretagne et des pays de l'Ouest*, 104:4, (1997), pp.41-50.

45   Paul de Sorbait, *Praxios medicæ, auctæ* (Vienna: George Matthew Lackhner, 1701), p.157-158.

46   André Corvisier, 'La Mort du Soldat' in *Revue historique*, 254 (1975), p.14.

47   Friedrich Wilhelm von Bessel, *Entwurf eines Militair-Feld-Reglements* (Hanover: H.E.C. Schlüter, 1778), p.309.

assuming that the campaigning season began in May. Cases would run fairly low until mid to late August, when the 'great sickness commonly begins'. How 'great' the sickness might be and how long it might last would be 'impossible to compute' because of variables like weather and when the campaigning season might end. In 1743, the sickness rate had been as high as 25 percent and in 1745, less than four percent, 'which was', Pringle admitted, 'remarkable'. Jean-François Vaidy, a regimental surgeon, writing of his experience in the Napoleonic Wars, hazarded a generalization that the best that could be planned for in wintertime was at least five percent sickness (marginally higher than Pringle's figure) doubling to 10 percent on campaign. But Vaidy warned that this figure might be 'fearfully increased' if the army is very numerous, concentrated, encamped on wet ground, suffering privations and discouraged (Vaidy perceived an intimate connection between morale and sickness), or lacking confidence in their leaders.[48] Nonetheless, Pringle risked generalizations, and asserted, for instance, that if a campaign were to be protracted until the beginning of November, then the last fortnight's sick roll would exceed that of the first two months. From such statistical scraps it is possible to represent the seasonal pattern of disease, assuming that the campaigning season begins in mid-May.[49] As is evident from Image 1.2, Ravaton, the chief surgeon of the French military hospital at Landau, came up with similar figures.[50]

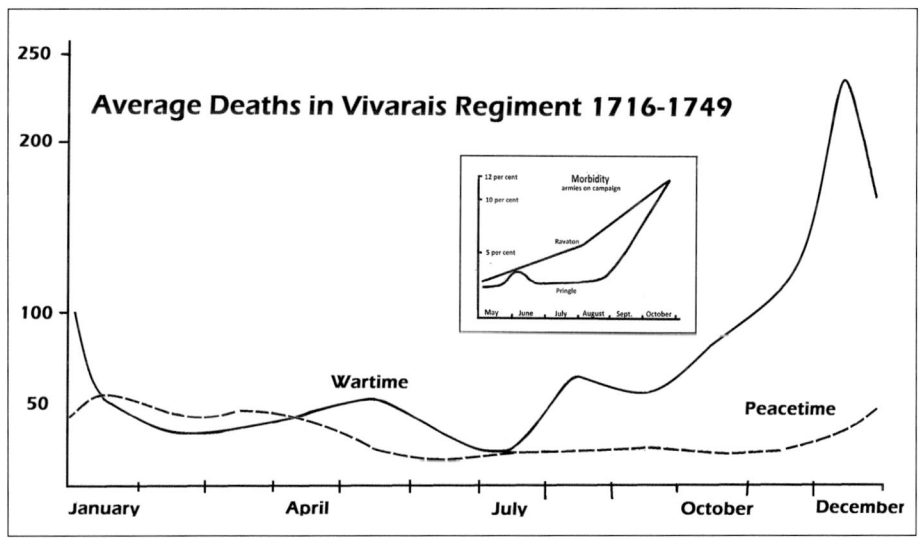

1.2 Seasonal patterns of morbidity and mortality.

So, deaths through sickness in wartime produced quite a different seasonal rhythm to deaths in peacetime. Morbidity and mortality spiked in the late summer

48   James Johnson, *Medico-Chirurgical Review* (London: S. Highley, 1833), p.430.
49   John Pringle, *Observations on the diseases of the army, in camp and garrison* (London, Millar, Wilson and Payne, 1752), pp.144-146.
50   Hugues Ravaton, *Chirurgie D'Armee,* (Paris: Didot le Jeune, 1768), p.635.

and autumn, as can be seen from hospital ration figures (Perpignan and *Bas Rhin*) or deaths (Almeida, Portugal) in military hospitals.[51] Quite when the peak rose, how high it spiked, and how quickly it subsided all varied from year to year and place to place. What were the diseases that produced this mortality spike?

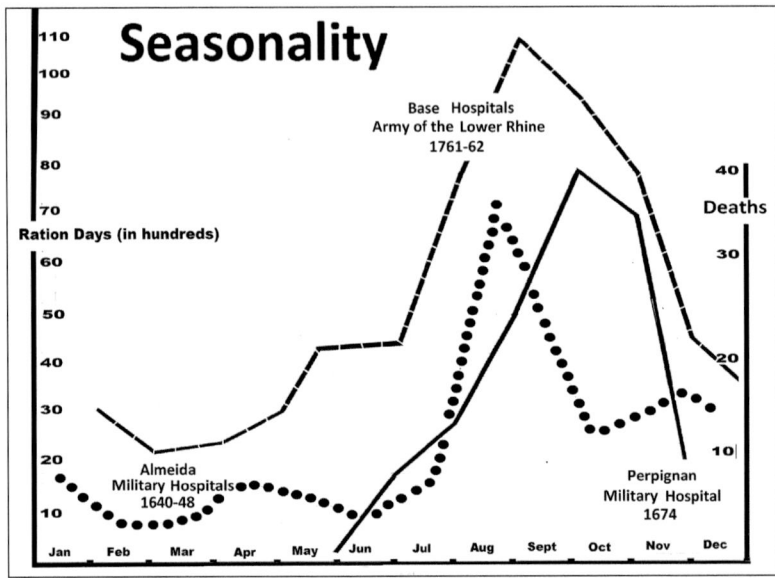

1.3 Seasonal patterns of mortality in army hospitals.

Fever and Flux

Galenic medicine showed a continuing vitality and contested the belief that ailments were individualized and had specific causes and mechanisms. Rather, 'there is but one fever in the world', as Benjamin Rush of Philadelphia insisted in 1796. It was more commonly held that distemper reflected some 'basic underlying state' and that the manifesting sickness could subtly shift from one form to another in response to changing environmental circumstances.[52] A remittent fever would probably, for instance, turn into a 'malignant' or 'putrid' fever as ever more dirt accumulated in a fetid hospital ward.[53]

51 'état general du movement journalier des soldats, cavaliers, entrés, sortis, morts, et journées en total dans chacun des hôpitaux sédentaires de l'armée du bas Rhin à commencer du 1er juin 1761 jusqu'au 1er juin 1762 SHD A¹ 3621 no. 288; 'Estat de la despance fait…pour la subsistence des malades', ADPO, C134; Augusto Borges, *Reais Hospitais Militares em Portugal 1640-1834* (Coimbra: Imprensa da Universidade de Coimbra, 2009), p.75.

52 Simon Finger, *The Contagious City: the politics of public health in early Philadelphia* (Ithaca NY: Cornell University Press, 2012), p.127.

53 Charles E. Rosenberg, *Explaining Epidemics* (Cambridge: Cambridge University Press, 1992), p.93.

A sample sick return in a 1758 military handbook reported 32 men hospitalized, of whom just three were wounded and over two-thirds were suffering from fever or dysentery, more commonly called 'flux'.[54] The imagined importance of the catch-all terms of fever and flux reflects reality as seen in wartime statistics, such as a British sick report from Portalegre in Portugal on 15 January 1763. The returns for Swedish garrison troops in Livonia also give top billing to 'fever' and its synonyms. 'Heated' fever and 'Haupt Krankheit' or 'skin-disease' probably denoted typhus, discussed below. However, scurvy nudges flux into third place. While situations might arise where other diseases were atypically prominent, like scurvy in this case or smallpox among American troops in the American Revolutionary War, most deaths could generally be blamed on fevers and dysentery.[55] Indeed, a physician who served on the notoriously sickly Danubian theatre recognised just these two 'diseases of camp', namely 'dysentery' and 'malignant fever'. The rest were 'either harbingers or followers of these two'.[56] Like him, my preferred approach would be to regard campaign sickness as a continuum with identifiable diseases at the beginning and end. It will nonetheless be necessary at times to superimpose modern diagnostic categories on old and vague ones, while ignoring warnings that this is 'pointless' or not 'logically possible'.[57]

Table 1.1 Sick Returns[58]

Livonia 1658-60						
Scurvy	Flux	Fever	'Heated' Fever	'Chest Disease' [Bröstsjuka]	Other	'Haupt Krankheit'
23	21	15	12	12	11	6

Portugal 1763	'Common' Fever	'Bilious' Fever	Flux
	73	14	13

---

54 Heinrich Wirz, *Einrichtung und Disziplin eines eidg. Regiments zu Fuß und zu Pferd* (Zürich: unknown publisher, 1758), p.227.

55 Ann M., Becker, 'Smallpox in Washington's Army: Strategic Implications of the Disease during the American Revolutionary War', *The Journal of Military History*, 68:2 (Apr., 2004), p.392.

56 Frederick Hoffman, *Dissertation on Endemial Diseases* (London: Thomas Osborne, 1746), pp.260-61 cited in Erica Charters, *Disease, War and the Imperial State: The Welfare of the British Armed Forces during the Seven Years' War* (Chicago, IL: University of Chicago Press, 2014), p.94; Bernardino Ramazzini, *De Morbis Artificum Diatriba*. (Utrecht: William Van De Water, 1703), p.296.

57 Chagniot, *Guerre et société à l'époque modern*, p.261; Andrew Cunningham and Ole Peter Grell, *The Four Horsemen of the Apocalypse: Religion, War, Famine and Death in Reformation Europe* (Cambridge: Cambridge University Press, 2001), p.300.

58 Margus Laidre, *The Great Northern War and Estonia: the trials of Dorpat, 1700-1708* (Tallinn: Argo, 2010), p.48. RCS Loudoun Papers (Medical), MS0192/3, fo 264.

'White' flux can often be equated with diarrhoea while 'red', or bloody flux, can be identified with bacillary dysentery (shingellosis) caused by the bacterium *Shigella dysenteriae* and tagged as 'red' because the characteristic intestinal ulceration bleeds into the stools. At the outset of the period under review, physicians considered that the balance or 'temper' of the four humours was vital in preventing 'distemper' which arises on a sudden change to any one of six conditions, namely, air, diet, sleep, exercise, evacuation, or the 'passions'. This Hippocratic/Galenic approach emphasised prevention by keeping the person in 'good humour' through moderation in all things, especially diet. Most laid the blame for flux on diet and recommended that the soldier should drink only wine (in moderation), milk or well-brewed beer, and avoid water, even from pure springs; bathing in or drinking cool water in hot weather was best avoided lest 'cold humours' and 'hot sources' be suddenly brought into contact within the body. Noting that fluxes peaked alongside the harvest, many Galenic physicians abhorred fruits in particular, but not all physicians were obsessed with diet to the exclusion of other possible causes.[59] Ramazzini, a Mantuan physician who pioneered the study of ailments associated with particular occupations, dutifully name-checked the authorities that pronounced on causes like bad food, tainted water, hard labour, long watches, rain, heat, cold, and sudden alarms [*inopinos terrores*]. 'Above all', he insisted that sickness was caused by the filth and uncleanliness [*neglectam munditiem*] of camps that tainted the air. He approvingly quoted Deuteronomy 23:12-14: 'Designate a place outside the camp where you can go to relieve yourself. As part of your equipment have something to dig with, and when you relieve yourself, dig a hole and cover up your excrement'. Ramazzini noted that Turkish soldiers, 'who are cleaner than ours', continued this admirable practice.[60] Towards the end of the period under review, physicians still harped on about 'spiritous liquors' and 'irregular living' but conceded that it was now a 'vulgar error' to suppose that fruit-eating caused dysentery. Probably influenced by the mechanical physiology favoured by renowned Dutch physician Hermann Boerhaave (1668-1738), physicians now issued warnings about the build up of 'putrescent' humours in the body during the heat of summer and the difficulty of venting these humours once wet weather blocked the pores. Heat followed by rain, then, explained explains why dysentery 'became frequent' in late July and persisted until the army went into winter quarters, typically in mid-October. A second cause was miasma, that intangible substance that could not be seen but could certainly be smelt, and which emanated in 'putrid streams' from latrines and animal carcasses.[61]

'Fever' is much harder to pin down because it was not just a symptom, but also a nebulous catch-all term. The ancient division into remittent, intermittent, and continued fevers was recognised, though many practitioners believed that each had the same cause and could mutate into another. An 'intermittent' fever is one

---

59   Johanne Friderico Allmacher, *De morbis castrensibus defendente* (Leyden: Rijksuniversiteit te Leiden, 1672), unpag.; Johannes Valentinus Wille, *De morbis castrensibus internis* (The Hague: Typis Matthiæ Godicchenii, 1676), pp.41-42.

60   Ramazzini, *De Morbis Artificum*, pp.294-295.

61   Donald Monro, *An Account of the diseases which were most frequent in the British military hospitals in Germany* (London: A. Millar, 1764), pp.57-58.

where temperature rises and falls in on/off cycles of paroxysms and remissions. J.G. Kramers, the noted protomedicus or chief physician to the Imperial forces during the War of the Polish Succession (1734-35), tabulated the various fevers and further subdivided 'continuous' into 'slow' and 'acute', the latter into 'benign' and 'malign'.[62] A continuous fever is one where temperature stays steady, declines slowly, or rises steadily, showing no signs of abating. The latter was denoted 'malignant' fever, and just got worse, progressively exhausting the patient and allowing no rest. 'Hungarian or Camp Fever' was by far the most important malignant fever, for present purposes.[63] The many other names derive from the fever's locales ('hospital', 'camp', 'gaol', 'ship') or most striking symptoms ('malignant', 'pestilential', 'petechial', 'spotted', 'putrid').[64] The term 'typhus' was not coined until towards the end of the period under study, and derives from the Greek 'typhos', which was used by Hippocrates to describe another symptom, namely that of stupor or delirium. Typhus was intimately associated with armies. Typhus was regarded as a new disease brought from the east mainly through war between Christians and Muslims.[65] The earliest recorded epidemic in western Europe broke out three decades later when the armies of Ferdinand and Isabella of Spain were infected by reinforcements from Cyprus while battling the Moors for possession of Granada.

Between 1620 and 1632, France, the Empire, United Provinces, and the Italian states were all hit by a typhus epidemic. That the epidemic coincided with the beginning of the Thirty Years War was no accident. [66]

Robert Koch (1843-1910) pioneered the classification of diseases by presumed causes: the mechanism and cause, respectively, of typhus is the human body louse (a more robust variety of the head louse species) sucking the infected host's blood and thereby ingesting *rickettsiae* bacteria which then multiply in the louse's gut.[67] When the original human host burns with fever, or cools with death, the louse will crawl to the bedding or clothes of another host, if possible. Louse-bites cause an allergic reaction in the host's skin, which becomes inflamed and itches, causing the person to scratch the area. *Rickettsiae* expelled in the louse's faeces can then penetrate the new host's skin as he or she scratches and rubs the faeces into breaks in the skin. Dried faeces in clothes or bedding can also be inhaled. Typhus is highly contagious to those who come very close to the clothes and blankets of living or recently deceased victims. As body lice live in the seams of clothing and require the warm habitat of a human's body temperature, they were common in cold weather where the hungry

---

62 Johann Georg Heinrich Kramer, *Medicina Castrensis* (Nuremberg: Peter Conrad Monath, 1735), p.7.

63 Stephan Benkotzi, *De Febre Hungarica seu Castrensi* (Erlangen: unknown publisher, 1759), p.xxi.

64 William Cullen, *Nosology: Or, a Systematic Arrangement of Diseases, by Classes, Orders, Genera and Species* (Edinburgh: William Creech, 1800), pp.39-41.

65 Hans Zinsser, *Rats, Lice and History* (New York: Leventhal & Black Dog Publishers, 1934), pp.185-186, 192, 201, 204.

66 Sabbatani, Sergio, 'Il tifo petecchiale. Storie di uomini, eserciti e pidocchi', *Le infezioni in medicina*, 14:3 (2006) p.167.

67 James Ronald Busvine, *Insects, Hygiene and History* (London: Athlone Press, 2015), pp.42-43.

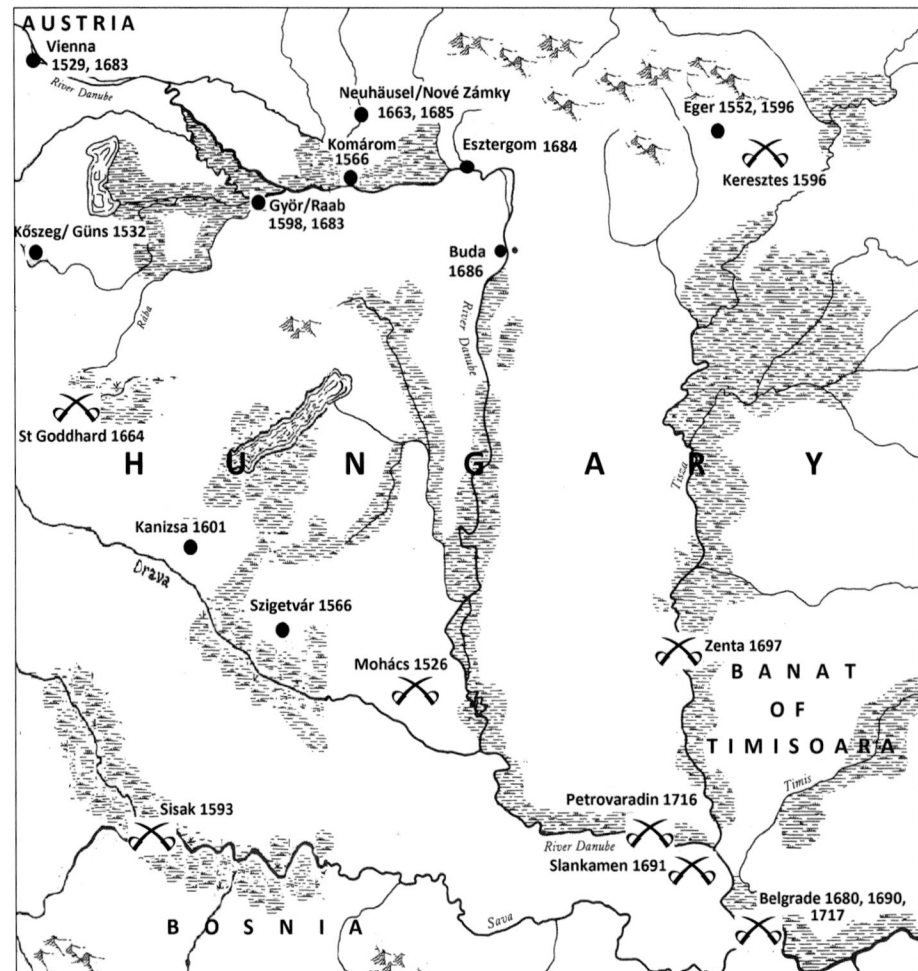

1.4 Danubian theatre.

and dirty huddled together for warmth.[68] Besides camps there were, of course, even more cramped carceral contexts like ships, gaols, hospitals, and workhouses, all of which were associated with typhus.

'Relapsing Fever' is a different disease from typhus in that the causative bacteria, *Borrelia recurrentis*, is a distinct one but its mode of transmission is virtually identical except that the second host crushes the engorged louse while scratching thereby rubbing the infected blood into a break in the skin.[69] It produced symp-

---

68   Charters, *Disease, War and the Imperial State*, p.94.

69   Smallman-Raynor and Cliff, *War Epidemics*, pp.57-58; Margaret Humphreys, 'A Stranger to Our Camps. Typhus in American History', *Bulletin of the History of Medicine*, 80:2, (Summer, 2006) p.272.

toms similar to typhus, except for the severe jaundice, which gave rise to the 'yellow' adjective.[70] This gave rise to the 'yellow' descriptor in the *fiabhras buí* of the Irish Great Famine. Conversely, *Rickettsia prowazekii* was known as *fiabhras dubh* ['black fever'], because the victim's face was sometimes suffused by blood.

Typhus was, opined Pringle, 'the most fatal distemper incident to army' and aside from bubonic plague it was the deadliest epidemic disease likely to afflict an army. The symptoms were fourfold: rapid onset of high fever (a 'burning heat'), headache, prostration and an outbreak of purplish rash (by days 3-4) on the trunk and limbs.[71] The rash comprised spots rather than vesicles, which helped distinguish typhus from smallpox and scarlet fever. Typhus was 'usually' accompanied by constipation.[72] Contemporaries complained of how often this 'Hungarian Camp Fever' was confused with other camp fevers, and so this diagnostic problem remains.[73] Outram thought a retrospective diagnosis drawing a distinction between typhus, relapsing fever and typhoid fever (discussed below) would be 'impossible', so he lumped them together.[74] While admitting the difficulties, it is possible to disentangle three categories of campaign/camp disease based on the close observations of contemporary physicians and surgeons. Dezon's 1741 *Lettres sur les Principales Maladies* which was a 'key text' of 18th century medicine, spotted the tell-tale seasonal footprint of three successive (albeit overlapping) sicknesses among the French troops in Italy in 1734.[75]

Table 1.2 Dezon's Categories of Seasonal Diseases

July to October	August and September	October to about December
'Dysentery'	'Malign Fever'	'Malign and Burning Fever'
	lethargy, heaviness of the head, black-outs, heart troubles, a bitter taste in the mouth.	usually culminating in delirium

In describing a 1748 outbreak among British troops in the countryside around Frankfurt-am-Main, Pringle also categorizes three more or less successive diseases in which his first and third categories are similar to Dezon's dysentery and 'malign and burning' fever above. However, his intermediate 'new disease' is similar to

---

70 W. Bonser and W. MacArthur, "Epidemics during the Anglo-Saxon period, with appendix: Famine fevers in England and Ireland" in *Journal of the British Archaeological Association*, 9: pp.48–71.

71 Ernst Gottfried Baldinger, *Von den Krankheiten einer Armee: aus eignen Wahrnehmungen in dem letztern* (Langensalza: Johann Christian Martini, 1765), p.192.

72 Cowan, *Typhus in History*, pp.9-26.

73 Isaiah Ulmann, *Dissertatio medica inauguralis De febre maligna Hungarica vulgo Castrensi* (Heidelberg: J.C.L.Hornung, 1731), p.2.

74 Outram, 'Warfare and the military mortality crises of the Thirty Years' War', p.159.

75 M. Dezon, *Lettres sur les Principales Maladies...* (Paris: Lambert & Durand, 1741), pp.5, 26, 194; Erica Charters, 'Colonial Disease, Translation, and Enlightenment: Franco-British Medicine and the Seven Years', in Frans De Bruyn and Shaun Regan, (eds.) *The Culture of the Seven Years' War: Empire, Identity, and the Arts in the Eighteenth-Century Atlantic World* (Toronto: University of Toronto Press, 2014), p.75.

Dezon's only in that it appeared in or about the middle of August.[76] What might this 'autumnal or bilious ('bilious' denotes the yellow-green colour of vomit and, sometimes, watery stool) remitting fever' have been?

The Middle Disease

Unhelpfully, Pringle blurs the three categories. *His* 'Hungarian disease' is 'bilious' fever that begins in the camp and, as patients crowd into hospitals, turns malignant from the 'foul air'. Moreover, Pringle also claims that the onset of dysentery is 'frequently' marked by a 'bilious' fever.[77] Richard Brocklesby, who succeeded John Pringle as Surgeon General of the British Army in 1758, also saw a 'relation' between flux and bilious fever because they tended to break out at the same time and often 'changed one into the other'. Bilious fever was, he opined, most prevalent in 'swampy grounds' like Zeeland in the United Provinces or in parts of Hungary, which then reached as far south as Belgrade.[78] In light of Brocklesby's remarks can the elusive middle disease be equated with what we now call malaria?

The word 'malaria' was unknown in the English language until 1748 and thereafter it commonly denoted that 'bad air' which supposedly gave rise to ague, congestive fevers, bilious fevers and intermittent fevers.[79] *Plasmodium vivax* is one of the species of *Plasmodium* that cause malaria in humans and is carried by the female *Anopheles* mosquito which, when feeding on humans, injects saliva to prevent blood clotting. Whereas the deadlier *P. Falciparum* survives only in the warmest regions of Europe like southern Iberia, *P. Vivax* is 'less fussy', and can become endemic in cooler places like the Netherlands and is happiest in bogs and fens when drought evaporates ponds or streams to small pools.[80]

Malaria was endemic in parts of the Low Countries, and the polders of north Brabant will form the subject matter of a specific case study of malaria. The French army in Flanders was ravaged by *paludinisme* in September 1703, 1706, and 1712, and most of the twenty-five feverish officers in Cambrai hospital in September 1712, for example, were afflicted with malaria.[81] Nine suffered from 'Tertian Fever' in which the paroxysms of chills, sweats and fever fell on every other day; in other words there was a day's intermission or remission between episodes. The five men suffering from a Double Tertian enjoyed no such interval, but their fever was

---

76   John Pringle, *Observations on the diseases of the army, in camp and garrison* (London: Millar & Wilson, 1752), p.24.

77   Pringle, *Observations*, pp.195, 234.

78   John Gardiner, *Observations on the animal oeconomy, and on the causes and cure of diseases* (Edinburgh: Royal Society, 1789), pp.352, 358.

79   Fiammetta Rocco, *The Miraculous Fever-Tree* (New York: HarperCollins, 2016), p.35.

80   Charles C. Mann, *1493: Uncovering the New World Columbus Created* (New York: Random House, 2012), pp.82-83, 87.

81   Monique Lucenet, 'Les épidémies dans l'infanterie au cours de la première moitié du XVIIIe siècle' in *Forces armées et sociétés, Actes du Colloque du 1er au 5 avril 1985* (Paris: Centre d'histoire militaire et d'études de défense nationale, 1987), pp.215-216; Estat', Cambrai, September 1712 *Archives Guerre* A¹ 2383 no. 138.

somewhat distinguishable from the two cases of continual or continued fever by its circadian rhythm. One unfortunate suffered from a malignant fever and eight from an unspecified fever.

The long war between Habsburgs and Ottomans along the Danube and the lower reaches of that river's tributaries was mostly fought in a landscape of 'marsh, open water, and tracts of firmer ground with the margins of each constantly shifting'.[82] Imperial troops sustained heavy losses through 'swamp fever' [*sumpffieber*], and, to further confuse matters, this is sometimes identified with the *Morbus Hungaricus*, which actually was, as we have seen, typhus.[83]

The middle disease could also have been typhoid, a disease caused by ingesting water or food contaminated by faeces. By and large a person with typhoid usually experienced a gradual onset (the onset in typhus was more abrupt) of headache, fever, and pains in the joints and bones, after an incubation period of a week or two, In a few days, most of the body would be covered in a rash. Next might follow a decline into apathy, delirium, and coma (hence *typhos* forms the common word root of typhoid and typhus). The sequence was not invariable, and the best known victim of typhoid, Prince Albert, complained on 22 November 1861 of sleeplessness and rheumatism. By the 29th he was suffering chills and fever, and by 1 December he had lost his appetite and was vomiting. On 7 December he slipped into delirium and irritability. On 13 December, his complexion took on a dusky hue, and on the next day he died.[84]

The symptoms that most set typhoid apart from flux, namely, 'continued' fever, apathy/delirium and purple-reddish spots on the body, all serve to confuse it with malignant fever or typhus. Indeed, eighteenth century Bills of Mortality grouped 'Spotted Fever and Purples' together, alongside 'fever', 'malignant fever', and 'scarlet fever'.[85] A distinction between typhoid and typhus lies in the fact that the latter was somewhat more of a winter, or inclement weather, disease and was somewhat deadlier. To judge from statistics relating to the British army in India in the closing decades of the 19th century, the typhoid case fatality rate ran at between a quarter and a fifth, whereas in the typhus epidemic of 1914-15 in Serbia, the fatality rate ran at 36 percent.[86] Typhoid is best differentiated post-mortem by characteristic ulceration of the small intestine: this is more helpful than it may seem, because surgeons like Pringle increasingly carried out autopsies.[87] Typhoid can also be confused with

82   John Stoye, *Marsigli's Europe 1680-1730* (New Haven, CT: Yale University Press, 1994), p.120.
83   Melchior Landersdorfer, 'Das Schicksal der bayerischen Soldaten im Türkenkrieg' (dissertation; Technische Universität München, 1984), p.59: F.X. Laiffe, 'Die Seuchen während der Belagerung von Wien und während des letzten Türkenkrieges 1683–1699' in *Archiv für Hygiene und Bakteriologie* 119: 1937, p.80.
84   Richard Adler and Elise Mara, *Typhoid Fever: A History* (Jefferson, NC: McFarland & Co., 2016), p.82.
85   William Black, *Observations Medical and Political on the Small-pox...* (London: J. Johnson, 1781), p.208.
86   Logan Waller Page, et al., *How to prevent typhoid fever* (Washington D.C. Office of the Surgeon General, 1911), p.5; George C. Kohn, *Encyclopedia of Plague and Pestilence: From Ancient Times to the Present* (New York: Infobase Publishing, 2008), p.6; V. Soubbotitch, 'A Pandemic of Typhus in Serbia in 1914 and 1915', *Proc R Soc Med.* 1918; 11, p.33.
87   Cowan, *Typhus in History*, pp.9-26.

dysentery as when one physician speaks of a 'dysenteric flux' manifesting a bilious and putrid fever.[88]

It is possible to differentiate typhoid when the case notes are detailed enough. For instance, the army of the Comte de Lorges had been camped at Bruchsal, near the heavily fortified frontier town of Philippsburg on the Rhine, since 6 June 1695. On 21 June De Lorges personally reconnoitred the routes for the march to a new camp and that same day, he was felled by sickness.[89] So grave was the illness that he could not be moved, and his hungry army awaited the outcome in countryside that had been picked clean. Bulletins on De Lorges' condition came from a fretful *commissaire de guerre*, from *Maréchal* de Joyeuse, De Lorges' second-in-command, and from De Lorges' devoted son-in-law, the Duc de Saint-Simon. For the first five days, De Lorges slipped in and out of consciousness, shivering and suffering from a 'continuous double tertian' fever that exhibited 'remissions' but no 'intermission'[90] Nonetheless, the patient was administered quinine, the specific remedy for intermittent fevers, and the tremors worsened to the extent that his palsied hand could not even grip a pen.[91] On the 26th, when the patient's fever 'redoubled', he lost consciousness, and his paroxysms then stretched to eight hours. Three doses of opium drops were credited with stimulating notable bowel movements [*des grandes evacuations*], whereupon De Lorges regained consciousness.[92] By the 30th, nine days after he had fallen ill, he was reported to be 'entirely out of danger', if a 'little' feverish. He was imbibing cordials and taking opium drops, and his fever was 'now breaking out in purples' or 'purple fever' [*fièvre pourprée*], as it was named in other bulletins.[93] This rash was acclaimed as a sure sign that he would recover, and by 5 July, he was well enough to be evacuated to Landau.[94] It would be another six weeks before he recovered completely.[95] De Lorges was almost certainly struck down by typhoid. The onset seems uncharacteristically sudden, but the Maréchal, burdened by the cares of command, may have shrugged off the earlier symptoms. Otherwise the symptoms can be checked off, continued fever, rash and constipation. Moreover, the time of year also suggests typhoid rather than typhus.

In the case of large groups and vague or terse descriptions, the best approach is to carefully examine the circumstances of a particular outbreak, such as location,

---

88   Michel Du Tennetar, *Lettre à M. P***, doct. méd., sur les flux dyssentériques, épidémiques en Lorraine* (Nancy: P. Barbier, 1777), p.7.

89   *Mercure Historique et Politique,* July 1695 (The Hague, 1695), p.25: *Mercure Galant,* June 1695 pp.327, 333.

90   Intendant de la Grange to Barbézieux, Nider-Nainsen, 21 June 1695, SHD A¹1322, no.80.

91   *Maréchal* Joyeuse to Barbézieux, Nider-Nainsen, 25 June 1695, SHD A¹1322, no.89: De la Grange to Barbézieux, Nider-Nainsen, 25 June 1695, SHD A¹1322, no.90: Commissaires de guerre to Barbézieux, Nider-Nainsen, 25 June 1695, SHD A¹1322, no.91.

92   La Grange to Barbézieux, Nider-Nainsen, 28 June 1695, SHD A¹1322, no.99: Maréchal de Joyeuse to Barbézieux, Nider-Nainsen, 28 June 1695, SHD A¹1322, no.101.

93   Desbordes to Barbézieux, Nider-Nainsen, 30 June 1695, SHD A¹1322, no.109: La Grange to Barbézieux, Nider-Nainsen, 30 June 1695, SHD A¹1322, no.112: Joyeuse to Barbézieux, Nider-Nainsen, 30 June 1695, SHD A¹1322, no.113.

94   Lucy Norton (ed.), *Memoirs of Duc de Saint-Simon 1691-1709* (Warwick NY: Carelton Books, 2007), pp.66, 71.

95   *Mercure Historique et Politique Mois d'Août 1695* (The Hague, 1695), p.158.

timing, morbidity, and mortality. Smallman-Raynor and Cliff, for instance, considered what happened to the British force of 40,000 that disembarked on the island of Walcheren in the Scheldt Estuary in July 1809. By 3 September, some 8,000 troops were in hospital, with the numbers rising to 9,000 in late October. Such was the extent of morbidity that by the end of the expedition, 40 percent of the force had contracted the disease. Smallman-Raynor and Cliff convincingly rejected the commonplace assumption that the disease was malaria, noting that malaria alone would not account for the severity of the disease. However their conclusion, that the outbreak was a combination of malaria, typhus, typhoid, and dysentery, is unhelpfully vague.[96] While evaluating camp(aign) diseases holistically, my case studies will be more specific by distinguishing between different diseases, or different phases of the same disease.

The case studies are grouped and sequenced according to the tactical context. Chapter 2 will consider the diseases that arose during, or because of, eight-week long encampments at Saint-Jean-Pla-de-Corts in Roussillon (1674) and Dundalk in Ireland (1689). These were long pauses, even considering the ponderous and tentative nature of *ancien régime* manoeuvre. A camp was seldom occupied for long. For instance, in the 1674 campaign, the main French army occupied 33 different camps in five months of campaigning across the southern Spanish Netherlands.[97] The reason why an army typically lumbered onward after about 4-5 days in each place was because it had eaten up all the nearby horse forage, but it also left all the 'Filth and Nastiness' of the camp behind.[98]

Chapter 3 will deal with fortress warfare. By the period under review, sieges tended to be shorter than before because of mutually supporting trenches and artillery batteries inching forward, more firepower, and a greater readiness to launch bloody assaults across open ground to overrun the covered way, the thickened outer skin of Baroque fortification. A garrison overwhelmed by a quick attack in this manner typically suffered more casualties from action than from sickness. That said, heavily fortified, competently commanded, and well-manned fortifications still cost time to capture and the examples in question, including Belgrade in 1717 and Philippsburg in 1734, dragged out for many weeks: the imperial besiegers remained in the same camp for over three months, long after they had captured Belgrade. Chapter 3 also presents siege warfare as experienced within the walls. Strictly speaking, the 1689 Siege of Derry was not a siege-in-form but a blockade punctuated by only one serious assault. After the Battle of Poltava (1709) Sweden's Baltic empire was picked apart by a coalition in which Peter the Great's Russia played the leading role. The Russian siege of Riga (1709-10) was another long blockade distinguished from all the other siege operations by an outbreak of plague within the city. The final case study serves as a reminder that the thematic distinction between camps, sieges, marches

---

96   Smallman-Raynor and Cliff, *War Epidemics*, p.106.
97   *Cartes des Marches & Campemens de l'Armée du Roy pendant la Campagne 1674* (1680), BNF, département Cartes et plans: http://catalogue.bnf.fr/ark:/12148/cb33281721x, pp.2, 122.
98   Donald Monro, *An account of the diseases which were most frequent in the British military hospitals in Germany, from January 1761 to the return of the troops ...*(London: A Millar et al., 1764), p.345.

and hospitals cannot be watertight: the Siege of Philippsburg (26 May-18 July) was followed by long marches up and down the Rhine, dispersal into winter quarters and mass hospitalization.

Chapter 4 analyses that most challenging operations of all in terms of sickness, the march through hostile territory. It was not considered discreditable for an army to abandon its sick if forced to retreat but the consequences for the wretches left behind were often dire. In May 1706 the Comte de Tessé abandoned his siege of Barcelona so suddenly that he left behind some 5,000 sick and wounded men from his army of 15,000. To his credit, the English commander the Earl of Peterborough took responsibility for the patients and saved them from having their throats cut by his *miquelet* (partisan) allies. Tessé was not culpably negligent or hard-hearted, and it was commonplace to abandon those too weak to walk, because there were never enough carts and draught animals to carry them.[99] The walking sick might set off, but be hard-pressed to keep up with an army in precipitate retreat. On the other hand, if the army was advancing across friendly territory then all might be well. For example, in March 1734 a 21,000-strong Spanish army set out on a long, though unopposed, march from Livorno south through Tuscany and the Papal States towards Naples. During that time the army left a 'large number' of sick on each day's march (in all 4,000 men) all the way from Livorno – the port of disembarkation – through Tuscany, to the Papal States and Naples.[100] Arrangements for hospital treatment were made with convents, fraternities and individual contractors and 'very few' of the sick died, boasted a Spanish official. Indeed at the time he made this boast on 24 May, 1,300 recovered soldiers had re-joined the ranks and as many again were expected to arrive in a few days.[101]

The first case study in Chapter 4 was a victory of sorts in that a Russian army penetrated and ravaged the Tartar stronghold of Crimea in 1736. The cost was high, excessively so, not least because of the huge distances involved: the approach march to Or Kapi or Perekop (the fortress guarding the neck of the Crimea) from the Dnieper army's base was all of 252 miles long. The second is that of a 326-mile-long counter-clockwise circuit in 1737 by Imperials from Belgrade to Niš, Radujevac, Orşova and, finally, to winter quarters in Timisoara. That year's campaign was a setback for Vienna, the latter part of the gruelling march was a retreat, and the whole war was a disaster in which the Habsburgs ended up ceding Belgrade and Serbia back to the Ottomans. The final case study serves as another reminder that the contexts often overlap, whether camp, siege or, march. By December 1742 a French army had been besieged in Prague for nine months, provisions were running low and the sick roll lengthening. At nightfall on 16 December the Duc de Belle-Isle,

99   Philippe-Henri de Grimoard (ed.) René de Froulay de Tessé, *Mémoires et lettres du maréchal de Tessé* (Paris: Treuttel and Würtz, 1806), Vol.II, pp.220, 222, 225; Fraciades Fleurus Duvivier, *Observations Sur la Guerre de la Succession* (Paris: J. Corréard jeune, 1830), Vol.I, p.346; E. Gruber Von Arni, *Hospital Care And the British Standing Army, 1660–1714* (Aldershot and Burlington, VT: Ashgate, 2006), p.162.

100   Pietro Colletta (trans. S. Horner), *History of the kingdom of Naples, 1734-1825* (Edinburgh & London: Constable & Hamilton, 1858), Vol.I, pp.30, 35.

101   Cristina Borreguero Beltrán, 'The Spanish Army in Italy, 1734', *War in History* (October 1998), 5, p.414.

French commander, quietly slipped a column of 14,000 men out of the city in the biting cold. He made for Eger (Cheb), one hundred miles to the west, all the while harassed by enemy hussars. He had to leave 6,000 sick and convalescent men behind and lost more along the way though sickness and frostbite.

Chapter 5 will evaluate hospitals. If disease arose from miasma or diet, many physicians nonetheless accepted that it could spread by proximity or contagion and would have had the sick put in a separate tent well away from their healthy comrades.[102] The field hospital and the base hospital, far to the rear marked a further step in isolating the patient. By 1708 Louis XIV maintained fifty such base hospitals: most of them on his north-eastern *pré-carré*. Pre-modern hospitals provided food, shelter and a chance to convalesce from accident and to be relieved of routine complaints likely to respond to rest and treatment. Alternatively, hospitals might be like pest-houses, serving to isolate the infectious sick, keeping them clean, dry, warm, and out of sight while acting as 'gateways to death' or even breeding iatrogenic disease or (in layperson's language) hospital infections.[103] It is generally accepted that a new type of hospital emerging from the 1790s facilitated 'more systematic responses' to new diseases as attending physicians benefitted from opportunities for repeated observations of symptoms and trials of cures.[104] However, practices like experimentation and statistical evaluation which are generally linked with this medical modernity were the products of 'long term evolution' in which medicine was 'transformed' well before the French Revolution. Military medicine was very much part of that change.[105]

The chapters on camps, sieges and marches will necessarily discuss hospitals in passing but Chapter 5 will focus on four relevant and richly documented examples. The first concerns the base hospital at Perpignan in 1674 following the outbreak of a camp epidemic discussed in Chapter 1. The second concerns the base hospital of Cremona and its satellites which accommodated the thousands of French soldiers who sickened in Piedmont during the winter of 1734-35. The third case study evaluates the British medical response to diseases, including the 'flux' and 'hospital fever' that broke out after the Battle of Dettingen (27 June 1743) in Bavaria. Surviving records present a multi-layered picture of the main hospital at Feckenheim, near Hanau, of a 'flying hospital' near Wied, and of a regimental hospital. The final example concerns the British expedition to central Portugal in 1762 in which the troops suffered heavily from disease, but sustained only a handful of casualties in action. The sick returns and medical correspondence relating to this expedition were preserved in the papers of John Campbell, 4th Earl of Loudon, the commander-in-chief, and provide an exceptionally complete account of a base hospital at Lisbon,

---

102   Roger French, *Medicine before Science: The Business of Medicine from the Middle Ages to the Enlightenment* (Cambridge: Cambridge University Press, 2003), p.163.

103   Roy Porter, *Blood and Guts: A Short History of Medicine* (London: Penguin Books, 2003), pp.136-139; Lindelman, *Medicine and Society*, p.160.

104   William H. McNeill, *Plagues and Peoples* (London: Penguin, 1979), p.219.

105   Lindelman, *Medicine and Society* p.163; Geoffrey L. Hudson (ed.) *British Military and Naval Medicine 1600-1830* (Amsterdam: Rodopi, 2007), p.9, citing Laurence Brockliss and Colin Jones, *The Medical World of Early Modern France* (Oxford: Clarendon Press, 1997).

a general hospital at Santarem, and many 'flying' and 'temporary' hospitals in far-flung outposts such as Abrantes, Montalvão, and Portalegre.

In sum, this study will categorize, quantify and, finally, evaluate. What were the killer epidemic diseases of European armies in wartime between the 1670s and the 1760s? What strategic, tactical, and logistical constraints and conditions were likeliest to produce a severe epidemic? Can one map modern disease categories onto the symptomatic descriptions of 'flux' and 'fever' with their attendant adjectives? How many soldiers did these diseases afflict, and how many did they kill? How did authorities frame and respond to the massive public health challenge involved? Did morbidity and mortality rates improve, worsen, or stay the same, and what part did changes in camp hygiene and medical treatment play in shaping outcomes?

2

Camps

The two case studies in this chapter have been chosen because they are, for their time, well documented. The same commander, Friedrich Hermann von Schönberg, or Schomberg, commanded in both instances which were 15 years and a thousand miles apart.

Saint-Jean-Pla-de-Corts (1674)

What follows is the story of a two-month long encampment by a French army on the Pyrenean frontier. This abnormally long duration must be considered a prime cause of the epidemic that ravaged the army. To grasp why Schomberg sat so long in one place it is necessary to consider the strategic backdrop, logistical constraints, and tactical contingencies that framed his decisions. Culturally and linguistically, the inhabitants of Roussillon looked over the mountains rather than to that abstraction, the French state, into which the northern counties of Catalonia had been absorbed as recently as 1659.[1] Taking advantage of renewed war between France and Spain in 1672-78, groups of natives plotted to assist Spanish troops massing just across the border to march on Perpignan, the regional capital The conspiracy was thwarted but it stoked the suspicions of Schomberg, French military governor in the aftermath of the plot, that locals were 'very disaffected' and that he was in an 'enemy country'.[2]

Rather than march on Perpignan, in May 1674 the Duke of San Germán, viceroy of Catalonia, lay siege to Fort Bellegarde which sat on a precipitous slope over the Coll del Portell/Le Perthus, a mountain pass about twenty miles inland from the Mediterranean coast.[3] Schomberg arrived on 21 May, having called up militia bands from Roussillon, Languedoc, and further afield to supplement his small army of regulars. However, he still had only 9,000 men to San Germán's 12,000 when Fort

1   David Stewart, *Assimilation and Acculturation in Seventeenth-century Europe: Roussillon and France, 1659-1715* (Westport Conn: Greenwood Press, 1997), pp.105-106.

2   Alice Martet, 'Les Conspirations de 1674 en Roussillon: Villefranche et Perpignan' in *Annales du Midi: revue archéologique, historique et philologique de la France méridionale,* 86:118 (1974), p.275.

3   Gatien de Courtilz de Sandras, *Histoire de la guerre de Hollande* (The Hague: H van Bulderen, 1689), Vol.I, p.77; Antonio Espino Lopez, *Las Guerras de Cataluña* (Madrid: EDAF, 2014), pp.84-86,241.

2.1 Roussillon. Key: 1: Perpignan. 2: Maureillas. 3: Céret 4: Elne. 5: Saint-Jean-Pla-de-Corts. 6: Le Boulou. 7: Fort Bellegarde. Source: Charles Inselin, 'Le Roussillon: Le comté de Roussillon', (Paris: Mr de Beaurin, 1710-1746) *BNF* GE DD-2987 (660).

Bellegarde capitulated, sooner than expected, on 1 June.[4] Keeping up the momentum, San Germán next descended as far as Maureillas-Las-Illas, and envisaged bringing his main body west to follow the River Tech upstream and take, in turn, Céret and Fort-Les-Bains. This would have given the Spanish control over a second Pyrenean pass. It was a bold scheme and had San Germán succeeded it would have gone hard on the French to prise him out of the Tech valley.[5]

Meanwhile Schomberg waited until 20 June until his army was stronger before marching up the Tech Valley.[6] He reviewed his army at Elne and counted about 17,000 men: 3,000 cavalrymen, 9,000 regular infantry and 5,000 militiamen.[7] The

---

4   M. Jacques Freixe, 'Le Passage de Perthus' in *Société Agricole Scientifique & Litteraire des Pyrénées-Orientales*, 54 (1914), p.201; Perpignan 17 June 1674, *Gazette De Lyon* (Lyon, July 1674), p.347.

5   Lopez, *Las Guerras de Cataluña*, pp.84-86, 241.

6   Pierre Vidal, *Histoire de Perpignan: des origines au XIXe siècle* (Perpignan: Barré et Dayez, 1988), p.243.

7   D. M. J. Henry, *Histoire de Roussillon comprenant l'histoire du Royaume de Majorque* (Paris: Imp. Royale, 1835), Vol.II, p.471; Jacques Basnage, *Annales des Provinces-Unies* (The Hague:

latter were drawn from Roussillon and Languedoc (from districts as far afield as Usès and Montauban, some 200 kilometres away) who rendezvoused at Elne between 21 June and 5 July. More would come in dribs and drabs, an 835-strong battalion (from Vivarais, in the Cevennes, on the furthest extremity of Languedoc) on 17 July, 4,000 militiamen from the *bandes* of Navarre and Béarn in late August, and a last increment of 450 from Languedoc. A contemporary estimate citing a final cumulative strength of 11,000 militiamen sounds about right.[8] At least 23,000 men would ultimately pass through Schomberg's army, though the actual peak strength was probably nearer 17,000.[9]

Table 2.1 Schomberg's Army Strength

Regular Infantry	9,000
Militia	11,000
Cavalry	3,000
Total	23,000

A fortnight later Schomberg made a characteristically cautious bid to relieve Fort-Les-Bains but got no closer than the village of Saint-Jean-de-Pagès [Saint-Jean-Pla-de-Corts] which he reached on 5 July. Leaving Catalan militiamen and *miquelets* around Fort Les Bains, San Germán pulled back most of his little army of 5,000 regulars to the Plain of Sant Jordi where he drew them in battle array to block the gap between the Pyrenean foothills and the Tech. There followed the only pitched battle of the entire campaign.[10] The mayor of Céter revealed to Schomberg that the Spanish were about to abandon the town. Schomberg gave orders for the army to be drawn up in readiness at dawn but, in that 'hurry up and wait' phenomenon familiar to anyone who served in an army, the unfortunate soldiers were stood-to under arms from two o'clock in the morning of 27 July. Schomberg remained asleep in his tent leaving Comte Lebret, his second-in-command, harangue the troops. As dawn broke, Lebret could see mules apparently bearing loads towards Le Perthus and lest he lose the chance to fall on what he assumed to be a fleeing enemy, he sent

---

C. Le Vier, 1726), Vol.II, p.57;'Êtats', Elne 21 June to 5 July 1674, ADPO, C134; 'Tagebuch Über den feldzug in Roussillon vom jahr 1674' in J.F.A. Kazner, *Leben Friederichs von Schomberg, oder Schoenburg* (Mannheim: Schwan & Götz, 1789), pp.87-90. A muster of 29 May returned 2,365 cavalry and dragoons.

8   'Comptes', (1674) ADPO, C134; Melchior Vogüé, Une famille vivaroise, histoires d'autrefois racontées à ses enfants, par le Mis de Vogüé,... (Paris: H. Champion, 1912) I, pp.316-317; Carlier to Louvois, Perpignan, 26 May 1674, SHD A¹ 415, no. 47, Du Pillo to Louvois, Perpignan 26 May 1674, SHD A¹ 415, no. 46; Schomberg to Louvois, Camp at Saint-Jean de Pages, 1 July 1674, SHD A¹ 415, no. 64; Carlier to Louvois, Camp at Saint-Jean de Pages, c. 26 July June 1674, SHD A¹ 415, no. 73; Schomberg to Louvois, Camp at Saint-Jean de Pages, 30 August 1674, SHD A¹ 415, no.92; Sauvé de Caissel, *Relation de Ce Qui s'Est Passé En Catalogne* (Paris: G. Quinet, 1678), p.63; Mège, Alexandre du, (ed.), De Vic, Claude and Vaisette, Joseph, *Histoire générale de Languedoc...*(Toulouse: J.B.Paya, 1846) Vol.X, p.190.

9   Freixe 'Le Passage de Perthus' p.201.

10 Freixe 'Le Passage de Perthus' p.208

two regiments of cavalry across the Tech. They passed through one defile, only to be shot down by musketeers lying in ambush in ravines and sunken roads. Charles Comte de Schomberg, the general's eldest son, brought foot soldiers to help the cavalry break off and pull back, but the militiamen and some regulars fled in 'panic fear'.[11] San Germán then pursued the French back to their camp where the older Schomberg, roused by the sound of musket fire, drew up a cavalry reserve along the northern bank of the Tech. His reserve left a gap for their fleeing comrades to pass through and held the line.[12] Schomberg lost 1,000 men killed and 300 taken prisoner, according to a Spanish source; the prisoners included the commander of the cavalry and also Comte Charles.[13] The French admitted to losing 500 men and official propaganda brazenly asserted that Schomberg had won at San Jordi and driven Saint German from Roussillon.[14] Privately, French sources admitted the reverse, but publicly they took their lead from Schomberg in blaming Lebret's impetuosity and crediting Schomberg's *sang-froid* with salvaging a reverse from a rout.[15]

Quite apart from revealing Schomberg's skill in deflecting blame, the encounter at San Jordi would define the rest of the campaigning season by immobilizing both sides in a stand-off. Giving up hopes of taking Fort-Les-Bains, San Germán built a fort upstream overlooking the bridge near Céret in order to stop Schomberg from attempting to ford the Tech. He also built fortified lines along the crest of the heights that loomed in an arc to the south of the Tech over Saint-Jean, while his outposts reached the banks of the river.

The chateau and the church of Saint-Jean both sat atop a tongue of high ground that stretched from the foothills to the north as far as the Tech. Both buildings doubtless sheltered the forward out-guards of Schomberg's camp and, to be sure, they needed the cover because they lay within 'musket shot' (by convention 120 *toises* or over 200 metres) of the Spanish sentinels and came off worst in exchanges of fire with the longer-range Spanish muskets.[16] The main body of the French, for want of tents, threw up huts of straw and brushwood among the olive groves on the hill to the north of Saint-Jean.[17] The plan of a battalion camp in Orrery's 1677 *Art of War* depicts a typical camp layout.

11   *Le Mercure* (Amsterdam, 1677,) p.347; Léon Lecestre (ed.), *Mémoires de Saint-Hilaire* (Paris: la Société de l'histoire de France 1903-16) Vol.I, p.162.

12   Basnage, *Annales,* p.547.

13   Freixe 'Le Passage de Perthus', p.203.

14   *Gazette De Lyon* (Lyon, July 1674) p.350.

15   Schomberg to Louvois, Camp at Saint-Jean de Pages, 27 June 1674, SHD A¹ 415, no. 60; Camille Rousset, *Histoire de Louvois* (Paris: Didier, 1864), Vol.II, p.112; Schomberg to Louvois, Camp at Saint-Jean de Pages, 27 June 1674, SHD A¹ 415, no. 60.

16   Jean Boisseau, *Nouvelle Description du comté de Roussillon, ensemble d'une partie des monts Pyrénées ou confinent la France et l'Espagne* (1639) Bibliothèque nationale de France, GED-2910; Roussel, Claude, La Principauté de Catalogne et le Comté de Roussillon (1697) in *BNF* GE DD-2987 http://catalogue.bnf.fr/ark:/12148/cb411139544; Nicholas de Fer, Le Roussillon (1706) *BNF* CPL GE DD-2987 (659), http://catalogue.bnf.fr/ark:/12148/cb40583889h Carte militaire de la Province du Roussillon (1758) *BNF* MS-6441 (214) http://catalogue.bnf.fr/ark:/12148/cb42059122j.

17   Freixe, 'Le Passage de Perthus' pp.205, 207; De Caissel, *Relation*, p.41.

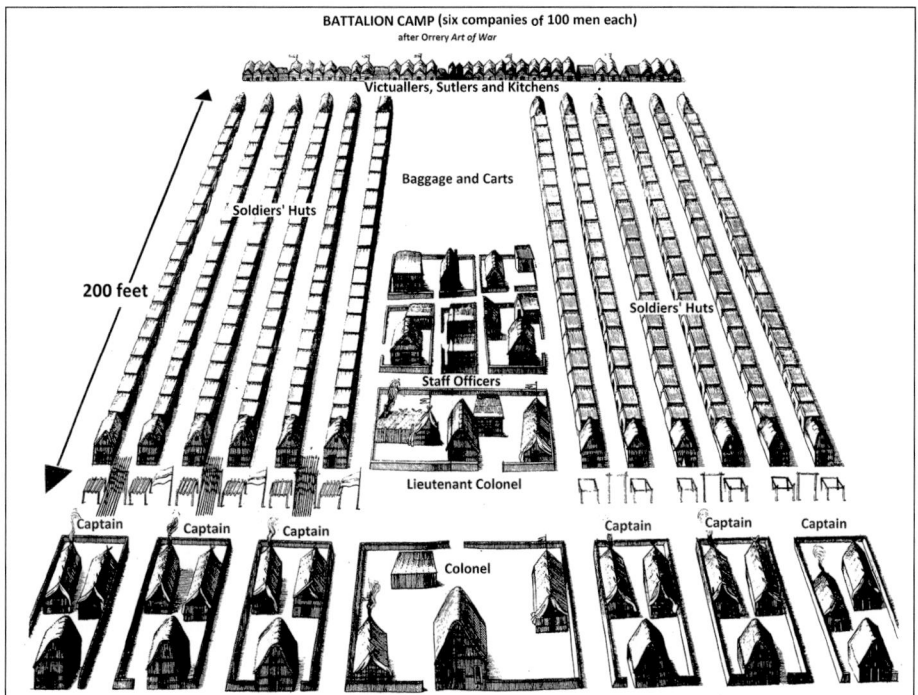

2.2 Plan of a Battalion Camp after Orrery, *Art of War*.

Senior officers enjoyed reasonably spacious quarters while the private soldiers were crammed by twos or threes into little bothies aligned with the hut of their respective captains.[18] The battalion's footprint was 100 yards wide and 80 deep, which gave just over one square yard of space for each of the 600 men. Encampments as a whole presented a decidedly linear, aspect since the battalions were aligned one beside the other. A detail from a plan of Schomberg's 1675 camp shows the first and second camp lines and illustrates the overall linearity.[19] The prescribed 500 paces between these lines had to be left uncluttered for manoeuvre and so did not form part of the battalion's living space.[20]

After San Jordi, Schomberg was warned by Secretary of State for War the Marquis of Louvois to take no risks [*faire le moins mal que vous pourrez*] and just hold his ground with the apparent intention of blocking San Germán from further advance, denying foraging ground to his cavalry and eventually forcing him back over the

---

18 Roger Boyle Earl of Orrery, *A treatise of the art of war* (London: Henry Herringman, 1677), p.90.
19 'Plan de Bataille autour de Maureillas en 1674' *BNF* Gallica. Notwithstanding the title, the map depicts the 1675 campaign.
20 Louis de Gaya, *L'Art de la Guerre* (The Hague: Adrian Moetjens,1689), pp.57-60.

Pyrenees.[21] In addition to holding the bridge upstream the Spanish held the bridge at Le Boulou, two kilometres downstream of Schomberg, while the latter posted sentinels in a fort near Le Boulou covering the high road along which the French resupply convoys passed from Perpignan.[22]

Despite these precautions, Schomberg was not able to completely interdict raids and forages; for example, on 30 July, near Perpignan, a troop of Spanish cavaliers swooped on a train of 150 mules laden with munitions and provisions.[23] He could, however, hold San Germán's main army in place so long as he remained and posed a potential threat to the 'Linea de Tech' as, for instance, on 11 July when he paraded his whole army in the open facing the fortified lines. Spanish artillery rained case shot down on Schomberg's unfortunate troops and 'made him pay dearly for his vain demonstration'.[24]

In *Kabinettskriege* one seldom witnesses a purposeful Clausewitzian strategy to destroy the enemy army and conquer his core territory. Regimes usually fought not to destroy each other but for limited territorial gains, so it was safest to 'occupy, entrench, and wait'.[25] A general who could keep his army in being and subsist off enemy territory was reckoned successful. Schomberg failed on both counts. He was immobilized on the French side of the Pyrenees by an army half the size of his own for two whole months, which was a perilously long time to linger at any one camp site.[26] On 8 September he finally decamped and pulled back to somewhere between Saint-Jean and Elne, where he encamped for another twenty days, before retreating to Elne. Schomberg's abrupt departure was forced on him in the main because his army was melting away at Saint-Jean. By 20 September, twelve days after retreating from Saint-Jean, he had slightly less than 5,000 men left who were fit to serve: 2,400 lay in hospital, and another 600 or so were sick in camp. In other words, only 8,000 men were left and 15,000, or 65 percent of the total strength, had disappeared in just two months.[27]

21   Louvois to Schomberg. Versailles 16 July 1674 in Henri Griffet, (ed.), *Recueil de lettres, pour servir d'éclaircissement à l'histoire militaire du regne de Louis XIV* (Paris: Antoine Boudet, 1760), Vol.II, p.441; Schomberg to Louvois, Camp at Saint-Jean de Pages, 27 June 1674, SHD A¹ 415, no. 60; Schomberg to Louvois, Camp at Saint-Jean de Pages, 1 July 1674, SHD A¹ 415, no. 64.

22   M. La Cainte, 'The Science of Military Posts' in *The Monthly Review Or Literary Journal Enlarged* (London, 1762), pp.21-21; Sandras, *Histoire de la guerre de Hollande*, p.187.

23   Freixe, 'Le Passage de Perthus', p.206.

24   Freixe, 'Le Passage de Perthus', pp.206-207; Feliu de la Peña y Farrel, *Annales de Cataluña* (Barcelona: Jayme Sur, 1709), Vol.III, pp.363-365; De Caissel, *Relation*, pp.44, 61.

25   Sebastian Le Prestre de Vauban (ed. George Rothrock), *A Manual of Siegecraft and Fortification* (Ann Arbor: The University of Michigan Press, 1968), p.3; Lynn, *The Wars of Louis XIV*, pp.362-363.

26   Kazner, *Leben Friederichs von Schomberg*, pp.87-90.

27   Schomberg to Louvois, Camp at Saint-Jean de Pages, 30 August 1674, SHD A¹ 415, no.92; 'Estat', Lexe, 20 September 1674; *ADPO* C.134; Carlier to Louvois, Camp at Saint-Jean de Pages, 8 July 1674, SHD A¹ 415, no. 68; Carlier to Louvois, Perpignan, 10 October 1674, SHD A¹ 415, no. 109; Schomberg to Louvois, Camp at Saint-Jean de Pages, 6 September 1674, SHD A¹ 415, no. 95; Schomberg to Louvois, Camp near Elne, 30 September 1674, SHD A¹ 415, no. 105.

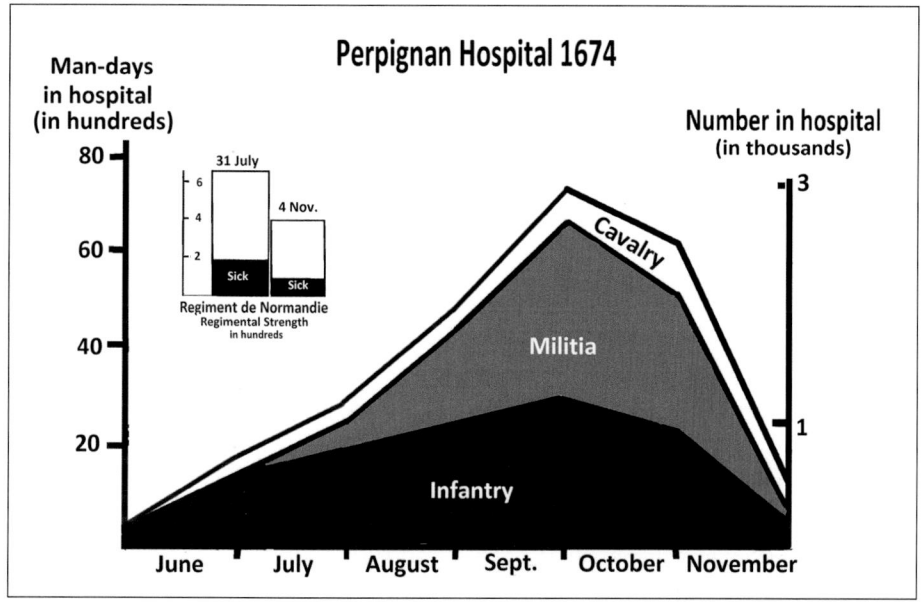

2.3 Numbers in Perpignan Hospital 1674.

In making his excuses two days before pulling back from Saint-Jean, Schomberg explained to Louvois that San Germán knew full well 'that desertion and sickness has reduced the [French] militia to almost nothing' and that the other troops were 'greatly diminished' by sickness.[28] Schomberg made no mention of losses in action, but he lost at least 1,000 men at San Jordi and in ambuscades laid by the *miquelet* leader Josep de La Trinxeria.[29] In fact San Germán believed Schomberg to be stronger than he actually was. Schomberg believed the same of San Germán even though the latter's little army would be worn down to 3,500 infantry effectives by October.[30] Schomberg reckoned the final death toll from sickness at 9,000 men, or 39 percent of his total cumulative strength.[31] The estimate tallies with musters taken on 31 July and 5 November respectively from which it is possible to extract before and after statistics for twelve companies of the Normandie Regiment.[32]

The strength of these twelve companies fell from 649 to 384, yielding a loss of 265 soldiers which was equivalent to 41 percent of the July strength. One can extrapolate from the 139 Normandie soldiers hospitalized on 31 July that 265 deaths through sickness would be credible, having regard to the trend of hospital admissions assuming an average stay of about three weeks, and conservatively assuming

---

28 Schomberg to Louvois, Camp at Saint-Jean de Pages, 6 September 1674, SHD A¹ 415, no. 95.
29 Alain Ayats, *Les guerres de Josep de La Trinxeria (1637-1694): la guerre du sel et les autres* (Perpignan: Trabucaire, 1997), pp.341, 343.
30 Lopez, *Las Guerras de Cataluna*, p.86.
31 Kazner, *Leben Friederichs von Schomberg*, Vol.II, nos.33 and 34; Matthew Glozier, *Marshal Schomberg, 1615-1690: 'The Ablest Soldier of His Age'* (Brighton: Sussex Academic Press, 2008), p.91.
32 'Extrats des revues pour servir au payement de la subsistence des troupes', ADPO, C220.

that only half of the patients died (although mortality was actually running at three-quarters by December).[33] However, Normandie and other regular battalions were bled by desertion (though not as badly as the militia regiments) and it seems safe to cut from 41 to 35 percent the estimate of the men of the twelve companies of Normandie who perished of sickness during those three months.[34]

The daily rations issued to the general hospital at Perpignan suggest that the militia and regular infantry fell sick and were hospitalized in rough proportion to their relative numbers, but one cannot discount anecdotal evidence that the militiamen were more liable to run away than the regulars and so the relative numbers may be unclear. By late August, if Schomberg can be believed, 'most' of the militiamen had 'run away in to the mountains'.[35] Most of these deserters would no doubt have felt justified because they had signed on for two months service and suspected (quite rightly) that they would be forced to stay in the ranks through various tricks like leaving them stranded in isolated outposts in hostile countryside or forcibly enlisting them as regulars.[36] Wastage through sickness and desertion was heavier among the *bandes* than among the regulars and in the final analysis, Schomberg's estimate that he lost about 39 percent of his men through sickness across the whole campaigning season is probably close to the mark.

While we are unusually well informed about the numbers who died of disease, details of the distemper(s) are scant. Schomberg's remark that gout was widespread among the officers betrays his tendency to dwell on trivial matters, while Intendant Étienne Carlier's observation that the *maladies* were 'frequent, violent and malignant' is unhelpfully vague.[37] Another account exaggerates the death toll: Fear caused the militiamen diarrhoea [*cours de ventre*] which quickly worsened to bloody flux. The *maladie du païs* and dysentery swept away so many that of the 11,000 who joined the army, more than 9,000 died in Roussillon'.[38] A third account, too, seems to think that only the militiamen were struck down by the *flux de sang*.[39]

No distemper was 'so common among soldiers' as dysentery but the *maladie du pays* was more mysterious.[40] The literal equivalent in English was the (and it was always the definite article) 'country disease' that was especially prevalent

---

33   The 12 weeks from the end of July to the beginning of October when hospital admissions were at their highest levels would have seen a complete turnover every three weeks, or on four occasions: so, 139 x 4= 556. Halved to accommodate a conservative estimate of 50 percent hospital mortality, this figure gives an extrapolation of 228 dead. If 265 represents 41 percent, then 228 represents 35 percent.

34   Carlier to Louvois, Camp at Saint-Jean de Pages, 7 August 1674, SHD A¹ 415, no.81.

35   Schomberg to Louvois, Camp at Saint-Jean de Pages, 19 August 1674, SHD A¹ 415, no. 88:

36   Mège, *Histoire générale de Languedoc*, p.190; Jacques Gébelin, *Histoire des milices provinciales (1688–1791)* (Paris: Hachette, 1882), p.25.

37   Schomberg to Louvois, Camp at Saint-Jean de Pages, 19 July 1674, SHD A¹ 415, no. 70; Carlier to Louvois, Camp at Saint-Jean de Pages, 8 July 1674, SHD A¹ 415, no. 68.

38   De Caissel, *Relation*, p.63.

39   Lecestre, *Mémoires de Saint-Hilaire*, p.163.

40   Melchior Landersdorfer, 'Das Schicksal der bayerischen Soldaten im Türkenkrieg: Krankheiten, Hunger, Marsch- und Gefechtsverluste, Militärsanitätswesen' (Munich: München, Techn. Univ., Diss., 1984), p.43; Johann Storchens, *Theoretisch und practische Abhandlung von ... Kranckheiten* (Nuremberg: M.G. Grießbach, 1735), p.203.

in a particular country, having been generated by the 'vicious constitution' of that region.[41] This might be 'consumption' in England or *'Fluxes of the Belly'* in Ireland as when Oliver Cromwell reported from Ireland in 1650 of a colonel 'lately dead of the Country-Disease'.[42] The term was sometimes used in that sense in French but far more often *maladie du pays* denoted acute homesickness and depression of the kind that afflicted raw recruits serving in an unfamiliar environment.[43] The malady began as a 'moral' or psychological affliction when the recruit 'lost sight of his church tower and of his relatives', though the further he marched from home the more it was conceived to be a physical illness brought on by change of air. Accustomed to a world in which he knew and was known to everyone, a rural soldier was forced to make the abrupt transition to military life.[44] This rupture could cause profound mental distress and manifest itself physically through a pathological homesickness, referred to by contemporaries as *mal du pays* or *nostalgie*.[45] The latter was first described in 1688 by Johannes Hofer who noted that the malaise mainly afflicted young countrymen who had been forcibly enlisted.[46] The militiamen at Saint-Jean fit all three categories. Most young men secured exemptions, many fraudulent, from the lottery and so the *miliciable* were those poorest, least well connected, and altogether most dispensable. So when the commune of Saint-Sulpice-de-la-Pointe (some 20 kilometres north-west of Toulouse) produced its assigned quote of seven soldiers for the Bataillon d'Albi these youths had been forcibly enlisted.[47] Moreover the militiamen were 'very young' and, complained Schomberg, left barefoot and in rags by their captains.[48]

Prevalence, incidence and mortality can help identify the killer disease(s). On 12 August Schomberg belatedly admitted that he had a 'good many' sick to be sent to

41   Francis Glisson, *A treatise of the rickets being a disease common to children* (London: P. Cole, 1651), p.172.

42   Robert Boyle, *An experimental discourse of some little observed causes of the insalubrity and salubrity of the air and its effects* (London: Sam. Smith, 1685), pp,19-20; Thomas Carlyle, *Oliver Cromwell's Letters and Speeches: With Elucidations* (London: Chapman and Hall, 1846), Vol.II, p.90.

43   Antoine Francois Prevost d'Exile, *Histoire generale des voyages* (The Hague: Pierre de Hondt, 1753), Vol.XI, p.69; Pierre Favier, *Quaestio medica proposita ... seu anxio patriam petendi desiderio vulgo maladie du pays* (Avignon: F. Mallard, 1713).

44   Jean Colombier, *Préceptes sur la santé des gens de guerre, ou Hygiène militaire*, (Paris: Lacombe, 1775), pp.146-147.

45   M.S. Anderson, *War and Society in Europe of the Old Regime: 1618-1789* (Leicester: Leicester University Press, 1988), p.123; Childs, *Armies and Warfare in Europe*, p.73.

46   George Rosen, 'Nostalgia: a 'Forgotten' Psychological Disorder', *Psychological Medicine*, 5:4 (Nov, 1975), p.44; Jean Chagniot, *Guerre et Société à L'Époque Moderne* (Paris: Presses Universitaires de France, 2001), p.142; Michèle Battesti, 'Nostalgia in the Army: 17th-19th Centuries', *Frontiers of Neurology and Neuroscience*, 38 (April, 2016), p.26; Lisa O'Sullivan, 'The Time and Place of Nostalgia: Re-situating a French Disease', *Journal of the History of Medicine and Allied Sciences*, 67:4 (October, 2012), p.628.

47   Pascal Roux, 'Le recrutement de la milice royale au XVIIIe siècle: l'exemple du bataillon d'Albi (1740-1771)' in *Annales du Midi, 108: 216* (1996), pp.464-469, 478; Edmond Cabié, *Notices communales, Saint-Sulpice-de-la-Pointe* (Toulouse: A. Chauvin, 1876), p12.

48   Schomberg to Louvois, Camp at Saint-Jean de Pages, 12 July 1674, SHD A¹ 415, no. 69.

Carlier's hospital at Perpignan.[49] By then 1,200 soldiers were hospitalized, mostly for sickness, though they must have included some wounded after San Jordi. Medieval Perpignan, capital of the Kingdom of Majorca, was endowed with imposing convents and churches, one of which was the large Franciscan convent complex of monastic buildings enclosing two cloisters.[50] The hospitalized soldiers occupied one of these many buildings. Seven weeks later, on 22 September, the number of hospitalized sick reached 2,000, 2,400 a week later, and 3,000 (or over 37 percent of the whole strength) after Schomberg broke camp and disgorged the sick from the camp into the base hospital.[51] The very rapid acceleration in late September followed by a precipitous fall due to cooler weather in October is characteristic of dysentery, or, taking camp disease as a continuum, stage one rather than stages two (typhoid) or three (typhus).

However, the fall-off in the numbers of sick is exaggerated by the fact that in or about October patients began to be transferred to smaller hospitals closer to home with hundreds transferred to the Hospital of St. Paul in Narbonne to take just one example.[52] Moreover, evidence of civilian deaths in Perpigan indicates that the crisis lasted through November and into December. Garrison towns were likely to be hit by diseases carried by soldiers quartered or – worse – hospitalized in their midst because the 'hospital infected the air of the said town'.[53] The number of deaths in Notre-Dame-de-la-Réal parish (the eponymous church lay only 500 metres from the hospital) ran between two and three times greater between March and December 1674 than for the average of the two years before and after.[54]

Table 2.2 Burials Notre-Dame-de-la-Réal parish

	Mar	Apr	May	Jun	Jul	Aug	Sept	Oct	Nov	Dec
1674	5	17	21	10	25	33	26	33	28	12
1672-3 & 1675-6	6	3.5	5.25	5	9	10	12.5	13.5	10.5	8.25

Finally, the sheer lethality of this disease points to typhoid rather than dysentery. Dysentery was the 'deadliest and most common' of the major epidemic diseases

49   Schomberg to Louvois, Camp at Saint-Jean de Pages, 12 August 1674, SHD A¹ 415, no. 84: Carlier to Louvois, 26 May 1674, SHD A¹ 415, no. 47; Carlier to Louvois, Perpignan 23 June 1674, SHD A¹ 415, no. 58.

50   Agnès Bergeret, et al., 'Le couvent des Franciscains de Perpignan: données historiques et archéologiques' in Catafau Aymat et al. (eds.), *Un palais dans la ville: Perpignan des rois de Majorque* (Canet: Éditions Trabucaire, 2014), pp.305-6.

51   Alain Ayats, 'Armees et Santé en Roussillon' in Jean-Marcel Goger and Nicolas Marty, *Cadre de vie, équipement, santé dans les Sociétés Méditerranéennes* (Perpignan: Presses Universitaires de Perpignan, 2005), pp.128-129.

52   A grant of 1,200 *livres* was awarded on 16 January 1675 to cover the 'bons soins' given to sick and wounded soldiers from Roussillon in 1674. Hippolyte Faure, *Hospices de Narbonne. Classement des archives antérieures à l'année 1790 ...* (Narbonne: Collard, 1855), p.56.

53   Ayats, 'Armées et Santé', p.130.

54   APDO, Registres de sépulture, paroisse Notre-Dame-de-la-Réal Perpignan (1659-1680) 9NUM112EDT1040_1041, ff 15-17, 20-25, 27-33, 38-40, 45-8.

bringing as heavy cumulative toll but it was nowhere as deadly as typhoid in any single epidemic.[55] In the case of the Normandie Regiment sickness point prevalence on 31 July (26 percent) and on 4 November (14 percent) straddles the three months of greatest incidence and, as discussed, up to 40 percent of the mustered men perished of sickness. This scale of mortality seems rather too high to attribute to dysentery alone, when one considers a somewhat analogous situation.

The culmination of the 1693 French campaign in Catalonia came when the Duc de Noailles captured (30 May-10 June) the coastal town of Rosas.[56] He set up camp afterwards at nearby San Pedro Pescador, apparently planning to press on to Gerona, but he was forced to call off operations because of epidemic dysentery. The chief physician dosed his dysenteric patients with Ipecacuanha, a root crop native to the Brazilian forests, which was valued by natives as a remedy for dysentery. This new treatment did not work (Ipecacuanha is best used in syrup form as a potent and effective emetic) and the physician fell back on a concoction of milk and *ferments* of wine which supposedly cured 'almost all' the sick.[57] It did nothing of the sort. Noailles decamped two months later, on 10 August, and re-crossed the Pyrenees to rest near Le Boulou at which point it becomes possible to quantify the death rate among two components of his army.

A company of Scottish Jacobite *emigrés* counted 96 men at the beginning of the Siege of Rosas, on 20 May 1693. Ten were killed or fatally wounded in the trenches but 'many' more fell sick every day from 'muddy' water and an outlandish diet of 'sardines, horse beans and garlic'. On the short march to encamp at San Pedro Pescador the weaker troops fell behind because of the 'extraordinary heat' and 'want of water'. When the Scots eventually returned to Roussillon they looked like 'shadows and skeletons' nineteen of them, or about a fifth of the whole strength, died of sickness in the hospitals that awaited them there.[58] A recently formed regiment of Irish Jacobites which was encamped beside the Scots also likely lost one fifth of its strength.[59] In other words, the death of one fifth of the troops is about the worst one might expect from a dysentery epidemic so, the loss of two-fifths at Saint-Jean points to an outbreak of typhoid as well as dysentery.

Can the Saint-Jean epidemic be identified as dysentery, or as dysentery accompanied (or followed by) typhoid? The evidence is inconclusive and the answer elusive. This uncertainty need not inhibit our search for a cause or causes because the cause may be one and the same for dysentery and typhoid. A 'cause' is 'something that makes a difference in the outcome while all else is held constant'. In real life it is impossible to hold all else constant and one seldom encounters a 'sufficient' cause

55   François Lebrun, 'Les crises démographiques en France aux XVIIe et XVIIIe siècles' in *Annales. Économies, Sociétés, Civilisations* 35:2, (1980), p.210.

56   *Mercure Galant* (July, 1693), pp.155-161.

57   Bernard Le Bovier de Fontenelle, *Œuvres* (Paris: Chez Brunet, 1752), Vol.VI, pp.524-545.

58   Anon. 'Memoirs of the Lord Viscount Dundee' in *Miscellanea Scotica* (Glasgow: R. Chapman, 1820), Vol.III, pp.76-85.

59   Duc de Noailles to Barbézieux, Pescador Camp, 2 July 1693, SHD A¹ 1237, no. 48.

that will inevitably produce disease but rather 'component' causes that, while necessary, will not produce disease on their own.[60]

Speculation as to the causes of the epidemic at Saint-Jean ran to sudden changes of the sort discussed in Chapter 1, namely in diet (unripe grapes were blamed), air and the 'passions'. Étienne Carlier, *Intendant de l'Armée* charged with provisions, complained to war minister Louvois that food was 'extraordinarily dear' at the camp because the convoys were being attacked on land and sea while barks from Narbonne and Marseilles carrying grain were regularly attacked by Majorcan brigantines.[61] The troops went two days without bread and yet were forbidden on pain of death to take food from the country people: Schomberg hanged a dragoon for stealing a sheep.[62] Not only was food scarce and dear, but many soldiers lacked the money to buy victuals because the captains embezzled their wages: whereas soldiers were usually supplied with a ration of bread deducted from their pay, they had to buy other provisions like meat, cheese and wine out of their own pockets. At the very end of the campaigning season Schomberg was still bemoaning the frauds [*chicanes*] perpetrated on the soldiers in camp.[63] Only De Caissel claimed that provisions were abundant:[64]

> Want which [usually] brings sickness to an army was certainly not a problem for us. Everyone had money, especially the militiamen who had been paid a bounty of five pistols to enlist. Moreover, there were plenty of foodstuffs all around [and] wine sold for six sols *le pot de camp* and 9 sols for a pound of meat of 36 ounces.

De Caissel's claim of abundance is undermined by the inflated prices he quotes. A musketeer's basic pay of five sols a day would not buy the *pot* (about 1½ litres) of wine that was one component of the soldier's notional daily ration, together with meat and bread.[65] Belief in the link between diet and dysentery was strong in the late 17th century. Johann Dietz, a surgeon's mate, recalled falling sick of dysentery at the Siege of Buda (1686)

> But now I lay in my tent expecting my end. I was very feeble and exhausted; and quite forsaken, having no one who would fetch me a drink of water, so I had to pay dearly for service. By chance a musketeer was passing by who had a wooden skewer of pickled gherkins. I called out to him: 'Friend,

---

60   Penny Webb and Chris Bain, *Essential Epidemiology: An Introduction for Students and Health Professionals* (Cambridge: Cambridge University Press, 2016), pp.202-203.

61   Ayats, 'Armees et Santé en Roussillon', p.127.

62   Anon. *La Conduite de Mars* (Rouen: unknown publisher, 1711), p.90.

63   Schomberg to Louvois, Camp at Saint-Jean de Pages, 12 July 1674, SHD A¹ 415, no. 69; Schomberg to Louvois, Camp near Elne, 30 September 1674, SHD A¹ 415, no. 105.

64   De Caissel, *Relation*, p.61.

65   John A. Lynn, *Giant of the Grand Siècle: The French Army, 1610-1715* (Cambridge: Cambridge University Press, 1997), p.149; Denis Diderot, et al. *Encyclopédie, ou Dictionnaire raisonné des science, des arts et des métiers* (Berne and Lausanne: Société typographique, 1780), Vol.XXVIII, p.385.

give me some too; I'll pay for them! 'But he would not, saying: 'If you want anything send to the Imperial camp on the Danube.'

Dietz crawled out of bed, bought a hat-full of gherkins and struggled back to his tent:

> There was one of my comrades, who asked me where I had been, for he had not thought to see me back again. I told him what had happened. 'Well,' he said, 'that is the last nail in your coffin; so prepare yourself.' I lay down, begging him to cover me up. This he did, as well as he could. He was still a true friend to me; it was he who had kept me going with apples, during the march. But then I had cured his arm, which had been shot through. Well, as soon as I laid myself down I fell asleep. He thought I was dead. I slept for some six or eight hours. Then it was as though I were newly born. The pain and purging had ceased; there was no fever; in summa, I was well again.[66]

Some physicians swore by one of the four 'cold seeds' which included cucumbers and courgettes and, doubtless, the surgeon's mate had latched on to this notion.[67]

Scrimshaw, Taylor, and Gordon's 1959 landmark paper made the case that malnutrition resulted in increased susceptibility to disease, and that infection adversely affected nutritional status. Most obviously, infections impose a nutritional cost; fever, for instance, increases the metabolic and energy demands while diarrhoea causes the loss of nutrients. The interactions were characterized as synergistic with the combined effects of malnutrition and infection being worse than the sum of the individual effects of either one alone.[68] On that basis one would expect that war-related malnutrition would help spread disease rapidly through a weakened population.[69] However, this simple causal relationship may not exist and the relationship between malnutrition and increased susceptibility to disease may be relative, not absolute, and for many diseases it may not even be a major factor.[70] However, a 'direct connection' between malnutrition and dysentery can be shown and nutritional status can potentially influence the duration, severity and case fatality rates of diarrhoeal diseases, though whether a hungry person is more susceptible and likely to 'catch' the sickness in the first place, is less clear.[71]

66   Bernard Miall, (ed.) *Master Johann Dietz* (London: George Allen & Unwin, 1923), pp.64-66.
67   Thiers de Marconnay, *Nouvelles découvertes en médecine, ou Ancienne médecine développée* (The Hague: P.Gosse & J.Neulme, 1731), pp.7-8, 12-13, 24, 63, 125.
68   Charlotte G. Neumann, 'Interaction of Malnutrition and Infection: A Neglected Clinical Concept' in *Arch Intern Med.* 137:10 (1977), pp.1364-1365.
69   Quentin Outram, 'The Demographic Impact of Early Modern Warfare', in *Social Science History*, 26:2, (2002), p.246.
70   J. Walter and R. Schofield, *Famine, Disease and the Social Order in Early Modern Society*, (Cambridge: Cambridge University Press, 1997), pp.18-21.
71   Livi-Bacci Massimo, *Population and Nutrition: An Essay on European Demographic History*, (Cambridge: Cambridge University Press, 1990), p.39; Outram, 'The socio-economic relations of warfare and the military mortality crises of the Thirty Years' War', p.169.

We know that the ultimate causes of the *flux de sang* were the piles of human and animal ordure which probably lay around the camp perimeter. The received wisdom was that the miasma generated by rotting cadavers could grow so much that 'malign particles are borne into the inner parts of the body' [*vitae penetralia*].[72] Military authorities were aware of this nuisance and, for example, a 1585 English code specified that no soldier shall 'ease himself or defile the Campe or Toune of Garrison, save as in such places as is appointed for that purpose'.[73] James Turner in 1683 spoke of a 'custom' of going to a spot 'marked by a long pole and a wisp of straw at the top of it' one hundred paces outside the camp perimeter. Porzio commended the practice of digging latrines at a distance from the camp, but admitted that 'our men [he served with Habsburg armies] often ease Nature beside the very Tents of their Generals'.[74] Paintings of camp scenes from mid-century tend to support neither Turner or Porzio and will show soldiers squatting outside the perimeter fortifications.[75] The Turks dug 'great pits' as latrines, and screened them off from view echoing the advice offered in Deuteronomy 23:12-14 (King James Version): 'Thou shalt have a place also without the camp, whither thou shalt go forth abroad… when thou wilt ease thyself abroad, thou shalt dig therewith, and shalt turn back and cover that which cometh from thee.[76] In 1683 Turner asked 'whether pits may not be dig'd for souldiers to do the work of nature in'? He left the question unanswered, pleading that 'the debate of it cannot be very savoury'.[77]

The housefly would be the prime suspect as a vector in transmitting infection from filth to foodstuffs, as discussed in a later chapter. However, there is no indication that swarms of flies posed a problem at Saint-Jean though such vivid descriptions are not uncommon at other encampments. Typical is the eyewitness who describes scavenging in the abandoned Turkish camp after the Battle of the Kahlenberg (1683) and the relief of Vienna when a swarm of flies so dense that 'that the air was darkened thereof' lighted on his horse, completely blanketing the beast.[78]

Tainted water, not flies, must have been the disease vector. The Tech in summer flows sluggishly past Saint-Jean as a shallow puddle among islets of gravel and shingle.[79] Moreover, if Spanish sharpshooters made it perilous for the grooms to lead their horses to the Tech it must also have been difficult to draw potable water for thousands of men from the river.[80] The soldiers, then, must have drawn at least some

72   Ramazzini, *De morbis artificum diatriba*, p.224.
73   C.G. Cruickshank, *Elizabeth's Army* (Oxford: Oxford University Press, 1966), p.302.
74   Gregory Hanlon, *Italy 1636 Cemetery of Armies* (Oxford: Oxford University Press, 2016), p.174.
75   Pieter Snayers (c.1650) 'Belagerung von Valenza del Po 1635', Deutsches Historisches Museum Berlin DHM Inventar-Nr: Gm 94/2; Matthaus Merian (1660) 'Abbildung des Schwedischen und Pollischen Feldlager am Weixel, San, und Niger flus da die Schwedische noch ubrige Volcker Ein geschlossen gehalten worden gescheten im Martio Anno 1656'.
76   Luigi Ferdinando Marsili, *Stato militare dell' Impèrio Ottomanno, incremento e decremento* (The Hague: Pierre Gosse, 1732), pp.80-81.
77   Sir James Turner, *Pallas armata, Military essayes of the ancient Grecian, Roman, and modern art of war* (London: Richard Chiswell, 1683), p.294.
78   Landersdorfer, *Das Schicksal der bayerischen Soldaten im Türkenkrieg*, p.55.
79   Lecestre, *Mémoires de Saint-Hilaire*, p.163.
80   Freixe, 'Le Passage de Perthus', p.207.

of their drinking water from the streams that ran into the Tech, such as the Rivière de Les Aigues which would have dried up to a putrid trickle under the intense summer sun.

Furthermore, it was quite hot. Regional records indicating the date that the grape was ready for wine-making tell us that the summers from 1672 to 1675 were cool, with the average date of ventange or grape harvest noted at 2 October. But the summer of 1674 was somewhat warmer than the five-year average, as suggested by the fact that the ventange, in Montpellier, was fixed for 26 September: every ten days represents a degree of temperature (centigrade) more or less. That said, the temperature was unexceptional for the century as a whole and was certainly not freakishly high: the killer heat wave of 2003 brought the ventange all the way back to mid-August.[81] Heat and drought do not, of themselves, create a vector of transmission from latrines to food or drinking water. When excreted, the harmful organisms in faeces quickly perish as the stool dries out in conditions of high temperature, low humidity, and strong ultraviolet light. Breathing in airborne dust, even if the particles include desiccated stool, is unlikely to cause sickness. However, the intense heat inevitably precipitated the thunderstorms so characteristic of that region. On average, such storms occur five times in August and virtually all summer rainfall results from the accompanying downpours.

To explain what must have happened at Saint-Jean it is helpful to consider an analogous experience almost 180 years later and ten thousand miles away. During the gold rush in the Australian colony of Victoria, a physician noted how dysentery did not break out in the squalid diggings during the dry season: 'So long as the perfect dryness of Australia, a dryness which parches and scorches everything, lasted, the excreta of the thousands of miners, which had been deposited for the most part in the immediate vicinity of the gold workings, were perfectly harmless and innocuous'.[82] However, with the onset of rain in March 1852 the gold fields were struck with 'a clap' of epidemic dysentery. The physician, still imprisoned by miasmic paradigm, surmised that 'the factors of the dysentery poison were set to work' once the turds were moistened. Applying this insight to Saint-Jean, the stools accumulating near the camp were harmless in dry weather but must have been swept along in the run-off from torrential downpours and thereby contaminated the water supply.

This will be the least conclusive of the case studies. We do know that Schomberg was forced to retreat after a three-month logistical stalemate during which time only a handful of his troops were killed in action, one third deserted, one third perished of sickness, and one third survived. Of the last category, a third of that third lay sick.[83] This was disaster reminiscent of the Thirty Years War when, for instance,

81   Emmanuel Le Roy Ladurie, *Histoire du Climat Depuis l'An Mil* (Paris: Flammarion,1983), pp.61, 66; Emmanuel Garnier, 'Les sociétés méditerranéennes à l'épreuve du climat 1500-1850', *Sud-Ouest Européen* 32 (2011), pp.19, 21; Joseph Jean Nicolas Fuster, *Des changements dans le climat de la France: histoire de ses révolutions* (Paris: Capelle, 1845), pp.262-3, 383.

82   Stephen Curtis Candler, *A Theory of the Causation and Suggestions for the Prevention of Dysentery* (London: Henry Renshaw, 1873), p.133.

83   'Estat', Lexe, 20 September 1674 ADPO C.134; Carlier to Louvois, Camp at Saint-Jean de Pages, 8 July 1674, SHD A¹ 415, no. 68; Carlier to Louvois, Perpignan, 10 October 1674, SHD A¹ 415, no. 109; Schomberg to Louvois, Camp at Saint-Jean de Pages, 6 September 1674, SHD

two-thirds of the French army that marched to the relief of Metz in 1635 was lost through 'desertion, disease and starvation'.[84]

We can infer that the proximate cause of that disaster at Saint-Jean was drinking-water from streams befouled by run-off from animal and human waste. One must be less confident about the nosology and, specifically, whether this disease was dysentery alone, or dysentery combined with typhoid and the mysterious *maladie du pays*.

'Raw' recruits and 'seasoned' veterans: the culinary metaphors assume that the soldier who survived a campaign or two was steadier in action and much less liable to die of disease than he had been on enlisting. The farm boy whose life was spent within sight of his native village would have had relatively little acquired immunity to crowd diseases. A virulent sickness, probably dysentery, was already present in the army mustering near Perpignan in May. The existence of this epidemic even before the march to Saint-Jean is a reasonable inference from the five-fold jump in deaths among the civilian population in Perpignan, and doubtless the soldiers quartered among them. In other words, the militia recruits had no prior exposure to the strain of dysentery that drove this mortality surge. Three-quarters of those sent, unwillingly, to the general hospital died and those left in the camp continued to sicken. Carlier was probably not an embezzler but his management of the hospital was so poor that one imagines he must have envisaged it as a place of confinement rather than care, still less cure.

Dundalk 1689

Saint-Jean was an episode in the Franco-Dutch War (1672–1678), Louis XIV's second major war, and this chapter will discuss an epidemic in a peripheral theatre of the Sun King's third major war, namely the War of the Grand Alliance (1688-1697). In 1688 William of Orange, *stadholder* of the United Provinces, invaded England and drove his uncle and father-in-law James II from the throne. Thereby William secured English and Scottish naval and financial resources, when England declared war against France on 7 May 1689, in the looming war between Louis XIV's France and an eponymous Grand Alliance of just about every other state in western and central Europe. In March 1689 James, at his patron Louis XIV's insistence, landed in Ireland. James saw Ireland as a base whence to descend on Britain, once his army captured the last major enemy enclave in Derry. However, his main army failed to take Derry, and another was annihilated at Newtownbutler County Fermanagh. To cap Irish woes, Schomberg considered by many 'the ablest soldier of his age', who had left the French service in disgust at the persecution of the Huguenots, disembarked an army of reconquest at Belfast Lough on 13 August 1689.[85] By then, in a

---

A¹ 415, no. 95; Schomberg to Louvois, Camp near Elne, 30 September 1674, SHD A¹ 415, no. 105.

84   David Parrot, *Richelieu's Army: War, Government and Society in France, 1624-1642* (Cambridge: Cambridge University Press, 2001), pp.115, 534.

85   Glozier, *Marshal Schomberg*, p.vii.

decade which stood out for wet summers and very cold winters, the campaigning season would soon be drawing to a close.[86] Schomberg frittered away the next fortnight in besieging Carrickfergus Castle, even though William expected Schomberg to strike a knock-out blow to the tottering Jacobite regime: at this point James could hardly put more than 7,000 soldiers in the field.[87] Schomberg eventually set out and penetrated as far south as Dundalk County Louth by 7 September (Old Style) 1689.[88] He went no further but camped near there for the next two months.

Schomberg began with 13,000 foot (comprising 14 English, three Huguenot, and two Dutch battalions) and 1,500 horsemen consisting of his personal Huguenot cavalry regiment, three English cavalry regiments, and an English dragoon regiment.[89] At Dundalk he would be reinforced by more units from Britain, together with locally raised Protestant cavalrymen from Enniskillen and infantrymen from Derry so that he mustered nearly 18,000 men at Dundalk on 18 October, with the rest of the 22,850 regular troops left behind in Ulster garrisons.[90]

A camp was usually not occupied for such a long time. For instance, the main French army occupied 33 different camps in five months of campaigning across the southern Spanish Netherlands in 1674.[91] The reason armies lumbered onward after about four to five days in any one place was because the forage within range of the camp had been consumed. Horses ate like horses. Schomberg and his apologists advanced superficially convincing reasons why he did not press on. One reason given was that his soldiers had no bread for four days after arriving at Dundalk and had to wait until ships laden with meal anchored off camp, ovens were built, and bread baked.[92] The staple was then affordable, at less than a half-day's pay for a two-day bread ration.[93]

86 Jan de Vries, *The Economy of Europe in an Age of Crisis, 1600-1750* (Cambridge: Cambridge University Press, 1988), p.12.

87 John.G. Simms, 'Schomberg at Dundalk, 1689', *Irish Sword*, 10:38 (1971), p.15.

88 Kazner, *Friedrichs von Schonburg*, p.301.

89 Simms, 'Schomberg at Dundalk', p.16.

90 Charles Dalton (ed.), *English Army Lists and Commission Registers 1661-1714* (London: Eyre & Spottiswodde, 1896), Vol.III, pp.ix, 106-23; *CSPD: William III February 1689-April 1690* (London: H.M. Stationery Office, 1895), p.273; Eric Gruber Von Arni, *Hospital Care and the British Standing Army, 1660-1714* (Aldershot: Ashgate, 2006), p.63; Robert Parker, *Memoirs of the most Remarkable Military Transactions* (London: S. Austen, 1747), p.2; George Story, *A True and Impartial History of the Most Material Occurrences in the Kingdom of Ireland* (London: Richard Chiswell, 1691), p.41; John Childs, *The Williamite Wars in Ireland 1688-91* (London: Hambledon Continuum, 2007), pp.134, 148, 195; Harman Murtagh, 'The Organization of King William's Army in Ireland, 1689-91' *The Irish Sword*, 70 (Winter, 1990), pp.69-71, 77-79.

91 Cartes des Marches & Campemens de l'Armée du Roy pendant la Campagne 1674 (1680) BNF, onale http://catalogue.bnf.fr/ark:/12148/cb33281721x, pp.2, 122.

92 Story, *Impartial History*, p.18; *CSPD: William III February 1689 April 1690*, pp.257, 278.

93 *CSPD William III February 1689 April 1690*, p.257. Bread cost 3d. per lb. where the standard daily ration was one and a half pounds John A. Lynn, 'Food, Funds and Fortresses: Resource Mobilization and Positional Warfare in the Campaigns of Louis XIV' in *ibid*, (ed.), *Feeding Mars: Logistics in Western Warfare from the Middle Ages to the Present* (Boulder, Colorado: Westview Press, 1993), p.140.

Some of his colonels found it 'incomprehensible' that he did not press on against the 'tattered, cowardly, beaten Irish army' gathering at Ardee but Schomberg now insisted that he had to keep communications with the North open.[94] Moreover, the troops needed new boots.[95] As William nagged him to 'hazard something', Schomberg offered to hold his position at Dundalk with infantry alone, while sending the cavalry away to forage. He also tried to placate William with a fatuous scheme to march part of his army 83 miles inland to take Jamestown County Leitrim, a crossing point on the Upper Shannon. He now blamed his problems on his colonels especially the Anglo-Irish ones, in a manner strikingly reminiscent of his complaints about officers at Saint-Jean: 'If our Irish colonels were as capable in war as they are in committing pillage and not paying the soldiers here, your Majesty would be better served'. Commissary Shales was incompetent and so Schomberg was still short of wagons and provisions. Treasurer Harbord 'makes great profit out of the musters, the hospital, the artillery and the payment of troops', so that the only unit that received regular pay was his own phantom troop of dragoons which consisted of Harbord himself, two clerks and a standard.[96] Schomberg's final plea was that the roads were few, the country alternately waterlogged or hilly, and some of the enemy troops were well-disciplined, all were well-fed, all were securely ensconced at Ardee County Louth (12 miles to the south-west) and they were 'at least' double his number'.[97]

The latter was the real explanation for Schomberg's halt. He firmly believed that the Irish had by now assembled a huge host of 40,000 fighters.[98] The true state of affairs was less fearsome. After a flurry of recruiting, the Jacobite field army mustered 22,000 poorly-armed men by the middle of October, but such was the disorganisation and dejection of the Jacobites in the meantime that Schomberg would have taken Dublin by a rapid march.[99] So James Fitzjames, Duke of Berwick, believed and he should know because he led a cavalry rearguard skipping a day's march ahead of the shambling Williamite army.[100] The French envoy, D'Avaux, could not understand why the Williamites did not press on and live off the land which James had been too soft-hearted to ravage and strip bare.[101] In short, Schomberg proved 'tired, over-cautious and pedestrian'.[102]

94   Lord Lisburn to the Earl of Shrewsbury, Dundalk 25 September 1689, *SP 63/352* f.56; Schomberg to William III, Dundalk,15 September 1689, *SP 8/5* f.288.

95   Schomberg to William III, 6 October 1689; James Dalrymple, *Memoirs of Great Britain and Ireland* (London: W. Strahan and T. Cadell, 1773) Vol.II, pp.171-2; Kazner, *Friedrichs von Schonburg*, pp.284, 302.

96   Von Arni, *Hospital Care*, p.63

97   Schomberg to William III, Dundalk 8 October 1689, *SP 8/6*, ff.27r, 30r.

98   *CSPD: William III February 1689 April 1690*, p.251.

99   Simms, 'Schomberg at Dundalk', p.20; Robert, H. Murray (ed.), *The Journal of John Stevens* (Oxford: Oxford University Press, 1912), p.81; Commissaire Fumeron to Louvois 30 September (NS) 1689 in Sheila Mulloy (ed.) *Franco-Irish Correspondence* (Dublin: IMC, 1983–4), Vol.III, p.80.

100   James Fitzjames, *Mémoires du Maréchal de Berwick* (Paris: Moutard, 1780), Vol.II, p.62.

101   James Hogan (ed.), *Négociations de M. Le Comte DAvaux en Irlande, 1689-90* (Dublin: IMC, 1934), pp.465, 469.

102   Childs, *Williamite Wars*, p.173.

A Jacobite pamphlet described Schomberg's main camp:[103]

> Count Schomberg had disposed his Camp upon two Lines in the plain
> Ground, at the foot of the Hills which were Northward of Dundalk having
> the River before him. His Left Wing was secured by a large Arm of the Sea,
> which came up to the Town. To secure his Right Wing, which lay most
> Exposed, he made some Retrenchments, and put a strong Garrison into a
> Castle of my Lord Bellew situated upon a Rising Ground.

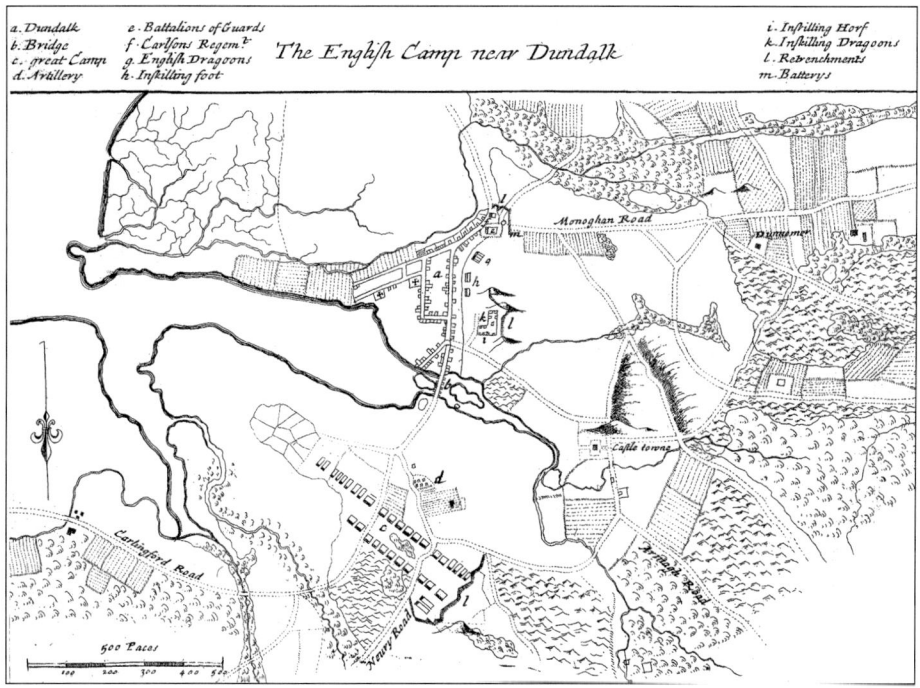

2.4 Dundalk Camp from Rev George Story's *Continuation*. Note that north is at the bottom of the
map and south on the top.

The two lines imitated the linear order of battle and stretched along a ridge from
Carn Beg (where 'l' is on Story's Map) to Dowdallshill with cavalry on the wings
and infantry in the middle. Schomberg chose to treat Dundalk, a walled town with a
pre-war population of between 2,000 and 3,000 people, as a bridgehead to be lightly
manned by Dutch infantry posted at a 'lesser camp' near the southern gate and by
Enniskillen horse and foot outside the walls.[104] The role of the latter was to act as

---

103 Anon., *A relation of what most remarkably happened during the last Campaign in Ireland*
(Dublin: James Malone, 1689) p.8.

104 Paul Gosling, 'From Dún Delca to Dundalk: the topography and archaeology of a medieval
frontier town A.D. c. 1187-1700' in *Journal of the County Louth Archaeological and Historical
Society*, 12:3, (1991), pp.258, 259, 262, 276, 284, 295-7, 304, 324-5; Harold O'Sullivan, 'The

out-guard and to deter soldiers in the Huguenot regiments from slipping across to the Jacobite lines because, on close enquiry, at least 160 of the Flemings, Germans, French, and Swiss in the three Huguenot regiments had turned out to be Catholics.[105] He also occupied Bellew's Castle (denoted as 'Castle towne' on Story's map) and its high ground as a headquarters and to command the nearby ford. Schomberg's deployment was distinctive and reminiscent of Saint-Jean, in that it was at once congested and scattered comprising as it did a cramped main camp together with many outposts.

Emboldened by Schomberg's timidity, James's Irish troops set up camp on 17 September just six miles away: their camp stretched between Knockbridge and Allardstown for nearly two miles along a ridge overlooking the Fane river.[106] Four days later, James's men marched even closer, almost to cannon shot, and stood for two or three hours.[107] Finally, after a scattered exchange of musket fire across the 'great bog' south of the town, the Jacobites pulled back.[108] Schomberg had let the Irish assert their dominance of no-man's land, however much Williamite sources boasted of subsequent patrols probing close to the Irish lines.

A council of war held on 2 and 3 October rejected the option of marching on the Irish camp because it was too strongly entrenched: 'whosoever gave the attaque it was odds against them'.[109] Taking a loop inland and behind the Irish camp was out of the question because the Williamites would then be moving further away from their supply ships. Rightly or wrongly, Schomberg would not press on without reinforcements of horse. Writing with the hindsight of seeing top-class infantry almost buckle under Jacobite cavalry charges at the Boyne next July, Story conceded that Schomberg may have had a point. Yet when more cavalry and dragoons did arrive on 9 October he sent them off, claiming there was not enough forage.[110] By now, this was likely true. Every day a horse needed about 20 lbs of dry fodder or 50 lbs of green fodder whereas the soldier consumed just two lbs of staples, supplemented by about a half pound of vegetables or protein.[111] Such was the equine predilection for fresh

---

Cromwellian and Restoration Settlement in the civil parish of Dundalk, 1649 to 1673' in *JCLAHS*,19:1 (1977), pp.42-7; J. Gavin, and H. O'Sullivan, *Dundalk: A Military History* (Dundalk: Dundalgan Press, 1987), p.12; James Buckley, (ed.) 'A Contemporary Letter Descriptive of Military Operations in County Louth in 1689' in *JCLAHS* I:3, (1906), p.37.

105 Fumeron to Louvois 20 September (NS) 1689 in Mulloy, *Franco-Irish Correspondence*, Vol.III, p.70; Kazner, *Friedrichs von Schonburg*, p.308; Col. La Caillemote to the Earl of Shrewsbury, Dundalk, 23 September 1689. *SP 63/352* f.52.

106 James Nihell, *A Journal of the Most Remarkable Occurrences that happened between His Majesties Army and the Forces under the command of Maréshal de Schomberg* (Dublin: James Malone, 1689), pp.4-7.

107 Fumeron to Louvois 30 September (NS) 1689 in Mulloy, *Franco-Irish Correspondence*, Vol. III, p.80.

108 Gavin and O'Sullivan, *Dundalk: A Military History*, p.15; Kazner, *Leben Friedrichs von Schonburg*, p.307; Anon., *A True and Impartial Account of their Majesties Army in Ireland* (London: Publisher, 1690), p.2.

109 Story, *Impartial History*, p.45

110 Kazner, *Leben Friedrichs von Schonburg*, pp.307, 311, 314.

111 J.F. De Chastenet, Marquis de Puységur, *Art de la Guerre par Principes at par Régles* (Paris: C.-A. Jombert, 1748), Vol.II, p.30; John Landers, *The Field and the Forge: Population,*

fodder there had to be large foraging expeditions every four days. By now the grass in the hinterland of the camp had been cut and foraging parties had to ride as far away as ten or twelve miles away, near the point of diminishing returns.[112]

Schomberg had, in effect, given up hope of advancing by week five of the 10-week encampment. On 16 and 17 October he duly sent off most of the remaining horse. Thereafter, he was staying until the Irish broke camp, so that they would not be able to pounce on him as he retreated. In this he succeeded. On 6 October the Irish pulled back and fixed a straggling camp further south and on 3 November they moved even further south and dispersed, leaving a strong garrison behind at Ardee.[113] A week later, Schomberg himself left the Dundalk camp, having first tried to evacuate all the sick by land and sea. That year's campaigning was over.

Quantifying death and sickness is not helped by unquantifiable remarks ('vast numbers' perished, 'several' men had been sent to hospital, regiments had 'wasted away' or 'grown pretty thin') that seldom distinguish between death and temporary incapacity due to sickness.[114] A muster of 26 September/6 October gives an opening strength of 18,208 Williamites.[115] When totted up, the various tallies and estimates of the Rev. George Story, author of the canonical *Impartial History* and chaplain in one of the worst-hit regiments, yields a figure of over 8,000 deaths.

Table 2.3 Deaths in Schomberg's Army[116]

Deaths	Location	Date
1,700	Dundalk	7 September-7 November
870	Hospital Ships	7-13 November.
c.2,000	Winter Quarters	Winter 1689-90
3,762	Belfast Hospital	Winter 1689-90

Story's guess as to how many perished 'in or about' Dundalk between 7 September and 7 November presumably included those who died at the hospital at Carlingford, 13 miles to the north-east. During the four days of evacuation it turned out that there would not be enough room on the ships for all the sick and many had to be taken in carts overland on 3 November: 'all the roads from Dundalk to Newry and

Production, and Power in the Pre-industrial West (Oxford: Oxford University Press, 2003), p.207.

112 Isaac Dumont de Bostaquet, *Mémoires Inédits* (Paris: Mercure de France, 1968), p.227.

113 Hogan, *Négociations*, p.532; Nihell, *Journal*, p.8; Murray, *Journal of John Stevens*, p.86.

114 Rev. J.S. Clarke, *The Life of James the Second* (London: Smith, Elder & Co.,1816), Vol.II, 382; Story, *Impartial History*, pp.21,24.

115 'Abstract of the muster of the army, taken at the camp at Dundalk', 26 September 1689, *SP* 8/5 f.322. Cavalry 7: Schomberg's, Villiers', Lord Delamere's, Coy's, Lord Hewett's, Lord Cavendish's and the Enniskillen regiment. Dragoons 2: Leveson's and Enniskillen. Infantry 22: Kirke's, Beaumont', Stewart's, Hanmer's, Wharton's, the Earl of Meath's, the Duke of Norfolk's, Lord Lovelace's, Lord Kingston's, Gore's, the Earl of Roscommon's, the Earl of Drogheda's, Earl's, Lord Lisburn's, Dering's, Herbert's, Ingoldsby's, Du Cambon's, De Meloniere's, De Caillemote's, Tiffin's, and Lloyd's.

116 Story, *Impartial History*, pp.38-40.

Carlingford were next day full of nothing but dead men, who ever as the wagons jolted, some of them died and were thrown off as fast'.[117] On Thursday the 7th most of the infantry regiments straggled northwards, braced against 'wind, raine and hail': 'several' fell out and 'so died'. A sickly Swiss *cadet* or gentleman-ranker in a Huguenot regiment was nearly one of them:

> Darkness caught up with us though our billet was still a distance away, and as my legs could not carry me any further I wanted to take the decision to stay the night in an old redoubt beside the highway. The officer did his best to persuade me to try and push on, but being completely worn out, I went inside the fort and was surprised to find two or three soldiers and a woman there, if I remember rightly. I believe they were at death's door, trying to absorb the last glimmers of heat emitted by some small embers, almost burnt to ashes. Their state shocked me, and restored my strength.[118]

Two days later, Schomberg led the rearguard from 'fatal Dundalk'. The 'several' who died on the march to Newry and the 'many' who subsequently passed away in winter quarters amounted, in Story's words, to 'more' than the number who died in and around Dundalk. This is entirely credible if one extrapolates from small known figures to larger unknown ones. Three colonels died of sickness at Dundalk, one (Henry Wharton) after three days lying in a 'violent fever' but three more colonels perished from fever or 'indisposition' between 24 November and 2 December, one at Lisburn and two at Chester.[119] A Huguenot cavalry *reformé* (an officer temporarily serving in the ranks) named De Bostaquet complained how sickness made 'terrible ravages' and caused the death of many of his comrades while they were in winter quarters: Bostaquet himself fell ill on Christmas Eve.[120] That epidemic disease broke out in quarters is unmistakably clear from the Church of Ireland burial registers for Blaris parish which included Lisburn, Schomberg's winter headquarters eight miles south-west of Belfast. Burials jumped from 48 in 1688 to peak at 188 in 1689 and 142 in 1690. Subtracting the 79 burials of military personnel between September 1689 and June 1690 these burials represent a doubling of background civilian mortality.[121]

---

117 Story, *Impartial History*, p.35-36

118 Pádraig Lenihan & Geraldine Sheridan, (eds.), 'A Swiss Soldier In Ireland, 1689–90', *Irish Studies Review*, 13:4, (2005), p.484; J.T. Dolan (ed.), 'Colonel Thomas Bellingham's Diary' in *JCLAHS*, 1: 2 (1905), p.55.

119 Edward Dering, Sir Thomas Gower, Carey Dillon Earl of Roscommon, Henry Wharton, George Viscount Hewytt, and Thomas Langston. Story, *Impartial History*, pp.50-1; John Debrett, *Debrett's Peerage of England, Scotland, and Ireland* (London: G. Woodfall, 1831), Vol.II, p.718; George Viscount Hewett died on 2 December 1689 see Sir Bernard Burke, *A Genealogical and Heraldic History of the Extinct and Dormant Baronetcies of England* (London: Scott, Webster, and Geary, 1838), p.261; Colonel Thomas Langston was buried on or about 6 December see Anon., *A Full and True Account of all the Remarkable Actions and Things that have happen'd in the North of Ireland since 15th of November to the 17th instant…* (London: Richard Baldwin, 1689), p.2.

120 De Bostaquet, *Mémoires Inédits*, p.231

121 Morgan, Valerie, 'Case Study of Population Change over Two Centuries: Blaris, Lisburn 1661-1848', in *Irish Economic and Social History*, 3 (1976), pp.11-12.

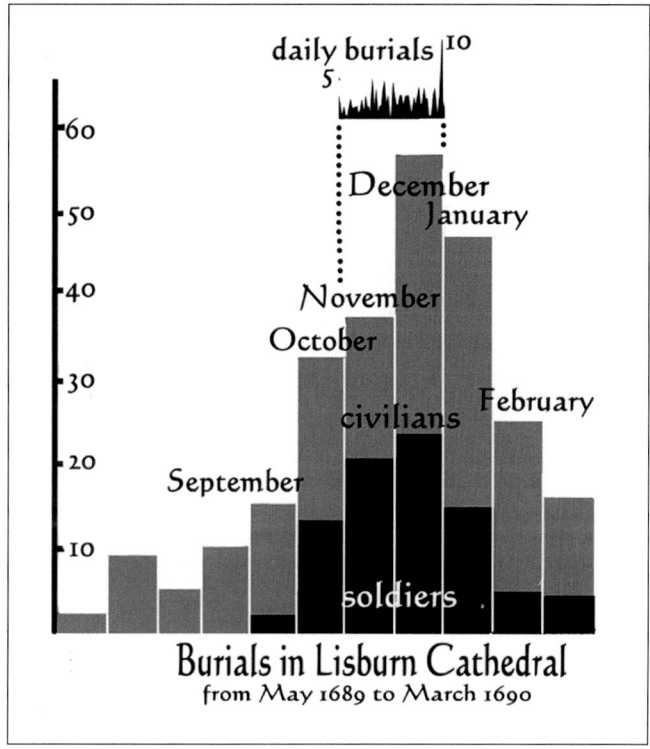

daily burials

December
January

November

October

civilians February

September

soldiers

Burials in Lisburn Cathedral
from May 1689 to March 1690

2.5 Burials in Lisburn Cathedral May 1689 to March 1690.

This is not quite as bad as Notre-Dame-de-la-Réal parish in Perpignan where the background mortality jumped two and a half times but is more comparable to, for instance, the Basse Meuse region of Spanish Flanders where late summer and autumn mortality more than doubled in the crisis years of 1674-1676 when the press and proximity of troops brought disease to civilians.[122]

The final category included those who died in the main hospital at Belfast which comprised converted storehouses.[123] The hospital was neglected and army paymaster Harbord pocketed funds set aside for it. According to Story, the hospital attendants reckoned that 3,762 patients died in the hospital. The tally is credible having regard to the peak number of 4,000 hospitalized in late November.[124] Overall, concluded Story, 'we lost nigh one half of the men we took over with us'.[125] His tally

---

122 Myron, P. Gutmann, *War and Rural Life in the Early Modern Low Countries* (New Jersey: Princeton University Press, 1980), pp.161-8.

123 Von Arni, *Hospital Care*, p.64.

124 William Smith to John Ellis, Belfast 14/24 November 1689 in 'Letters of Lord Longford on Irish Affairs 1689-1702', *Analecta Hibernica* 32 (1985) p.69; Robert M. Young (ed.), *The Town Book of the Corporation of Belfast, 1613-1816* (Belfast: Marcus Ward, 1892), p.331.

125 Story, *Impartial History*, pp.30, 35, 36, 39; 'Debates in 1689: November 23rd-30th', Grey's Debates of the House of Commons: volume 9 (1769), pp.438-66; URL: http://www.british-history.ac.uk/report; date accessed: 15 February 2007

is conservative when compared to almost all other reports. Crowing by Jacobite sources that this mortality manifested the 'finger of God' can be ignored, but not Williamite sources suggesting a much higher death toll.[126] Two soldiers of the Earl of Meath's Regiment thought, respectively, that three-quarters or more than two-thirds of the English troops perished 'like rotten sheep'.[127] On 21 October, William King, Dean of St Patrick's in Dublin, heard reports that 300-400 men a day were dying at Schomberg's camp and that he had already lost one quarter of his army.[128] The two soldiers were writing many years after the event; King was imprisoned in Dublin and had his news at second-hand, likely, from his gaolers. In any event, there is a tendency, as will become more apparent in later chapters, for anecdotal and impressionistic evidence to exaggerate the dimensions of a catastrophe, as compared to statistical data.[129]

Record-keeping tends to falter as a crisis worsens and in this case head counts were taken only for 26 September and 18 October.

Table 2.4 Infantry Musters[130]

	Effectives	**Sick**	**Morbidity %**	**Dead**
26 September	12,401	3,023	24.3	318
18 October	9, 857	4,102	29.3	895

126 John Thomas Gilbert (ed.), *A Jacobite Narrative of the War in Ireland, 1688-1691* (Dublin: Dollard, 1892), p.251.

127 Parker, *Memoirs*, p.20; Richard Kane, *Campaigns of King William and Queen Anne 1689-1712 and A New System of Military Discipline for a Battalion of Foot in Action* (London: publisher unknown, 1745), pp.2, 4, 42; De Bostaquet, *Mémoires Inédits*, p.228.

128 Hugh Jackson Lawlor (ed.), 'The diary of William King, D.D.: Dean of St. Patrick's, afterwards Archbishop of Dublin kept during his imprisonment in Dublin Castle, 1689' *JRSAI* (1903), p.71.

129 'Abstract of the muster of the army, taken at the camp at Dundalk', 26 September 1689, *SP 8/5* f.322. Cavalry 7: Schomberg's, Villiers', Lord Delamere's, Coy's, Lord Hewett's, Lord Cavendish's and the Enniskillen regiment. Dragoons 2: Leveson's and Enniskillen. Infantry 22: Kirke's, Beaumont', Stewart's, Hanmer's, Wharton's, the Earl of Meath's, the Duke of Norfolk's, Lord Lovelace's, Lord Kingston's, Gore's, the Earl of Roscommon's, the Earl of Drogheda's, Earl's, Lord Lisburn's, Dering's, Herbert's, Ingoldsby's, Du Cambon's, De Meloniere's, De Caillemote's, Tiffin's, and Lloyd's. List of the infantry regiments with names of their officers, engaged on service in Ireland and reviewed in the camp at Dundalk', Dundalk, 18/19 October 1689, *SP 8/6*, f.63; Same 22 regiments as on 26 September.

130 'Abstract of the muster of the army, taken at the camp at Dundalk', 26 September 1689, SP 8/5 f.322. Cavalry 7: Schomberg's, Villiers', Lord Delamere's, Coy's, Lord Hewett's, Lord Cavendish's and the Enniskillen regiment. Dragoons 2: Leveson's and Enniskillen. Infantry 22: Kirke's, Beaumont', Stewart's, Hanmer's, Wharton's, the Earl of Meath's, the Duke of Norfolk's, Lord Lovelace's, Lord Kingston's, Gore's, the Earl of Roscommon's, the Earl of Drogheda's, Earl's, Lord Lisburn's, Dering's, Herbert's, Ingoldsby's, Du Cambon's, De Meloniere's, De Caillemote's, Tiffin's, and Lloyd's. List of the infantry regiments with names of their officers, engaged on service in Ireland and reviewed in the camp at Dundalk', Dundalk, 18/19 October 1689, *SP 8/6*, f.63; Same 22 regiments as on 26 September.

Table 2.5 Villiers' Regiment of Horse[131]

	Effectives	Sick
26 September 1689	207	19
16 October 1689	180	90
13 November 1689	144	
6 June 1690	107	

Story's estimates can be knit onto those musters together with fragmentary data, such as the report to the House of Commons that 10,000 men went into winter quarters. The accompanying graph gives a sense of the scale, tempo, and duration of the crisis, though the later data points on the graph depicting the numbers of sick are tentative since they extrapolate from four examples of individual units, sub-units or identifiable categories.

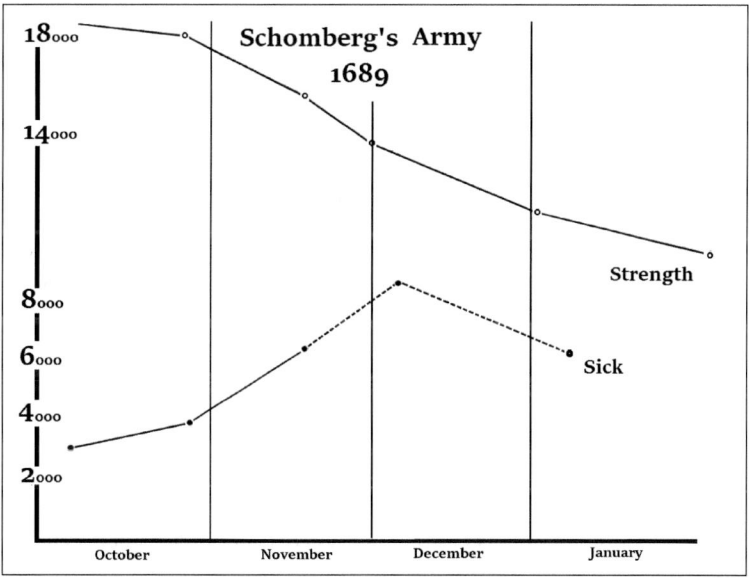

2.6 Schomberg's army 1689-90.

On 26 September, fourteen days after disembarking at Dundalk, Villiers' Regiment of Horse numbered 207 men in six troops, including the bedridden.[132] Two troops of Villiers' Horse, originally comprising 100 troopers, could made up together only

131 Abstract of the muster of the army, taken at the camp at Dundalk'.26 Sept. and 1 Oct. 1689, *SP 8/5* f.322. Unknown Corporal, Third Horse', CARDG:1730, http://www.qdg.org.uk/diaries.php

132 Abstract of the muster of the army, taken at the camp at Dundalk'.26 Sept. and 1 Oct. 1689, *SP 8/5* f.322.

48 effectives on 13 November.[133] By 6 June 1690, before reinforcements arrived, the regiment had but 110 men left. The regiment lost about 51 percent of its strength.[134] Gower's Foot, mustered in Newry County Down just after breaking camp, had one company with just sixteen effectives left out of an initial strength of about 50 men while the strongest had just 26.[135] On 23 November two-thirds of them were 'disabled to present a musquet'.[136] On 6 January 1690, thirty of the fifty surviving carters (100 had set out from London originally) were sick.[137]

To sum up: Story's 'nigh half' is a slight underestimate and fully half of the troops who marched south in early September 1689 were dead of dysentery and typhus by Christmas, or soon after. In the absence of plague (forty years had passed since what we now know to have been the final outbreak in Ireland) such apocalyptic mortality is hard to accept, not least because it demands almost unbelievably high morbidity. But such was the case. Luzancy reckoned hardly 2,000 men escaped falling sick while Story estimated that morbidity had already reached 80 percent in some companies by 20 October.[138] The soldiers perished of sicknesses which, if they did not originate in Dundalk camp, acquired a critical momentum there and peaked a fortnight or so after Schomberg broke camp. The plural 'sicknesses' is used advisedly because there were at least two major components of the epidemic.

What first struck was the 'country disease'. This phrase carries an entirely different meaning from the *Mal du Pays* of Saint-Jean and describes 'a violent Flux, attended with gripes' [intestinal pain]: 'The Loosness doth also greatly reign in Ireland, as well among those of the countrie as among the Strangers, wherefore the English inhabitants have given it the name of the country-disease'.[139] As the quote suggests: natives and newcomers were equally susceptible: the Irish Protestants of Lloyd's Regiment were 'also subject to illness as much as the others'.[140] Neglected, this could deteriorate to 'the Bloody flux' which 'killeth the most part of the sick, except they be carefully assisted with good remedies'. De Morsier states that most soldiers fell sick sooner or later, while others reckoned that 'hardly anybody has escaped'.[141] The universality of the affliction suggests a background disease like flux. A Jacobite poet, writing (in Latin) just four years later gloated that 'there raged 'gainst Schomberg's allies all/ Foul plague, a flux [*fluor*] of bowel, untreatable,/ Gnawing intestines with sharp bites of pain/'.[142]

---

133 'Unknown Corporal, Third Horse', *CARDG:1730*, http://www.qdg.org.uk/diaries.php.

134 'Unknown Corporal, Third Horse', *CARDG:1730*, http://www.qdg.org.uk/diaries.php.

135 Anon., 'The Dear Bargain; or a true Representation of the State of the English Nation under the Dutch' in Sir Walter Scott,(ed.), *A Collection of Scarce and Valuable Tracts...* (London: T. Cadell, W. Davies,1809-15), Vol.X, p.362.

136 Walter Harris, *The History of the Life and Reign of William-Henry, Prince of Nassau and Orange...*(Dublin: Edward Bate, 1749), p.247.

137 Dalton, *English Army Lists*, Vol.III, p.xi.

138 Glozier, *Marshal Schomberg*, p.218; Story, *Impartial History*, p.30.

139 John Oldmixon, *History of England* (London: Thomas Cox,1735), p.23; Gerard Boate, *Irelands naturall history* (London: Samuel Hartlib, 1652), p.183.

140 Dalton, *English Army Lists*, i, p.121.

141 Unk. to William III, [undated] [1690.], *SP 8/8* f.26; Glozier, *Marshal Schomberg*, p.218.

142 Pádraig Lenihan and Keith Sidwell (eds.), *Poema de Hibernia* (Dublin: IMC, 2018), Book 5, Lines 164-169.

As discussed in chapter one, flux was normally blamed on diet. It was six days after the Williamite army reached Dundalk that store ships berthed at Carlingford and disgorged 204 cart-loads of bread. Before then the army had slaughtered 2,000 sheep confiscated from enemy sympathisers and so the troops had not gone hungry, though the idea that they suffered from 'hunger-induced sickness' has persisted into modern history-writing.[143] Story blamed the flux on an unbalanced rather than inadequate diet: 'our ships not coming great scarcity of bread but plenty of flesh caused our soldiers to eat freely without bread and nothing to drink but water cast a great many into fluxes'.[144] Schomberg blamed 'new beer' rather than water but mainly griped about shortages of overcoats and boots which 'greatly contribute' to the sickness of the soldiers.[145] He also complained that they had not bothered to build themselves snug waterproof huts. Moreover, the English troops, were too 'delicately reared'.[146] The House of Commons, debating Commissary Shales's guilt, followed Schomberg's lead in decrying poor clothing. The cavalry, some members thought, escaped with 'little mortality' (in fact, they did not so escape) because of their cloaks and the Dutch infantry because they wore 'great-coats over their close-coats'.[147] Viscount Lisburn, one of the colonels, complained of 'extraordinary bad' weather and a 'cold' camp site which caused the men to 'fall daily sick in great numbers'.[148] Another correspondent writing on 25 October also bemoaned the 'stormy weather these ten days which I fear has done great mischief at the camp' by causing a bad flux' which could kill in 3-4 days'. He hoped that the soldiers were now 'seasoned' and the 'distemper' decreasing.[149]

The idea that Schomberg camped 'on marshy ground' and that marshy effluvia and miasma generated disease there grew after the fact and persists in modern scholarship.[150] However, the very name of the site occupied by the camp, Dowdall's Hill, confirms that the camp was not pitched in a marsh.[151] The camp might have sat, as De Bostaquet noted, on the edge of a 'marsh' [marais] but not in it. The mistake begins with Story's remark that 'we lay in a Hollow at the Bottoms of the Mountains', by which he meant that the army sat on ground that was not low-lying as such but only so compared to the range of hills further north running from Faughart to Carrickedmond. As discussed in Chapter 5, concern with tainted air or 'miasma' as a cause of disease would grow in the following decades. Later accounts, including

---

143 Story, *Impartial History*, p.18; John M Stapleton Jr. 'The Dual Monarchy in Practice...' in David Onnekink and Esther Mijers, (eds.), *Redefining William III: The Impact of the King-Stadholder in International Context* (Aldershot: Ashgate, 2007), p.81.

144 Buckley, 'Contemporary Letter', p.36.

145 Schomberg to William, Dundalk 27 September 1689 in John Dalrymple, *Memoirs of Great Britain and Ireland* (London: A., Strahan, and T., Cadell, 1773), Vol.II, appendix p.33.

146 Schomberg to William, Lisburn, 30 December, SP 8/6 f.142.

147 Anchitell Grey (ed.), *Debates of the House of Commons from 1667 to 1694* (London: D. Henry, R. Cave, J. Emonson, 1763), Vol.IX, pp.446, 448.

148 Lord Lisburn to the Earl of Shrewsbury, Dundalk 25 September 1689, *SP 63/352* f.56.

149 William Smith to John Ellis Belfast 25 October 1689 in Patrick Melvin (ed.), 'Letters of Lord Longford on Irish Affairs 1689-1702', *Analecta Hibernica* 32 (1985), p.69.

150 John Childs, 'The Williamite War 1689' in Thomas Bartlett, ☒ Keith Jeffery, (eds.), *A Military History of Ireland* (Cambridge: Cambridge University Press, 1997), p.200.

151 Story, *Impartial History*, p.39.

such memoirs as those of De Bostaquet and the Jacobite Lieutenant Stevens penned decades later, projected a miasmic assumption that the air was 'infected with pestilential vapours' onto a casual misreading of Story's 'hollow'.[152]

Among all these putative causes of the flux, (bad diet, thin clothes, tumbledown huts, 'exhalations' and 'emanations') what were the 'real' ones? A necessary but not sufficient condition was a critical number of afflicted soldiers. There is no need to hypothesize that Kirke's Regiment brought the sickness to the camp with them from Derry: sooner rather than later flux would have broken out. It spread because of three factors. In the first place, men suffering from dysentery were likely to be overcome by faecal incontinence and, imagined the Jacobite Latinist, 'each square became an open sewer'.[153] Ironically, matters would be worse if they reached the designated 'convenient places' outside the perimeter. Orrery's 1677 *Art of War* represents English practice when he stipulates that the designated place for the soldiers to 'do their Easements' should be 'either in the River or Brook, or in some Pits to be digged by every Regiment for that end'. Considering that contemporaries still regarded the Ottomans' 'great pits' to be a notable innovation, it is likely that the vicinity of water courses may still have served English, and European, armies.[154]

'For drink' recalled De Morsier, 'we had fresh beer and stagnant bog-water, and, in some places, spring water that soldiers brought to the camp to sell for a half *sou* a bottle.[155] At that price, the common soldier would have drawn from nearby pools of standing water. Then the rain fell. Colonel Bellingham noted weather conditions precisely and one can count four episodes of very wet weather from his journal. Between 28 September and 2 October Bellingham noted successively 'Very wett meather', 'Much raine', and 'much raine' and another four days of unrelieved 'stormy', 'very wett', 'sad' and 'bad' between 13-15 October, followed by three days of 'dreadfull' and 'dismall' weather between 18-20 October. Between 5-8 November another front of bad weather climaxed with 'wind, raine and hail' until Schomberg left 'fatal Dundalk' behind him.[156] This rain 'caused the flux' in the sense that the successive deluges must have run human waste off into the water sources. Typhoid fever was probably a component of the flux epidemic because it is an intestinal infection spread by ingesting food or, especially, water contaminated by *Salmonella typhi*. It is difficult to distinguish from dysentery given the lack of first-hand accounts of the epidemic's opening stages.

Finally, why did some units escape more lightly than others? Critics at Westminster lauded Dutch officers for taking care of their soldiers 'as their children' by having them build snug bothies with ample bedding of straw.[157] The likelier reason why the Dutch battalions escaped so lightly was because they were posted well away from the

152 Murray, *Journal of John Stevens*, p.106.
153 Lenihan and Sidwell (eds.), *Poema de Hibernia*, Book 5, Lines 164-169.
154 Luigi Ferdinando Marsili, *Stato militare dell' Impèrio Ottomanno, incremento e decremento* (The Hague: Pierre Gosse, 1732), pp.80-81; Orrery, *Art of War*, pp.83-84.
155 Lenihan and Sheridan, 'Swiss Soldier', p.484.
156 Dolan, 'Colonel Thomas Bellingham's Diary', pp.51-54.
157 'Debates in 1689: November 23rd-30th', Grey's Debates of the House of Commons: Vol. 9 (1769), pp.438-66; URL: http://www.british-history.ac.uk/report; date accessed: 16 February 2007.

filth of the main camp and close to a source of fairly clean running water, the mill race running by the southern defences of Dundalk.

The causes of camp dysentery and typhoid were identical, the prognosis comparable, and the signs and symptoms bewilderingly similar: Even the bloodstained faeces of bloody flux could be imitated by the intestinal bleeding of typhoid. The main significance of the dysentery/typhoid outbreak was that the many bedridden or enfeebled soldiers crowded together in tent, hut or hospital were vulnerable to Typhus.[158] As discussed earlier, this was a relatively new disease west of the Balkans and masqueraded under synonyms suggestive of congestion and dirt including 'jail-fever', 'hospital-fever', 'camp-fever', and 'ship fever'.[159]

As noted earlier, *Rickettsia prowazeckii* was spread by the powdery faeces of a human body louse which had fed off a human in the febrile stage of typhus. How could the insect vector flourish when 'it was a disgrace to be lousy'? The English royalist poet Abraham Cowley could envisage no worse death for the Civil War Parliamentary leader Pym than to imagine him on his deathbed in 1645 'like Herod eaten up with lice'.[160] One reason is that the seventeenth century marked 'a low point in European hygiene' when civilians did not bathe all over but, rather, washed their face and hands, brushed their hair and, crucially, changed linen and woollen garments 'frequently'.[161] Personal cleanliness meant 'clean clothing rather than clean skin'.[162] Demoralization, cold, wet, sickness added to the exigencies of wartime, could make the soldier neglect to pick the lice off his clothes, the usual method of vermin control. Paintings of camp scenes sometimes depict naked or near naked men hunkering on the outskirts and picking at their clothes. It would have been better still if the soldier could have changed his shirt.[163] This is where the emphasis on commissary failures may be relevant, and men may have died for want of a second shirt. Johann Dietz, a surgeon's mate with the Elector of Brandenburg's troops, described returning from the sack of Buda in 1686 to wait, famished and unpaid, in quarantine for four weeks near Frankfurt an der Oder because 'the Hungarian sickness hung round our necks like a curse...I was so full of vermin that I got no rest at night. On this account I had to creep stark naked into the hay at night, for only then could I get any rest'.[164]

Tobias Kober, a physician with the Imperial armies on the Danubian front asserted that the crawling of lice caused black bile to concentrate and thicken with harmful

---

158 Pringle, *Observations on the Diseases of the Army*, p.235.
159 Graham A.J. Ayliffe and Mary P. English, *Hospital Infection: From Miasmas to MRSA* (Cambridge: Cambridge University Press, 2003), p.38.
160 Keith Thomas, 'Cleanliness and godliness in early modern England' in Anthony Fletcher (ed.), *Religion, Cultures and Society in Early Modern Britain* (Cambridge: Cambridge University Press, 1994), p.72; Sarahson, 'The Microscopist as Voyeur', p.86.
161 Hanlon, *Italy 1636*, p.175.
162 Lisa T. Sarahson, 'The Microscopist as Voyeur: Margaret Cavendish's Critique of experimental Philosophy', in Melinda S. Zook and Sigrun Haude (eds.), *Challenging Orthodoxies: The Social and Cultural Worlds of Early Modern Modern women* (Aldershot: Ashgate, 2014), pp.71, 78, 79.
163 Raymond Crawford, 'Contributions from the History of Medicine to the Problem of the Transmission of Typhus', *Proc.Roy.Soc.Med.* 6 (1913), pp.9-10.
164 Miall and Consentius (eds.), *Master Johann Dietz*, p.87.

effects, but he drew no connection with *Languor Pannonicus* (yet another synonym for typhus) which he counted as a distinct sickness caused by the air, the mental strains of warfare, the hardships of camping on the hard ground, enduring extremes of heat and cold, and other such environmental factors.[165] Luca Porzio, serving on the same front, recommended that the soldier change his clothes every few days because 'nastiness' inhibits respiration and 'may by that means produce numberless disorders'. This potentially key observation is disposed of in a single paragraph but he discusses the Galenic non-naturals, such as irregular sleep and sudden shocks, at much greater length.[166]

There also lingered an ancient notion that lice were spontaneously engendered by the corrupted humours of those suffering from *phthiriasis* or the 'lousy-disease'. A Jacobite pamphlet described the sufferings of the Williamite soldiers with unwholesome relish and the 'lice and vermin which issued out of their plague-sores'.[167] The 'lousy disease' was believed especially appropriate for tyrants and enemies of religion. Given that William III was both, in Jacobite eyes, it is hardly surprising that Jacobite epicist speaks of: 'A second pestilence [which] soon came to birth, /Which worse hurts flesh and skin externally./ The grub, attacking fierce its lord, goes round/ Upon six legs, running all o'er, and bites/'.[168] More remarkably, the poet specifies a method of transmission when the lice-ridden patient 'asks for comrades' aid,/ And begs them strip his clothing off and then/ To char it with hot ashes and to burn/ From thence the lice, by scattering on hot coals./ Those who obey are followed by the plague's/ Living contagion, for the deadly flock/ Creeps up the knuckles and the arms of them/ Who make this recompense, and bring dire death'.[169]

Airborne transmission by the powdered faeces of the louse was probably more likely than the poet's scenario, since soldiers, especially those laid low with flux, spent so much time cheek by jowl in the cramped fug of tent or hut. All things being equal, human proximity is the key to disease transmission and such tents or huts were very cramped.

A contemporary illustration of a wedge tent or *canoniere* interior shows eight men sleeping top and tail and a ninth squeezed into the rounded back or bell.[170] The tent, excluding the bell, was nine *pieds* long and six wide: the French *pied* was slightly longer than a foot.[171] English four-man tents were proportionately smaller and no less cramped and it is not surprising that De Morsier saw four-man huts or

---

165   Tobias Kober, *Observationvm Medicarum Castrensivm Hungaricarvm Decades Tres* (Helmstad: Friedrich Lüderwald, 1685), pp.32, 49; J. E. McCallum, *Military Medicine: From Ancient Times to the 21st Century* (Santa Barbara, CA: ABC-CLIO, 2008), p.293.

166   Luca Porzio, *The Soldiers Vade Mecum* (London: R. Dodsley, 1747), pp.13-15.

167   'The Dear Bargain', pp.362-3.

168   Clarke, *Life of James the Second*, Vol.II, p.382; Lenihan and Sidwell, *Poema*, Book 5, lines 194-199.

169   Lenihan and Sidwell, *Poema*, Book 5, lines 194-199.

170   Puysegur, *Art de la guerre*, plate 10.

171   Guillaume Le Blond, *Essai sur la castrametation ou sur la mesure et le trace des camps* (Paris: C.A.Jombert, 1758), pp.98-99; Joseph de Fallois, *Traité de la castrametation et de la défense des places fortes* (Berlin: J.Decker, 1771) plate 1; De La Porterie, *Institutions militaires pour la cavalerie et les dragons* (Paris: Guillyn, 1754), p.386.

2.7 Tent interior: after Puységur, *Art de La Guerre.*

tents in which all those within lay dead.[172] The localised pattern of the epidemic, bypassing troops on the fringe of the main camp, indicates that the main focus of infection was among the English infantry who were posted in the centre of the two lines.[173] The pattern also suggests, on the whole, transmission from man to man and tent to tent.

There are few first-hand accounts of typhus. De Morsier fell sick in camp and 'could not stand upright'. Moreover, he was 'tormented by a burning fever from which my only relief was to rest my head and brow against the tent sodden from the incessant rain'.[174] The characteristic very high fever is reflected in yet another synonym for typhus namely *Hauptkrankheit* [lit. 'head-sickness'] De Morsier wintered at Moneymore County Derry and he recorded that in his billet 'a man named La Loubière passed away. He died of a hot fever; indeed the very night he died he was singing in his sleep, though feebly, having listened to us singing at the fireside earlier'.[175]

Though De Morsier blamed diet, he actually presents a fairly clear picture of typhus. So too does a petition by Lieutenant Thomas Chetwynd of Sir Henry

172 Jullien, 'Journal de Jean-Francois de Morsier', p.91.
173 Story, *Impartial History*, p.46
174 Lenihan and Sheridan, 'A Swiss Soldier', p.484.
175 Lenihan and Sheridan, 'A Swiss Soldier', p.485.

Ingoldsby's infantry regiment who 'lost the use of his limbs', as did many of the carters in the artillery train.[176] In severe cases of typhus clots form in the blood vessels and cut off blood supply causing peripheral gangrene and necrosis of fingers, toes, and even limbs. It is likely that typhus remained the main killer in Belfast hospital but conditions for soldiers in winter quarters (many of the officers had gone home) were no longer sufficiently squalid to perpetuate that disease. That said, soldiers in winter quarters and officers at home died in large numbers. The cavalry *reformé* De Bostaquet fell sick on Christmas Eve while quartered near Lurgan County Armagh. He was brought to the brink of death by a 'continuous fever' that lasted twenty-eight days, attended by raving delirium, looseness [*dévoiement*] and ulcerations. The latter probably signifies that he was coughing up bloody sputum.[177] De Bostaquet's sickness manifested so many symptoms and signs simultaneously, including pneumonic ones, as to be unclassifiable. Colonel Bellingham provides a second example when he records in his diary that he 'fell ill att night of a feavour' on 21 November and languished until 13 January. The after-effects of the fever included 'spitting of blood', when he coughed.[178] However, Bellingham's case history is too terse to admit of classification.

Anomie, the erosion of behavioural norms, is not readily identifiable as a 'cause' of flux and fever. Still, on his daily rounds to visit the sick in their huts, the chaplain of Gower's Regiment was horrified to see the living sick use their dead comrades 'to lay between them and the cold wind' or even 'to sit and lie upon', and so concluded that they were 'the hardest-hearted one to another in the World'.[179] Indifference to the dead and to the rituals of death was the most striking indication of this callousness. The sick who died while being evacuated to the hospitals at Carlingford were 'left in the high waye'.[180] Those who perished in the camp were dumped along the sea-shore at low tide or 'put thirty or forty in a hole'. The living patients were disturbed by this callous indifference and 'when they felt the approaches of death, they desired to see their own graves made, and begged their friends to bury them…'. [181] A lieutenant of the Queen Dowager's, or Lumley's, Regiment of Horse having disembarked at Carlingford took a walk along the strand and

> heard a voice, from among the dead bodies, calling to him, by the name of brother, for help, and going to the place, he found it was indeed his brother, who had been at the ships to buy some bread and cheese, but falling there, he had been robbed of it, instead of being helped by his comrades.

The luckless brother may have been left in the tents erected by the sea shore that accommodated the overflow from the hospital proper in Carlingford Castle. More

---

176 Petition of Thomas Chetwynd, c.24 December 1689 in Joseph Redington (ed.), *Calendar of Treasury Papers 1556-1696* (London: Longman, Green, Reader, and Dyer, 1868), p.88.; Dalton, *English Army Lists*, Vol.III, p.xi.
177 De Bostaquet, *Mémoires Inédits*, p.231.
178 Anthony Hewitson, *Diary of Thomas Bellingham* (Preston: Toulmin & Sons, 1908), p.98.
179 Story, *Impartial History*, p.30.
180 Dolan, 'Colonel Thomas Bellingham's Diary', *JCLAHS* 1:2, (1905), p.54.
181 'The Dear Bargain', p.363.

typical than Hobbesian predation was outright neglect. The hospital was 'grossly insufficient' and Harbord felt it necessary to apologize, after a fashion, to William: 'Had I but known as much of a hospital in the spring as I do now, I am assured that I would have saved two-thirds of the men that have died, and prevented many from being sick. I am heartily sorry that I have bought the experience so dear at those poore creatures' cost'.[182] Morsier subsisted on two bowls of gruel daily and a bare attic floor.

> I was sent to a castle called Karlinfort [Carlingford] where the sick were kept. All the places were already taken and all that was left for me was a pigeon loft above the house; two or three cadets and soldiers did their best to tidy it and we slept on the floor. Later we were given straw mattresses and blankets. My fever did not abate and this ill health made me long for home, but reflecting that such thoughts would do me further harm, I made the best of it and reminded myself that many were worse off than me. In this way I tried to make my condition more bearable, and managed fairly well on the two bowls of gruel we were brought every day. By God's grace I picked up a little, and when some sailors came from their ships nearby to sell their biscuits, I bought some, and, being then able to walk, I succeeded in procuring some more substantial food for myself. The sailors' trade did not last long, but I found a peasant's house about one or two musket shots away where he grew very nice white cabbages. I cooked them and seasoned them well every day for quite a while until I felt a little stronger.[183]

Morsier pulled through, one suspects, because he could scrape together enough coins to buy food from sailors and peasants. To modern sensibilities the fact that Schomberg left so many sick men behind when he evacuated the camp betokens callous indifference. A Jacobite officer described what he heard about the abandoned camp:

> a vast number of dead bodies was found there unburied, and not a few yet breathing but almost devoured with lice and other vermin. This spectacle not a little astonished such of our men as ventured in amongst them, seeing that raging with hunger some had eaten part of their own flesh and having yet their speech begged as a charity to be killed.[184]

An Irish visitor to the deserted camp recalled with horror that 'I myself saw' [*do dhearcas féin*] a hospital between Dundalk and Newry that the enemy had set on fire lest their sick encumber the army. 'What unparalleled barbarity to burn poor

182 Von Arni, *Hospital Care,* p.63; William Harboard to William III, Dundalk 23Oct. (OS) 1689, *SP8/6,* fo 77r.
183 Lenihan and Sheridan, 'A Swiss Soldier', p.484.
184 Murray, *Journal of John Stevens,* p.96.

sick creatures to ashes', he exclaimed.[185] However, it may have been the Irish who burnt the hospital to prevent infection after, one hopes, the patients had passed away. In practice there were never enough carts and draught animals to carry off all the sick and the hopeless cases were usually left behind. William III left many sick and wounded behind as his forces hastily pulled out of the siege camp at Limerick the year after Dundalk. While burning munitions to prevent them falling into Irish hands, the Williamites contrived to set their own hospital ablaze: 'Hence could be heard the groans and angry cries/Of those being burned, the curse and dissonant shout/From diverse mouths, just as is told there were/In Nimrod's citadel'.[186] Lieutenant Stevens also recalled this 'spectacle of horror' of 'miserable wretches [who] lay within half burnt and others that had more strength or were nearer crept out at the three doors'.[187]

The fact that Williamite sources are reticent (though Story notes that 'some few' were left) about abandoning the sick at Dundalk (and Limerick) suggests that they considered this discreditable. Perhaps they were uneasy not because the gravely ill were left behind but that no arrangements were made for their care such as leaving a surgeon and a skeleton staff of orderlies behind.

On returning to camp from Carlingford, De Morsier relapsed and barely survived the gruelling retreat from Dundalk to Newry until he stumbled across three or four dying comrades:

> Their state shocked me, and restored my strength, along with a nip of brandy that I asked the officer to give me from a bottle in which I was going halves with him; I was also sharing one with Lullin my messmate. I then pressed onwards.[188]

The episode is a reminder of how physical survival depended so much on a small tight group of comrades. The importance of small-group cohesion is a truism of modern military organizations with their fine-grained subdivision down to platoons and sections/squads, thirty and a dozen men respectively. Early modern armies, though, lacked that in-built cohesiveness, having no unit smaller than the company of about 50 men. The soldier looked to informal ties between messmates, fellow countrymen or kin: De Bostaquet, a Huguenot cavalier, frequently notes that so-and-so was a relative, as for example when he laments a 'friend' who died at Dundalk whose mother was a relative of his (De Bostaquet's) first wife.[189]

Schomberg's army was predisposed to incohesion and anomie. Partly this was a matter of language and national prejudices. The English disliked and envied the Dutch and Huguenots who seemed to monopolize William's favour and the conspiracy among the Huguenots fuelled their suspicions. The Dutch and Huguenots,

185   Breandán Ó Buachalla, 'Seacaibíteachas Thaidhg Uí Neachtain', *Studia Hibernica*, 26 (1992), p.44.
186   Lenihan and Sidwell, *Poema*, Book 6, lines 860-865.
187   Murray, *Journal of John Stevens*, p.185.
188   Lenihan and Sheridan, 'A Swiss Soldier', p.484.
189   De Bostaquet, *Mémoires Inédits*, p.228

for their part, tended to look down on the English as amateurish and untrustworthy. However, anomie also characterized relationships within and between the various English components and goes back to how that army was raised in the first place. In general, seigneurial recruitment remained important, especially so in the case of freshly commissioned captains and colonels raising entirely new units. Young men recruited from rural areas often contemplated enlisting only because the captain or colonel was a member of a local or regional seigneurial family.[190] Thus, he 'was spared what, at least for the peasant recruit, was the harshest and most traumatic experience of all, that of being suddenly thrust into a strange and frightening environment where he had no one to whom he could look for protection and took any personal interest in his welfare'.[191] To take a practical example: the recruit could hope to exert a moral claim for support from a captain or colonel who would have the resources to pay him from his own pocket during those frequent intervals when food and provisions ran short.

Though the English foot regiments were recruited in particular shires, six (Lisburn, Kingston, Meath, Roscommon, Drogheda, and Ingoldsby) of the seventeen colonels were Anglo-Irish *émigrés* who had few connections with those localities. The regiment of Adam Loftus Viscount Lisburn ('every day he drinks more wine than he can hold', noted an inspection report at Dundalk), for example, was recruited in Huntingdonshire. However, Lisburn and at least four of his company commanders (Richard Coote, Thomas Allen, Edward Osborne and Hyacinth Edgeworth) were Anglo-Irish and had no identifiable connection to East Anglia. Is it a coincidence that, with one exception, the regiments commanded by 'Anglo-Irish' notables were the sickliest ones? The exception was more apparent than real, because the regiment of Edward Brabazon 4th Earl of Meath had swallowed a large chunk of a pre-war regular regiment, including no fewer than 160 veteran private soldiers.[192] When Schomberg complained that his 'Irish' colonels had recruited 'boys on the cheap' (the enlistment bounty of 20 shillings was indeed low and would double in 1690) he does not mean that they were the gaolbirds and riff-raff of Jacobite propaganda, but that they were recruited by beat of drum at markets and fairs to serve under and alongside complete strangers and were desperate enough to be attracted by a miserly enlistment bounty, so miserly it would have to be doubled the following year.[193]

The received version of events is that Schomberg lost half his army to flux and fever because his troops were hungry, ill-clothed, and camped in boggy ground. Yet he was, somehow, blameless: 'the men's dying afterwards, this was not the General's fault', insisted George Story, who was present as a chaplain.[194] Commissary Shales

---

190 Guy Rowlands, *The Dynastic State and the Army Under Louis XIV: Royal Service and Private Interest (1661-1701)* (Cambridge: Cambridge University Press, 2002), pp.206-207; Tallett, *War and Society in Early Modern Europe,* pp.91-92.

191 Martin Smith Anderson, *War and Society in Europe of the Old Regime 1618-1789* (London, Fontana, 1988), pp.122-3.

192 Dalton, *English Army Lists*, Vol.III, pp.75-76.

193 Schomberg to William III, Dundalk 8 October 1689, *SP 8/6f.30;* 'The Dear Bargain'; p.361; Charles Messenger, *For Love of Regiment: A History of British Infantry 1660-1914* (Barnsley: Leo Cooper, 1994), p.4.

194 Story, *Impartial History*, p.46. 120

was the scapegoat for leaving the army short of carriage horses and the foot soldiers poorly fed, shod and dressed.[195] Having seen what happened at Saint-Jean one must either believe that time and again Schomberg was singularly ill-served by commissaries or that he must shoulder some of the responsibility. For all the maladministration and malfeasance, Schomberg's troops had, after week one of the camp at Dundalk, enough bread to eat. After week five his horses had eaten all the green forage. Between weeks one and five, therefore, Schomberg could have pushed on against a smaller army. Instead he elected to skulk behind earthworks. However, that is the wisdom of hindsight. Armies in the latter decades of the 17th century were battle-shy and manoeuvred to occupy positions from which they might fight (but usually did not) or force an enemy army to withdraw and expose a swathe of territory to be sprinkled with fortified garrisons or stripped bare. Battle, even a winning battle, was usually too costly to risk. The guiding principles were to avoid battle (except at a clear advantage), batten off enemy territory and, by marches and manoeuvres, stop the enemy doing likewise.[196] Schomberg was just an exceptionally cautious practitioner of that kind of warfare. Even if one accepts the necessity of his defensive posture, though, Schomberg is still open to criticism. If he feared to advance or retreat he could have moved camp in an ambit around the vicinity of Dundalk, but he did so only after nine weeks encamped on the ridge of Dowdallshill and Carn Beg. This was too long. John Pringle's landmark *Observations on the Diseases of the Army* would stipulate that armies should move camp at least twice in late summer when the 'flux' would begin spreading and so leave behind the dirty water, privies, rotten straw and the general 'filth of the camp'.[197]

Schomberg occupied comfortable quarters in Viscount Bellew's house at Castletown, away from the squalor of the main camp, and seems to have been in denial about the sickness problem. On 13 October 1689 he admitted to having 1,000 sick (the real figure was three times higher), and just over a week later he was trying to reassure William that there were not as many sick as he had been informed from other sources.[198] On the second-last day of that year he noted (prematurely) that 'the sicknesses begin to abate'. Consequently, it was quite late when a co-ordinated medical response put in train. On 23 October Dr Richard Lawrence, chief physician of the expeditionary force, called together all the regimental surgeons to discuss what to do about the 'Flux and Fever, which then were very violent'.[199] It was probably on medical advice that orders were given to put the sick aboard ships but these orders were not executed for another fortnight. Between 20 and 27 October the

195   'Debates in 1689: November 23rd-30th', Grey's Debates of the House of Commons: vol. 9, (1769), pp.438-66; URL: http://www.british-history.ac.uk/report; date accessed: 15 February 2007; House of Commons Journal, vol. 10, 27 November 1689', Journal of the House of Commons, vol. 10: 1688-1693 (1802), pp.295-6; URL: http://www.british history.ac.uk/report; date accessed: 16 February 2007; House of Commons Journal, vol. 10; 16 December 1689, Journal of the House of Commons; vol. 10; 1688-1693 (1802), pp.309-10; URL: http://'/www.british-history.ac.uk/report, date accessed: 16 February 2007.
196   Childs, *Armies and Warfare*, p.103.
197   Pringle, *Observations on the Diseases of the Army*, pp.102, 174.
198   Schomberg to William, Dundalk 3 and 12 October, Dalrymple, *Memoirs* pp.36, 43.
199   Childs, *Armies and Warfare*, p.44; Story, *Impartial History*, p.29.

whole army at last shifted to a fresh campsite in the vicinity of Dundalk. This move may have been prompted by medical advice, but it is more likely that the camp site was shifted because some huts were 'over flow'd with water'.[200]

Whose fault was the catastrophe? Of course, Schomberg had grounds to complain of his subordinates. The paymaster embezzled, the commissary was incompetent, and many of the amateurish officers who commanded his English regiments neglected their charges. There were exceptions and it is quite conceivable that Colonels Gower, Deering, and Wharton contracted typhus while visiting their bedridden men. It was always hard to get soldiers to leave the comforting fug of hut or tent in foul weather, but it was up to regimental officers to try. Schomberg did sent out parties to bring ferns for bedding into the camp but the soldiers were so 'lazy' that they did not bother to collect their bedding or keep themselves 'dry and clean'.[201] The fact remains that armies commanded by Schomberg suffered heavy losses through sickness not just at Saint-Jean and Dundalk: in August 1662 Schomberg led an English expeditionary force to Portugal in August 1662 where about a third of his foot soldiers died or deserted within six months.[202]

Conclusion

The disaster that began at Dundalk shares some points of comparison with Schomberg's earlier debacle at Saint-Jean. The context of both episodes was an uncommonly long encampment because of Schomberg's tactical preference for defence and for positional warfare. His defensive posture was more justifiable at Saint-Jean than at Dundalk. Striking, too, was Schomberg's denial and deftness in deflecting blame when denial was no longer possible. Moreover, both outbreaks began during weather events that were extreme, even for the place and season. The proximate cause of the outbreak was the same, namely, heavy rain sluicing manure and faeces into the water supply, though one cannot be certain if the resultant disease was dysentery or a combination of dysentery and typhoid. Much effort was expended on isolating the sick by consigning soldiers to hospitals but far less to curing or even caring them once they were admitted. Patients at Perpignan may have been even more crowded and neglected than those at Carlingford or Belfast, not to mention the hospital ships sailing to Belfast.

If staying put during an epidemic was bad, moving was worse. A move out of contact with the enemy ratcheted epidemics into catastrophes as the hopeless cases were left behind, the less sick died in jolting carts and the least sick, who could just about walk, straggled and fell out of the column to lie down for ever. This was so even though Schomberg's retrograde manoeuvres at Saint-Jean and Dundalk were carefully prepared and as successfully executed as these things could be.

So much for the similarities between Saint-Jean and Dundalk. There remains the key difference between one third and one half of an army perishing of sickness. Two

200 Hewitson, *Diary of Thomas Bellingham*, p.90.
201 Story, *Impartial History*, p.27.
202 John Childs, *The Army of Charles II* (London: Routledge and Kegan Paul, 1976), p.163.

explanations spring to mind. In the first place, the epidemic sequence at Saint-Jean was truncated in that typhus, the third phase of the camp disease continuum, does not seem to have broken out. Secondly, it was easier for unhappy soldiers to desert from Saint-Jean than from Dundalk and many of those who deserted would otherwise have died of sickness.

3

Sieges

The traditional model for infectious disease is the triangle of external agent (such as a virus, bacterium, or other microbe) a susceptible host, and an environment that brings the agent to the host or victim. Agent and host are necessary but not sufficient conditions. Sieges have two environmental characteristics that can complete the triad. The first is congestion, the second immobility.

Besiegers and, especially, besieged were packed cheek by jowl within masonry or earthen ramparts. The degree of constriction varied. The image below shows the comparative areas of three besieged cities (Derry, Vienna, and Riga), together with two siege camps (Belgrade and Philippsburg) and one field camp (Alte Veste) associated with a quasi-siege. For convenience, the scale is the French *toise* of about two metres. All the places are clearly defined by their enceintes, with the exception of Philippsburg. The latter had a countervallation (an encircling line whose salient angles pointed away from the besieged place), but no circumvallation. An inundated flood plain served instead to separate besiegers from besieged and the edge of the flooded area is denoted by a broken line. The image also shows the best estimates of the camp or town's populations, rounded to the nearest thousand.

Soldiers and townspeople in besieged places like Vienna or, above all, Derry (numbering about 100,000 and 20,000, respectively) were far more cramped than the occupants of a field or campaign encampment such as Wallenstein's laager at Alte Veste in 1632 would have been.[1] Alte Veste enclosed over 100,000 troops and camp followers in what one expert considers a 'not unmanageably congested' area of four square miles, while another reminds us that such a huge population must have produced four tonnes of human excrement every day, and so the camp must have been 'swarming with rats and flies spreading disease'.[2] As noted in Chapter 1, 'ambulatory cities' of ragged and rain-sodden canvas did not enjoy urban amenities like cesspits, sewers, water pumps, rubbish tips, or watertight houses. Of course, besieged towns quickly lost or overloaded most of these amenities, and, relatively

---

1   The pre-war population of Vienna was about 100,000. The wartime garrison of 11,000 regular troops and refugees from the hinterland may have counter-balanced the flight of citizens. John Stoye, *The Siege of Vienna* (Reading: Birlinn, 2000), pp.39, 104; Andrew Wheatcroft, *The Enemy at the Gate* (New York: Perseus, 2008) p.118.

2   Geoff Mortimer, *Wallenstein: The Enigma of the Thirty Years War* (New York: Palgrave Macmillan, 2010) p.155; Peter Wilson, cited in Lauro Martines, *Furies: War in Europe, 1450–1700* (New York: Bloomsbury, 2013), p.173.

3.1 Siege camps and besieged cities.

speaking, the inhabitants of besieged towns were even more cramped than soldiers and camp followers swarming in a besieger's laager. Consider the outline of Vienna and of Derry to see how grossly overcrowded they were (though outworks expanded Derry's footprint during the siege) compared to, for example, the main siege laager outside Belgrade, which sheltered an estimated 72,000 mouths. One can envisage how urban inhabitable space might be extended into upper storeys and cellars, but that would not be enough to make up for the huge disparity in the respective footprints. Contagion, the person-to-person transmission of morbid matter, must have been greatly facilitated by proximity.

The second relevant characteristic is that these were static operations that immobilized tens of thousands for quite long stretches of time. Up until the middle of the seventeenth century it had been even worse, and the relative advantage lay with the besieged who could sit behind thick bastioned ramparts for months and even years, as was the case at Ostend (1601-1604), to take just one example.[3] In the latter half of the century, the advantage had swung to the attacker. The improvement can be attributed to the systematization of sapping and diggings associated with Vauban (1633-1707), Louis XIV's chief siege master. Deploying massed firepower (including

---

3   Christopher Duffy, *Fire and Stone: The Science of Fortress Warfare, 1660-1860* (New York: Hippocrene, 1975), p.100.

that new terror weapon, the mortar) and throwing manpower at the breaches could also shorten the siege even more: at both the French and Anglo-Dutch sieges of Namur in 1692 and 1695 respectively the attackers enjoyed a numerical advantage of about six to one. Finally, defenders were increasingly unlikely to 'fight like Turks' to the 'last extremity' (even Turks were less inclined to do so), and a prudent governor capitulated when the enemy had dug himself into the 'covered way' which formed the toughened outer skin of Baroque fortresses.[4] All of the sieges under discussion lasted between six and 15 weeks, except for Riga (1709-10) which was an outlier in that it dragged on for 10 months. The longer the camp lasted, the greater the accumulated filth and the more dangerous the epidemiological environment.

Bearing the characteristics of constriction and immobility in mind, let us consider three case studies.

Derry 1689

In March 1689, Richard Talbot, Earl of Tyrconnell, James II's Lord Deputy in Ireland, sent a small army under Lieutenant General Richard Hamilton to Ulster to bring the rebellious Protestant Association to heel. Hamilton successively routed the Association's forces near Dromore, County Down (14 March), at Portglenone, County Antrim (10 April) and at Cladyford, County Tyrone (15 April), and forced the survivors to fall back on the walled city of Derry, which was virtually the last place in Ireland still holding out for William III.

It was a strong place. The city stood on what had originally been called the 'Isle of the Derry' and it remained essentially insular. A 1685 water colour map by Thomas Phillips shows a ridge nestling into a bend of the River Foyle on the north-east to south-east segment. The rest of the segment (the aptly named 'Bogside' of later days) was spongy ground which had been made passable in places by drainage.[5] Derry's cruciform plan imitates the geometric grid layout of the Roman *castrum* with straight roads radiating from each side of the central square or 'diamond' (as it is known in Ulster) towards gates in a 'very strong wall' impervious to anything but close range artillery fire.[6] A windmill marked the highest elevation of the island's crest, half a mile to the south-west of Bishop's Gate in the city walls. That was an obvious place for the besiegers to site their guns which is why the first wartime governor, the execrated Lundy, built a ravelin in front of Bishop's Gate.[7]

The opening move in any leaguer was to surround, or 'invest', the city. This the Jacobites duly did, but their ring was loose and their troops stretched thinly. The besieged, led by the inspirational Colonel Adam Murray, sallied out on 21 April

4   Marquis de Feuquières, *Mémoires* (Amsterdam: François L'Honore & Zacharie Chatelain, 1741), Vol.II, p.197.
5   B.G. Scott, 'Plans and economies: defending the Plantation city of Londonderry', *The Journal of Irish Archaeology* Vol.X, (2011), p.144.
6   Scott et al., 'Great guns like thunder', pp.70, 72, 88–9.
7   Richard, Doherty, *The Siege of Derry 1689: The Military History* (Gloucestershire: Spellmount Publishers, 2010), p.36.

to probe a weak point, about a mile north of the city where the Pennyburn River debouched into the Foyle. Lieutenant General François de Maumont, the officer in charge of the siege, quickly gathered as many horsemen as he could, scattered Murray's horsemen and pursued them back towards the walls of the city. Protestant musketeers in a nearby orchard then fired on the Irish horsemen, killing Maumont as well as his second-in-command.[8] The significance of the Pennyburn skirmish was twofold. By eliminating the top two officers in the chain of command, it left Hamilton, who was 'neither a great general nor a skilled siege commander'.[9] In the second place, Pennyburn confirmed the dominance of Jacobite cavalry over the countryside that surrounded the 'island' of the Derry. As late as 25 July, during the last days of the siege, hungry foragers, goaded by the sight of cattle grazing behind the Jacobite lines, broke out briefly. But the 'Battle of the Cows' ended when a cavalry counter-attack drove the foragers back.[10] The besieged would not be able to break out.

Nor could the besiegers break in. Aside from a small detachment on the east bank of the Foyle, they had about 7,000 men ensconced in a semicircle to cut off the landward side of the city: hardly more than the number of armed men within.[11] Twice the Jacobites tried to seize Windmill Hill. On the night of 5-6 May, 3,000 Jacobites appeared out of the darkness, drove off the pickets and set about entrenching over the ridge from the Bogside to the Foyle. The underlying plan was to constrict the garrison within the walls and deny them access to fodder and spring water. However, a Williamite counter-attack drove the Irish off the hill the next day.[12] Murray, belatedly recognising the weakness of Windmill Hill, completed the fortifications begun by the enemy and so secured an additional area larger than that enclosed by the city walls.

On 4 June, 84 days into the siege, the besiegers tried again. The main attack 'could have been more prudently managed' (a generous understatement that) by the Irish whose line of battle stepped forward slowly in broad daylight under heavy fire, only to find the 12-foot high earthworks impassable without scaling ladders.[13] They pulled back, after sustaining their heaviest casualties of the siege: 'Blessed be God! we had a notable victory over them, to their great discouragement', exulted Captain Thomas Ash within the city.[14] The final attack was made on 28 June when an improbably small party of 200 men assailed Butcher's Gate, facing the Bogside, but were quickly rebuffed. Just over a month later, HMS *Swallow* broke the boom across the

---

8   Doherty, *Siege of Derry 1689*, pp.96-97; D'Avaux to Louis XIV and to Louvois, Dublin 6 May
     1689, D'Avaux to Louvois, Dublin 12 May 1689 in J. Hogan (ed.) *Négociations de M. le Comte
     D'Avaux en Irlande 1689-90* (Dublin: Government Publications Office, 1934), pp.110, 117,
     139.

9   Carlo Gebler, *The Siege of Derry* (London: Little Brown, 2005), p.183.

10   Doherty, *Siege of Derry 1689*, p.191.

11   Gébler, *Siege of Derry*, p.171.

12   Doherty, *Siege of Derry*, pp.150-153; J. T. Gilbert (ed.) *A Jacobite narrative of the war in
     Ireland, 1688-1691* (Shannon: Irish University Press, 1972), p.79; John Childs, *The Williamite
     Wars in Ireland 1688-91* (London: Hambledon Continuum, 2007), pp.122-123.

13   Doherty, *Siege of Derry*, pp.105, 118-121; Gilbert, *Jacobite Narrative*, pp.77-8, 226.

14   John Hempton (ed.), *The siege and history of Londonderry* (Derry: Hempton, 1861), p.286.

Foyle, whereupon two merchantmen laden with beef, peas, flour, and biscuit sailed through. There was no longer any chance of starving Derry into submission, so the Jacobites decamped, on the night of 31 July.

If we take into account the numbers that perished in the three-month long stalemate, we are told that '… it was one of the most disastrous struggles of modern times'.[15] Hyperbole aside, in relative terms, the losses among the defenders (about the Jacobites we simply do not know) were heavy. Captain Joseph Bennet claimed that there were 12,000 'Men in Arms in the Town', and this may be true of the opening stage of the siege, after which Bennet was sent out of the city as a courier to slip through enemy lines.[16] A more credible figure of 7,020 rank and file, embodied in eight named regiments, is cited by Rev. George Walker, joint governor for a time.[17] The overall pattern is of a steep and accelerating fall in the size of the garrison.

Table 3.1 Garrison of Derry 1689[18]

19 April	7,020
8 July	5,520
13 July	5,310
17 July	5,114
22 July	4,973
25 July	4,892
27 July	4,465
30 July	4,300

The besieged came off best in most clashes, and no more than 100 of them were killed in action. Desertion certainly accounts for a component of those heavy losses, as at the beginning of the siege Hamilton had been naively lenient in letting soldiers and civilians pass through his lines when the normal practice was to drive so-called 'useless mouths' back to continue consuming the town's provisions. At the beginning of the siege, French envoy D'Avaux grumbled that every day Hamilton was letting 50-100 civilians slip out of the city, 'contrary to orders'.[19] We also know of five captains who left during the siege and a proportional number of men (perhaps

---

15   Thomas Witherow, *Derry and Enniskillen in the Year 1689* (Belfast: William Mullen, 1873), p.173.

16   Joseph Bennet, *A true and impartial account of the most material passages in Ireland since December 1688 with a particular relation of the forces of Londonderry* (London: John Amery, 1689) p.25; Anon. *An Account of the most remarkable occurrences relating to London-Derry with a relation of the signal defeat given to the French and Irish papists, May 5, 1689* (London, Richard Baldwin, 1689), p.1.

17   Rev. George Walker, *A true account of the siege of Londonderry* (London: Robert Clavel and Ralph Simpson, 1689), pp.16, 38.

18   Walker, *A true account*, pp.38-39, 41; Doherty, *Siege of Derry 1689*, p.207; Joshua Gillespie, *A Narrative of the Most Remarkable Events in the Life of William the Third* (Derry: M. Hempton, 1823), p.148.

19   D'Avaux to Louvois, 18 May 1689, Hogan, *Négociations*, p.159.

3-400 or so) doubtless also slipped away. Discounting depletion due to desertion and losses in action, sickness probably carried off just under 32 percent of the garrison.

What can account for such a grievously heavy death toll in just three months? Survivor narratives offer the traditional litany of Galenic 'conditions': John Mackenzie blamed the 'Feavers' and 'Flux' ('of which great Numbers died'), on 'want of Rest and Food', and on cold caught by terrified soldiers and civilians who fled outdoors to 'lie about the walls all night' for fear of bomb-strikes.[20] Stilted dialogue between governor Henry Baker and his successor John Michelburne, as represented in the latter's drama 'Ireland Preserved' is Galenic in tone:

> BAKER, I find myself much indisposed; and my being called out of my warm room, on that occasion, has, I fear, brought on a relapse of my sickness, which was severe enough in its first attack. I have some apprehension that it may be fatal. MICHELBURNE. God forbid; you have only caught cold on this late action, having been out from sunset to sunrise, but I hope it will pass over, by care not to expose yourself to the sharp winds of this wintry spring...[21]

Above all, survivor accounts dwell on hunger. 'Ireland Preserved' mentions 'hunger' ten times, 'sickness' thrice, and 'flux' or 'fever' not at all.[22] His co-governor George Walker emphasized hunger and included a price list of foodstuffs such as horse and dog meat from the days just before the relief. Walker famously concluded by telling of a 'fat gentleman' who went into hiding 'because he imagined that some of the soldiers, who were perishing by hunger, looked at him with a greedy eye'.

At first the food ration sufficed with each soldier getting a weekly issue of 'a Salmon and a half, two pound of Beef, and four Quarts of Oate-meal. Good strong Beer is also order'd to be sold at a Penny a Quart'.[23] But by the end, the soldier was cut to 'a half pound of tallow fried with a piece of Hide, and a pint of Meal daily'.[24] A source reliant on Major General Percy Kirke maintained that by the time his relief fleet broke the boom, the inhabitants had only 'began to want', and had been just 'for some days together' reduced to gnawing on horsemeat and a biscuit every day.[25] Kirke would have had a motive to downplay the hardships endured by the people in Derry, in order to defend himself against accusations of tardiness and timidity in

---

20 John Mackenzie, *A narrative of the siege of London-Derry* (London: Richard Baldwin, 1690), p.38.

21 Michelburne, 'Ireland Preserved', p.126.

22 John Graham, (ed). *John Michelburne, 'Ireland Preserved; or the Siege of Londonderry'*, (Dublin: Hardy and Walker, 1841), passim.

23 Anon., *An Account of the most remarkable occurrences relating to London-Derry with a relation of the signal defeat given to the French and Irish papists, May 5, 1689* (London: Richard Baldwin, 1689), p.1.

24 Anon., *An Exact account of the raising the siege of Londonderry and the deplorable condition the town was in, till happily reliev'd by Major-General Kirk* (London: R. Wood, 1689), p.2.

25 Anon., *Account from Colonel Kirk of the relieving of London-Derry* (Edinburgh: publisher unknown, 1689).

relieving the besieged city, yet other accounts corroborate Kirke. For 27 July Captain Thomas Ashe recorded in his diary:

> God knows, we never stood in such need of supply; for now there is not one week's provision in the garrison. Of necessity we must surrender the city, and make the best terms we can for ourselves. Next Wednesday is our last, if relief does not arrive before it. This day the cows and horses, sixteen of the first, and twelve of the last, were slaughtered; the blood of the cows was sold at four pence per quart, and that of the horses at two pence. There is not a dog to be seen, they are all killed and eaten.[26]

On the face of it, this makes grim reading but the fact is that the soldiers were put on short rations rather than no rations at all, and the last of the beeves and horses were slaughtered only three days before the city would be relieved. The supplies would hold out, barely, and no soldier perished of outright hunger. Close reading of the memoirs penned by John Hunter of Maghera, County Derry, who served as a private soldier, also suggests as much:

> I myself would have eaten the poorest cat or dog I ever saw with my eyes. The famine was so great, that many a man, woman, and child, died for want of food. I myself was so weak from hunger, that I fell under my musket one morning as I was going to the walls; yet God gave me strength to continue all night at my post there, and enabled me to act the part of a soldier as if I had been as strong as ever I was; yet my face was blackened with hunger. I was so hard put to it, by reason of the want of food, that I had hardly any heart to speak or walk.[27]

Hunger gnawed at Hunter, weakened him, but did not kill him. Civilians may very well have perished of hunger, but men under arms were issued with enough provisions to keep body and soul together, though one source claims that 'many hundreds' of soldiers also died of famine.[28] As discussed in Chapter 2, malnutrition certainly worsened the course of fluxes and fevers, but may not have increased the risk of infection in the first place.

Water rather than food was a more critical problem; indeed, water supply in Derry would long prove tight, even in peacetime. The River Foyle's waters were, and are, too brackish to be potable and before 1800 the inhabitants of the city had to carry water from wells without the walls since what could be drawn from pumps within was insufficient.[29] Later, until the mid-19th century, the growing city had to

---

26   Captain Thomas Ashe, 'Circumstantial Journal' in Hempton (ed.) *The siege and history of Londonderry,* p.300.
27   Witherow, *Derry and Enniskillen in the Year 1689,* p.157.
28   Anon., *An Exact account,* p.2.
29   Robert Simpson, *The Annals of Derry: Showing the Rise and Progress of the Town* (Derry: Hempton, 1847), p.214.

draw its clean water from reservoirs on the Waterside, the other side of the Foyle.[30] In wartime conditions, the water sources within the walls, always muddy, were contaminated, Carlo Gébler suggests, from lanes awash with human excrement.[31] This certainly happened in a comparable situation in Belgrade just six years earlier, when the soldiers relieved themselves in the streets and alleys despite municipal bye-laws to the contrary.[32] The nearest clean water sources to the besieged in Derry were St Columb's (*recte* Colmcille's) three wells. These are shown on Neville's 1689 siege map as lying about 60 metres from the double bastion on the south-western corner of the city, in the Bogside. Sixty metres was a great distance in a close siege, as the well lay at the bottom of a steep slope in the no-man's land beyond and below the outworks on Windmill Hill. As early as 14 May, George Walker complained of the 'great difficulty' in reaching the well '...which they often Fought for, and cost some of them their Blood. One Gentleman had a Bottle broke at his Mouth by a Shot; yet the Water of the Town was so muddied and troubled with our continual Firing, and so many going to it, that we were forced to run those hazards'.[33] A month later, the Irish seem at last to have woken up to the critical importance of St Colmcille's Well, and burrowed even closer, according to Captain Ash's diary entry for 20 June: They are come close to our skirts now, so that none without great hazard dare go to Columb-Kill's well for water.[34] Many did not run the risk: 'I could not,' groused John Hunter, 'get a drink of clean water'.[35] Evidently, he imbibed dirty water.

Inferences that the available water supply was contaminated gives the clearest pointer that typhoid must have been the major component of the epidemic that killed one third of the garrison in three months. Dysentery, as discussed in Chapter 2, could not deliver so high a case fatality rate.

Riga 1709-10

Peter the Great's destruction of the Swedish army at Poltava in 1709 serves as a reminder that even in an epoch dominated by the measured tempo of the siege, a truly decisive battle, both tactically and strategically, could still be fought. Following Poltava, a Russian army marched on Riga, the Baltic German city which comprised the greatest Swedish stronghold in Livonia, a territory that would straddle present-day southern Estonia and northern Latvia. Field Marshal Sheremetev laid siege to the city and had blocked up the River Dvina or Daugava by 27 October (or 7 November by the Russian calendar) 1709. He possessed a prodigious artillery train

---

30   'Report on the Londonderry Borough Improvement Bill' in *Parliamentary Papers* (London, 1847-48) (xxxi) pp.2-3; John Hume, *Derry Beyond the Walls: Social and Economic Aspects of the Growth of Derry* (Belfast: Ulster Historical Foundation, 2002), p.61.

31   Gébler, *The Siege Of Derry*, pp.225, 264.

32   Melchior Landersdorfer, 'Das Schicksal der bayerischen Soldaten im Türkenkrieg' (Dissertation; Technische Universität München, 1984), p.43.

33   Gillespie, *A Narrative of the Most Remarkable Events in the Life of William the Third*, p.115.

34   'The Trial of Lieutennat Colonel Robert Lundie', at http://thetrialoflundy.com/20th-june-1689/

35   Witherow, *Derry and Enniskillen*, p.157.

of 300 cannons and 63 mortars, and lined many of his guns along the banks of the River Daugava to deter any relief fleet that would try to sail the short distance upriver from the Swedish coastal fort of Dünamünde, or modern Daugavgrīvas. He could not take the city and citadel outright, because the ramparts and moats were too massive, and the garrison of 10,414 regulars too numerous.

From 25 November, Russian mortars began to hurl projectiles into the city.[36] On 12 December, a projectile sparked a conflagration that spread to the main gunpowder magazine, which was housed in one of the citadel bastions. The resulting explosion wrecked the nearby hospital, sheltering as many as 1,200 sick soldiers, and 'hurled 600 able-bodied soldiers into the air'.[37] The author of a siege journal recalled with horror seeing 'men's shoes and legs on all the streets, small children at the breasts of the mothers lying [dead] in the houses' after the massive explosion.[38]

Table 3.2 Bombs on Riga 1709-10[39]

Nov.	Dec.	Jan.	Feb.	Mar.	Apr	May	June
201	387	299	349	288	476	423	1,147

Bombs were a terror weapon that seldom actually decided outcomes. They continued to rain down steadily until June, when the tempo increased fivefold. However, other events proved more decisive. On 9 June 1710, a Swedish squadron arrived at Dünamünde and tried to sail upriver to Riga, but was driven off by the heavy gunfire of the batteries lining the shore. Riga was definitively cut off. By 7 June, the garrison was reduced to eating horsemeat for want of bread which was increasingly scarce, with cereal prices tripling between March and June.[40] Ominously, the Russians had twice (on 1 and 2 June) broken through the palisades at different points along the defensive enceinte.[41] The siege journal that comprises our main source finishes abruptly on 18 June, while the siege had 12 days yet to run (presumably the author died) and on 30 June negotiations began for the surrender of the city. On 5 July governor Stromberg capitulated, pressed by the burgers and clergy who were willing to surrender if they were promised their traditional rights and liberties. As it happened, the Russians would grant generous terms that retained traditional rights,

36 John Mottley, *The Life of Peter the Great, Emperor of All Russia* (London: M. Cooper, 1755), Vol.II, pp.41, 45; Robert I. Frost, *The Northern Wars: war, state and society in Northeastern Europe, 1558-1721* (Harlow: Longman, 2000), p.294.

37 Heinrich Anselm, *Historisches Labyrinth der Zeit: darinnen die Denckwürdigsten Welt...* (Leipzig: Gleditsch, 1718), p.1372, Bayerische Staatsbibliothek http://reader.digitale-sammlungen.de/en/fs1/object/display/bsb11197404_01396.html.

38 'Jaurnal öfver Staden Rijgas Belägringh' in Gustaf F. Floderus, *Handlingar hörande till Konung Carl XII:s historia* (Stockholm: unknown publisher, 1819-26), Vol.II, p.79.

39 'Jaurnal öfver Staden Rijgas Belägringh', in Floderus, *Handlingar*, Vol.II, pp.178, 181, 182,186,189, 196, 204.

40 A.V. Bulmerincq (ed.) *Aktenstücke und Urkunden zur Geschichte der Stadt Riga 1710-1740*, (Riga: J. Deubner, 1902-06), Vol.III, p.15. Biblioteka Uniwersytecka w Toruniu, http://www.kpbc.ukw.edu.pl/dlibra/plain-content?id=35439

41 'Jaurnal öfver Staden Rijgas Belägringh', in Floderus, *Handlingar*, Vol.II, p.204.

recovered privileges abolished by the Swedes, and recognized the pre-eminence of the German language and Lutheran confession. Moreover, Stromberg was also only too aware that the men in his charge were hungry, hopelessly cut-off, and being mown down by the 'pestilential disease'.[42]

'Pest' is often a synonym for plague, but was this disease really the plague? A wartime epidemic that reached the Baltic coast at Danzig (modern Gdańsk) in January 1709, swept east along the littoral to Königsberg (Kaliningrad) by August 1709 and thence north-east to Vilnius by late autumn 1709 and Courland (Kurzeme in western Latvia). Following Frandsen, I believe this Baltic epidemic was 'basically the same' as modern *Yersenia Pestis*, or, to put it another way, it belonged to one of the twelve *Yersinia Pestis* strains and biovars.[43]

Puzzlingly, no contemporary account written during the siege mentions plague as such. Colonel Gustav Ernst Albedyll's reports of 30 May and 6 June 1710 complain that his soldiers had no pay to buy food at the inflated prices and that the officers were hard-put to stop them from eating carcasses and from hunting cats and dogs. Of plague there was 'not one word'.[44]

So, was plague present at all? The disease minutely described by *Oberpastor* Bartholomew Depkin (he himself was struck down on 8 July) had a wide range of features, namely fever, fatigue, diarrhoea, and headache. If that was all, then 'by the grace of God there was hope for life'.[45] But if 'buboes, carbuncles and spots' appeared there would be little hope. Since buboes did not always appear, it is not surprising that initial outbreaks of the Baltic plague epidemic of 1709-10 were often described as 'hot fever'.[46]

What set plague apart from all the diseases discussed was its sheer lethality. The buboes were the most dramatic symptom of the plague, and in almost 60 percent of cases death followed between three and five days after they erupt. The pneumonic variant followed when *Yersenia Pestis* settled in the lungs, and that was 'almost invariably and rapidly fatal'.[47] On the face of it, the death toll of the garrison does not point to plague.[48]

---

42   Bulmerincq, *Geschichte der Stadt Riga*, p.15.

43   Karl-Erik, Frandsen, *The Last Plague in the Baltic Region, 1709-1713* (Copenhagen: Museum Tusculanum Press, 2010), p.42; Ann G. Carmichael, '1 Universal and Particular: The Language of Plague, 1348–1500' in *Medical History*, Supplement 27 (2008), p.17.

44   Frandsen, *The Last Plague*, p.13.

45   Frandsen, *The Last Plague*, p.44.

46   Frandsen, *The Last Plague*, pp.396-397.

47   J.N. Hays, *The Burdens of Disease: Epidemics and Human Response in Western History* (New Brunswick: Rutgers University Press, 2009), p.38.

48   'Jaurnal öfver Staden Rijgas Belägringh', in Floderus, *Handlingar*, Vol.II, p.172; F. Arfwidsson, *Försvaret av Östersjöprovinserna 1708-1710* (Celle: Gefleborgs Tryckeri Aktiebolag, 1936), p.400-401; Mottley, *Life of Peter the Great*, Vol.II, p.41; 'Oderint dum probent', https:// rusmilhist.blogspot.ie/2011/04/swedish-garrison-of-riga-10-july-1710.html. The figure of 12,000 cited by Mettig probably includes armed townsmen; C. Mettig, *Geschichte der Stadt Riga* (Riga: Jonk & Poliewsky, 1897), p.372. Bulmerincq puts the final Swedish strength as low as 1,500; Bulmerincq, *Geschichte der Stadt Riga*, p.15.

Table 3.3 Swedish Garrison Strength 1709-10

	30 September	9 November	10 July
Total	10,414	9,431	5,132
Sick		202	2,905

The loss of 51 percent of the regular troops in the garrison over nine months is by no means unprecedented, and bears comparison with, for example, the death toll at Dundalk over a shorter time span. Some of the 51 percent were killed in action, including the 600 men supposedly blown up by the magazine explosion in mid-December. As against that, the 10 July figures capture just a relatively early phase of an epidemic, which continued to rage in Riga until October, following the habitual summertime seasonal footprint of plague. Moreover, the rapid pace of the epidemic is captured by Alebdyll's returns for just five days, 1-5 June, when he reported that 132 all ranks had died in that time and 230 had fallen sick. Assuming that the tempo of mortality stayed constant (and it probably quickened), that would amount to 1,056 dead between 1 June and the day of capitulation. In other words, the garrison was still an estimated 6,188 strong on 1 June when sickness began to pose a grave threat, graver even than bombardment. Russian breakthroughs were now happening because the shrinking numbers of ambulatory Swedes were stretched too thinly. By the time of the capitulation, 49 percent of the survivors were sick, and most of the sick were doomed. If one had a later head count, from August, the death toll would have been far higher than 51 percent, at least 70 percent.

Frandsen concludes that plague reached Riga in mid May 1710 while Mettig's 1897 history of Riga seems to imply that the plague began *after* the capitulation and he embeds his conclusion in miasmic theory (Alexander Yersin had identified *Yersinia Pestis* only three years earlier): 'The fresh air that penetrated into the city seemed to stir up the pestilential miasmas and spread them in the debilitated constitutions of the inhabitants'.[49] Elsewhere, however, Mettig accepts that plague broke out before the capitulation in asserting that 'more than 20,000 inhabitants of the city perished of the plague *during the siege* and in the two [August and September] subsequent months'. Incidentally, this would imply that some 60-70 percent of Riga's population perished, which is the worst outcome compared to recent estimates (Table 3.4) for other Baltic urban centres.

Sheremetev reported cases of plague among his troops beginning on 14 May, presumably among those troops south of the Daugava, and he ordered his troops (less those infected, one imagines) to pull back north of the river and use the geographical barrier as a *cordon sanitaire*.[50] This precaution proved to be in vain: an anecdote from a Russian source speaks of a dog with two heads that swam across the Daugava from Courland. Two-headed dogs do not feature among the more common animal portents of plague. The Arab physician Avicenna warned his readers to look

49   Mettig, *Geschichte der Stadt Riga*, pp.376-77.
50   John T. Alexander, *Bubonic Plague in Early Modern Russia: Public Health and Urban Disaster* (Oxford: Oxford University Press, 2003), p.22.

for animal portents that would herald plague such as frogs, snakes, mice, and basilisks fleeing their holes in the ground as a pestilential corruption emerged from the earth to corrupt the air and then to be borne on the winds.[51] However, the hellhound Cerberus was associated with death and in Greek mythology, three-headed Cerberus guarded the entrance to Hades by the banks of the river Styx. The hellhound's swimming the river, then, symbolizes his bearing death from Hades or, in the present case, Courland. Sheremetev was harried with advice from Tsar Peter to keep healthy regiments apart from plague-ridden ones during the 'fever seasons' of summer and autumn; to isolate sick soldiers and to ply the healthy with wine and camphor. Notwithstanding the Tsar's advice, the Russian army suffered heavily and lost 9,800 men in the outbreak, so many that the assaults planned for May had to be postponed for a month.

The plague must have been carried from or through the Russian blockade by a deserter or refugee. The siege journal notes, for example, that on 4 May, 'at night a farmer arrived, escaped from the enemy'.[52] Perhaps he was the 'patient zero' of the plague epidemic in Riga. He would not be the last. The city council complained shortly after the capitulation that the plague had carried off so many townspeople that there were not enough left to repair the roofs of the houses damaged in the bombardment.[53] The claim was hardly an exaggeration and the plague, as noted above, carried off up to 70 per cent of the whole population.

Table 3.4 Population Loss from Plague[54]

Königsberg	20-25 percent.
Danzig	50-65 percent.
Reval/Tallinn	55-70 percent.
Riga	60-70 percent.

The plague was intimately bound up with the Great Northern War in that the movement of soldiers and refugees was the most important vector of transmission. This connection would continue after the capitulation of Riga, when the Russians permitted 114 Swedish households to sail to Stockholm bearing the pestilence across the Baltic with them.

In comparing Derry and Riga, can one generalize that the longer the siege and more cramped the place, the worse the epidemic? Simply totting up how many died relative to the initial strength of the garrison, Riga's experience was worse, with just over half the Swedes perishing (mainly of disease) by the time they capitulated. In

---

51 John Aberth, *An Environmental History of the Middle Ages: The Crucible of Nature* (London and New York: Routledge, 2013), pp.15-16.

52 Jaurnal öfver Staden Rijgas Belägringh' in Floderus, *Handlingar*, Vol.II, p.198.

53 Mettig, *Geschichte der Stadt Riga*, p.376.

54 Stefan Kroll, "*Die 'Pest' im Ostseeraum zu Beginn des 18 Jahrhunderts.Stand und Perspektiven der Forschung*" in Stefan Kroll and Kersten Krüger (eds.) *Städtesystem und Urbanisierung im Ostseeraum in der frühen Neuzeit* (Münster: LIT Verlag, 2006), p.137.

contrast, over a third of Derry's defenders had died before Kirke's relief fleet broke through the boom. Mortality at Derry was undoubtedly high and it was, not coincidentally, the most grossly overcrowded space of all those cited with, moreover, clear evidence that the water supply was inadequate and dirty. Riga's loss was spread out over three times the length of time and the accompanying graph shows that the gradient of falling numbers was comparable.

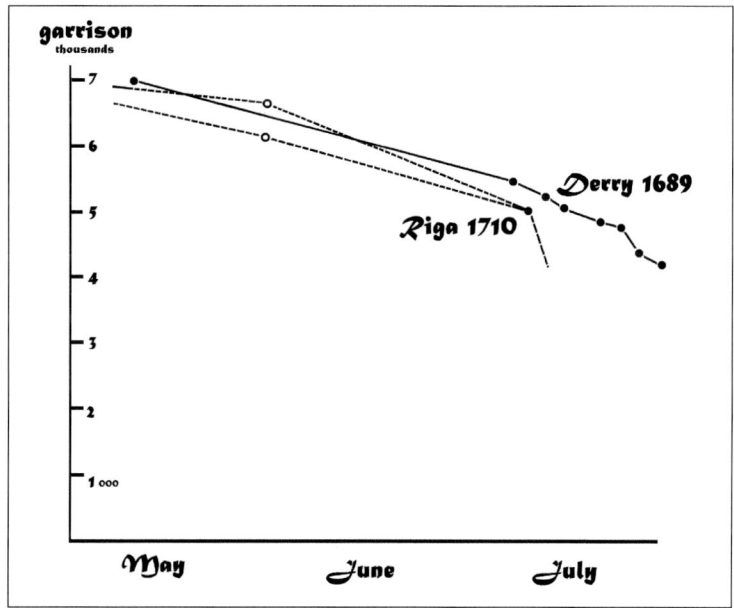

3.2 Garrison strength: Derry and Riga.

Yet the comparison tends to downplay the death rate in Riga in that the final data point of the line graph represents the strength at the time the garrison capitulated at the beginning of the bubonic plague epidemic. Given the very high morbidity among the Swedes by then, it is reasonable to posit that the fall in numbers accelerated after that point. Moreover, the positioning of the middle data point of the line is speculative. The estimated strength of the garrison on 1 June of 6,188 men is arrived at by back-projection from the tally at capitulation assuming the numbers of dead per day (shown in Table 3.7) remained constant but the daily death rate probably increased. That equally plausible reconstruction would yield a line with a steeper fall-off in numbers at Riga than at Derry.

In all, Riga probably had it worse.

Belgrade 1717

During the 1683-1699 phase of the long conflict between Habsburg and Ottoman, Elector Max Emmanuel of Bavaria seized Belgrade in 1688, only for Mustafa Kuprili to recapture it in 1690. Three years later, a 49-day Habsburg siege failed, leaving

Belgrade solidly in Turkish hands as their new military and administrative frontier headquarters. Emboldened by their victories over the Russians in 1711 on the Pruth River and over the Venetians in 1715 in the Morea, the Ottomans had renewed the war with the Habsburgs and in July 1716 Grand Vizier Ali Pasha led a large army 42 miles north-west from Belgrade against the Habsburg frontier post of Peterwardein [Petrovaradin], on the Danube. However, Eugene of Savoy (1663-1721) crushed Ali Pasha's army and followed up his victory by conquering the Banat of Temesvár which was the last Ottoman territory north of the Danube.

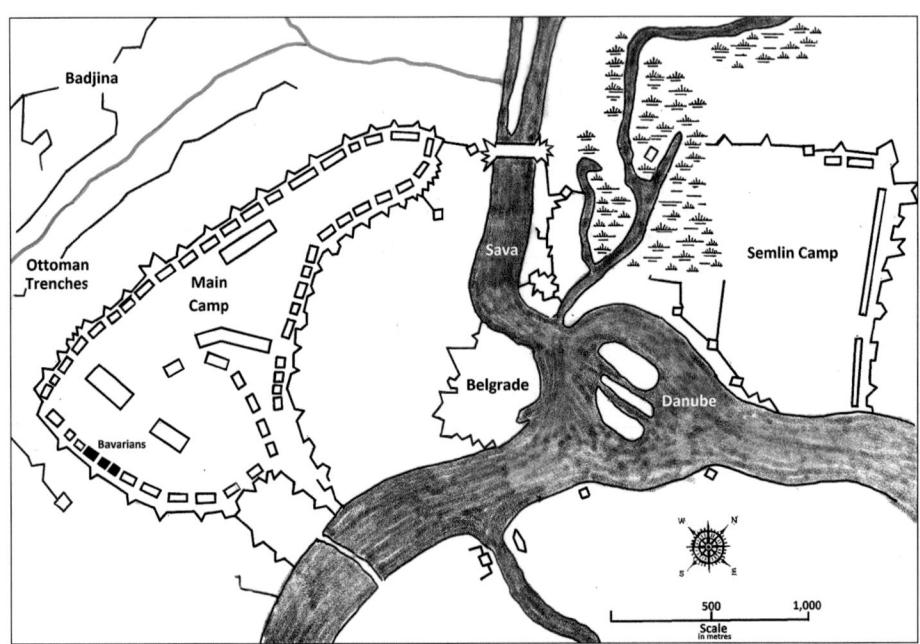

3.3 Imperial camp, Belgrade 1717.

Eugene had first fought for the Habsburgs at the Siege of Vienna in 1683, and had earned European renown by defeating the Ottomans at Zenta [Senta] in 1697. He was a peerless battlefield commander, with an unerring ability to foresee threats, identify fleeting opportunities, and react appropriately. As a siege commander, however, he was merely competent, as evidenced by the crude and bloody assaults he had thrown against Lille in 1708.

At the head of the largest army he had ever commanded, Eugene threw a bridge of boats across the Danube and forced his way over to Belgrade between 15 and 16 June. It would not be until 22 July that he had completed the lines of contravallation and circumvallation in the face of lively opposition from the 30,000-strong Turkish garrison. The contravallation, the lines bristling outwards, was a necessary precaution because, as Eugene knew, the Grand Vizier Khalil Pasha was on the march from Adrianople with a relieving army of no fewer than 150,000 men. By then Eugene's force numbered 116,480 men in all, or about 95,000 men in and around Belgrade itself.[55] Belgrade sat at the apex of a triangle formed by the confluence of the Sava and Danube, and Eugene's siege lines ran in a semicircle from the Danube to the Sava, enclosing Belgrade. In addition, his men built a pontoon bridge over the Danube and another over the Sava. About a quarter of Eugene's 95,000 men occupied the 'little camp' over the Sava at Semlin [Zemun] in order to protect the all-important bridge and supply route from Peterwardein.[56] Four battalions of foot, or about 2,800 men, were also posted to guard a bridge over the Danube.[57] That left some 72,000 men within the fortified *grosse lager* which belied its name and was quite cramped.[58]

Knowing that a Turkish relief army was on the way, Eugene did not begin sapping towards the city ramparts but dug-in and waited.[59] On the afternoon of 2 August, the Turks duly arrived and pitched their tents so that a carpet of green and red spread behind the crest of the peninsula, tucked away out of sight of the Christian army.[60] The latter's 'Great Camp' sat 'in something like a small valley overlooked on one side by the town ramparts and on the other by knolls where the relieving army was encamped'.[61] Massed guns and mortars fired non-stop from the higher ground so that nowhere was safe from falling bombs or from cannon shot ricocheting along the sun-baked earth. Eugene declined to allow his tent to be pitched somewhere less conspicuous, even after one of his own servants was killed by a cannon ball as he was entering it, though he prudently moved the magazine further away from his own tent.[62]

55   Anon., *Die grossen Thaten…in dem Königreich Ungarn* (Nuremberg, 1717) pp.7-8, p.32; J. Odenthal, *Oesterreichs Turkenkrieg 1716-1718* (Düsseldorf: G.H.Nolte, 1938), p.80.

56   Anon. *Campagnes de … Prince Eugene en Hongrie* (Lyon: Thomas Armaulry, 1718), p.197; Anon., *Lettres historiques, contenant ce qui se passe de plus important…',* vol. 52 (Amsterdam: Adrian Moetjens, July 1717), pp.26, 65; François C. Le Roy de Lozembrune, *Histoire de la guerre de Hongrie pendant les campagnes de 1716, 1717 et 1718* (Vienna: Graetfer, 1788), pp.127, 132; Anon., *Ausführliche Beschreibung des Ungarischen Feld-Zugs Anno 1717* (Nuremberg: Johann Albrecht, 1717), p.31, BSB. https://reader.digitale-sammlungen.de/de/fs1/object/display/bsb10352837_00001.html

57   *Designation und Explication über die Schlacht so zwischen dem Keyser[lichen] und Türck[ischen] Lager bey Belgrad auf Röm[ischen] keyser[lichen] Maj[estät] Seiten unter Com[m]ando Sr Durch[laucht] Prinzens Eugeny von Savoyen den 16 Aug. 1717.* A reliable map names and depicts all the units. In the small camp were 30 infantry battalions and 18 cavalry squadrons depicted and in the large camp 108 and 123 respectively thus (allowing 700 men for every infantry battalion and 140 men for every squadron) making 95,000 in total. 'Lager vor Belgrad', Bibliothèque nationale de France, CPL GE DD-2987 (5903).

58   Marquis de Villette to Madame de Maintenon, 17 July 1717, Belgrade, in Honoré Bonhomme (ed.), *Madame de Maintenon et sa famille, lettres et documents inédits…* (Paris: Didier et Cie.,1863), p.160.

59   *Le Nouveau Mercure,* Paris, September 1717, p.157.

60   Nurdan Melek Aksulu, *Die Hohe Pforte, Türkenkriege, Konflikte und Beziehungen zwischen Abendland* (Norderstedt: Wolf & Sohn, 2009), p.159.

61   Eleazar De Mauvillon, *Histoire du Prince François Eugene de Savoie…* (Amsterdam: D'Arkstee & Merkus, 1740), pp.139. 152.

62   *The Daily Courant,* London 23 August 1717 no. 4941, p.1.

Though he lay ill from a tertian fever (doubtless malarial), with his army sand-wiched between enemy forces almost double his own, Eugene nonetheless projected calm resolve. However, Alessandro Marquis de Maffei one of Eugene's generals, and a fellow-Italian, did not share his commander's optimism:

> The position of our camp is bizarre. We are besieging a place with a powerful garrison, we are at the same time besieged by a formidable army, on our right we have the Save, on our left the Danube so that we are locked up in a cage [and] we must conquer or die.[63]

Eugene's plan had apparently been to fortify his camp with virtually impregnable retrenchments and wait for eight days after which shortage of forage would force the bloated Ottoman relief army to decamp.[64] Eugene thought his troops had consumed the forage for six or seven leagues about but he 'soon learned otherwise', a French volunteer ruefully noted.[65] For the next fortnight, the Turks burrowed ever closer inwards. Their 175 artillery pieces could hit 'almost the whole of our [the Imperial] front' and on the night of 13 August, the grand vizier doubled the fire against the imperial camp. His troops had dug their approach trenches within musket shot and were piling up fascines in apparent preparation for a storm.[66] Eugene ordered his guns and mortars to fire on Belgrade, 'to make the Turks believe, he design'd to give an Assault to it' and a lucky shot touched a powder magazine within the fortress, setting off a massive explosion that killed 3,000 Turks.[67] By now, 14 August, Eugene was on his feet again, and, seeing his troops so 'hard pressed' and 'cramped', he chose to attack his attackers.[68] Shortly after midnight, on 15 August, two lines of Imperials crept silently uphill towards the Ottoman batteries, shielded by darkness and mist.

Even by the standards of Eugene's dare-devilry, this was a desperate throw of the dice. Many contemporaneous accounts, and most later ones, conclude that he must have taken the gamble because his army was wasting away through sickness and his camp was 'nothing more than a hospital'.[69] Another explanation is that Eugene was anticipating an imminent attack.[70] Waiting passively was not his style.[71]

---

63   Maffei to unk., Camp before Belgrade, 9 Aug 1717, in BayHStA Kasten Schwartz 1308 Bayerisches Hauptstaatsarchiv.

64   Lozembrune, *Histoire de la guerre de Hongrie*, pp.127, 132. Maffei, Camp before Belgrade, 9 Aug 1717 in BayHStA Kasten Schwartz. 1308, Bayerisches Hauptstaatsarchiv.

65   'A French volunteer', Imperial Camp, 15 August in Mauvillon, *Histoire du Prince François Eugene de Savoie*, pp.156-157.

66   Franz George Friedrich von Kausler et al. *as Leben des Prinzen Eugen von Savoyen, hauptsächlich aus dem Militärische*n (Freiburg im Breisgau: Herder, 1838), Voi.II, p.120.

67   Anon., *The Political State of Great Britain* (London: J. Baker, 1717), Vol.XIV, p.226.

68   *Le Nouveau Mercure*, Paris September 1717 p.160.

69   Anne-Marie Cocula (ed.), Jean Marie de La Colonie, *Mémoires De Monsieur De La Colonie*. (Paris: Mercure de France, 1992), pp.533, 551.

70   Jean Nouzille, *Le Prince Eugene de Savoie et le Sud-Est Europe en 1683-1736* (Paris: Honoré Champion, 2012), p.154.

71   Anon., *Ausführliche Relation des Herrlichen Sigs* (Munich: Matthias Riedl, 1717), np.

The attack did not go according to plan. The horsemen on the right wing stumbled into fresh trenches which the Turks were digging that very night and thereby forfeited the advantage of surprise. They struggled through to the old trenches, were repulsed and pressed forward in a see-saw struggle that lasted until dawn broke, when they took, and held, the trenches.[72] The crisis of the battle occurred when the front line of infantry followed the cavalry of the right wing and veered off, thereby exposing a gap in their front lines. Eugene quickly spotted the danger and threw in the second line infantrymen, armed with flintlocks and well-drilled in musketry, who mowed down the Turks in close-quarter volleys but were almost overwhelmed by ever more enemy soldiers pressing over the bodies of their fallen comrades. Eugene next led the cuirassiers and hussars of the cavalry reserve to the charge and they fell on the Turkish flank. Still, on the Badjina Heights the élite Janissaries stubbornly guarded the 18-gun grand battery that poured shot into the Imperial lines. A final attack, in which the three Bavarian regiments took part, took the Badjina Heights around nine o'clock in the morning, and Khalil Pasha's army fled.[73]

With his troops threatening to mutiny, Mustafa Pasha negotiated safe passage for the men of the garrison and their families, in return for surrendering the city. The Peace of Passarowitz (July 1718) brought the Habsburg to its maximum expansion as far as Orşova [Oršava] and the Iron Gates about one hundred miles downriver of Belgrade.

How many of Eugene's men fell sick during the siege, what were the sicknesses, and what caused these diseases?

Eugene's reports to the Hofkriegsrat and the Emperor make no mention of disease, even as he himself lay sick.[74] Such reticence is comparable to Schomberg's evasions at Saint-Jean and Dundalk, and suggests commanders considered camp epidemics as somehow reflecting badly on them.

In contrast, unofficial primary sources infer a full-blown catastrophe. Examples of such sources would be an account from an unnamed French volunteer published in the *Nouveau Mercure* that same year and La Colonie's memoirs which would appear twenty years later.[75] According to such sources, the original strength had been 90,000-100,000 troops, but on the day of the battle, Eugene could scrape together only 30,000 to 50,000 men for the attack, after leaving a skeleton garrison of 10,000 at Semlin and in the lines.[76] In other words, by the day of the battle, at

---

72   Anon., *The Political State of Great Britain*, Vol.XIV, p.232.
73   Nicholas Henderson, *Prince Eugen of Savoy* (London: Weidenfeld & Nicolson, 1966), pp.227-8.
74   Moriz Edlen Von Angeli, *Feldzüge Des Prinzen Eugen Von Savoyen* (Vienna: Gerold, 1876), Vol.II, pp.119-131.
75   *Le Nouveau Mercure* (September 1717), p.163; Cocula, *Memoires de Monsieur de La Colonie*, p.533.
76   Jean-Baptiste Joseph Damarzit de Sahuguet d' Espagnac, *Histoire de Maurice, comte de Saxe* (Paris: Saillant and Nyon, 1775), Vol.I, p.47; M.I. Schmidts, *Geschichte der Deutschen...Kaiser Karl VI. Vom Jahr 1715 bis 1740* (Vienna and Ulm: August Lebrecht Stettins, 1803), pp.4-5; *The Daily Courant*, London 23 August 1717 no. 4941, p.1; Jon Manchip White, *Marshal of France: The Life and times of Maurice, Comte de Saxe* (London: Hamish Hamilton, 1962), p.38; Nouzille, *Le Prince Eugene de Savoie*, p.155.

least one third of Eugene's army was disabled by sickness. Historians increasingly relied on this second category of primary sources and presented a lurid picture of a camp suffering the 'shocking ravages' of dysentery for four weeks before the attack.[77] During that time, men were buried 'by the hundreds' every day, and there was no battalion that did not have a burial ground behind it covering at least as much space as the battalion's lines.[78] Right before Eugene attacked, he was supposedly losing nearly 20 men every hour through dysentery.[79]

Hard statistical evidence casts doubt on this second category of primary sources. A *Tabelle* covering eight of the battalions encamped in the 'Little Camp' near Semlin on 5 August shows unexpectedly low morbidity point prevalence, with 22.6 percent of the troops sick, at the very most.[80] One might object that conditions across the Save may have been less cramped, morbidity correspondingly low, and the Semlin regiments atypical. But the contingent of Bavarians, led by Lieutenant General Allesandro Maffei, surely was representative in that the contingent's three infantry regiments were posted in the middle of the 'Great Camp'.[81] Yet the Bavarians demonstrated even lower morbidity, of just over 14 percent, than the regiments across the Save.[82] This morbidity should not be considered negligible and Maffei, for one, complained that the sickness rate was 'extraordinary' because 600 men lay sick in his six battalions.[83] 'Today is the thirteenth day since we were encircled', lamented Maffei, 'the troops are much worn out and disease gets much worse every day'.[84] And worse: the sickness spread, even after the Turks had been driven off, because the army remained in the big camp, which was now but 'a graveyard or hospital', the

77 Pierre Massuet, *Histoire de la Derniere Guerre* (Amsterdam: François L'Honore, 1737), p.333.

78 De Lozembrune, *Histoire de la guerre de Hongrie* pp.161-2; Anon. 'Remarques et Observations dans la campagne 1717' in Ludwig Matuschka, *Feldzüge des Prinzen Eugen von Savoyen: Der Türken-Krieg 1716-18* (Vienna: Gerold, 1891), VOL XVII, p.125. Von Kausler, *Das Leben des Prinzen Eugen von Savoyen*, p.620.

79 Charles Joseph Prince de Ligne, *The Life of Prince Eugene, of Savoy: From His Own Original Manuscript* (London: J. Davis, 1812), p.65.

80 Of the strength of 5,012 (including over 400 servants) 313 were 'auswärts krank' or 'sick elsewhere', absent or detached. Those sick in camp numbered 820 or 17.45 of the whole. Matuschka, *Feldzüge Des Prinzen Eugen von Savoyen*, pp.125, 144.

81 *Ausführliche Beschreibung des Ungarischen Feld-Zugs Anno 1717*, p.32; Gaspar Rad, *Designation und Explication über die Schlacht so zwischen dem Keyser[lichen] und Türck[ischen] Lager bey Belgrad auf Röm[ischen] keyser[lichen] Maj[estät] Seiten unter Com[m]ando Sr Durch[laucht] Prinzens Eugeny von Savoyen den 16 Aug. 1717*, BNF Cartes et plans, GE D-26051.

82 Maffei *Mémoires*, p.242: At the begining of the campaign the Crown Prince's two battalions numbered 1,439, Von Lerchenfeld's two battalions amounted to 1,395 men and the two battalions of Foot Guards present made up 1,441. In all the contingent numbered 4,275 men, somewhat short of the paper strength of 4,800. By mid-August 600 Bavarians were laid low with sickness and corpses were buried in every hole and corner of the camp. Joseph Schuster, *Studien zur Geschichte des Militärsanitätswesens im 17. und 18. Jahrhundert, mit besonderer Berücksichtigung der kurbaye* (Munich: J. Lindauersche Buchhandlung, 1908), p.21. Maffei to unk., Camp before Belgrade, 9 Aug 1717 in BayHStA Kasten Schwartz 1308. Maffei to unk, Camp before Belgrade, 13 Aug 1717 in BayHStA Kasten Schwartz 1308.

83 Maffei to unk., Camp before Belgrade, 9 Aug 1717 in BayHStA Kasten Schwartz 1308.

84 Maffei, Camp before Belgrade, 13 Aug 1717 in BayHStA Kasten Schwartz 1308.

air of which was infected by 'carcasses and carrion'.[85] 'The soldiers all fall sick and all the sick die', concluded Maffei with pardonable exaggeration. On 1 September, the great Camp was finally abandoned and a new camp pitched near Semlin. By then the Bavarians had no fewer than 720 lying sick in grim conditions: *Commissar* Jäger complained that the Imperial authorities were uncaring but that 'it pierced his soul' to see the sick and wounded 'in a miserable state': 'Most' he went on, 'have no straw and blankets and there are but 60 beds put into peasant huts [*Raizen-haüser*] for 700 to 800 patients, no drugs or dressings and no money to buy brandy and other necessaries'. Maffei expected that most of them were bound 'for the next world', but he cautiously expressed hope that the numbers of sick would begin to fall, once the army left behind the 'infected air' of Belgrade Camp.[86]

The numbers did not diminish. On the contrary, by 2 October, when the army broke up into winter quarters, Maffei loaded 1,179 Bavarian sick on to boats for evacuation upriver to Belgrade, whence they were taken by wagons to their winter quarters at Trenčín, in what is today western Slovakia.[87] By then too, 862 Bavarians had perished of sickness.[88] Lugubrious as ever, Maffei foretold disaster befalling troops marching for three weeks across 'a sort of desert', where 'we can have no hope of help'.[89] In the event, conceded Maffei afterwards, the Bavarians completed the march 'much more happily' than he had anticipated because of unexpectedly benign October weather.[90] That said, the infantry rolls were 'full of sick' after the march and by May 1718 and the start of the next campaigning season only one quarter of the Bavarians (to extrapolate from the experience of Maffei's own regiment) remained.[91] However, an unquantifiable proportion of this loss must have been due to desertion now that the regiment was quartered so temptingly close to home. This study must therefore remain focused on the siege experience, and grounded in statistics that capture epidemic morbidity and mortality.

The strength of the Bavarian contingent was 5,600 in mid-July and 860 had perished of sickness by the beginning of October: the case fatality rate amounted to some 15 percent in two and a half months. As revealed by these mortality figures (and the morbidity statistics above), camp sickness was not nearly so grave as many contemporary accounts imply, even if Maffei considered the mortality 'extraordinary'. Perhaps the death toll was somewhat higher than ordinary (whatever *that* was), but it was still far less than the losses during and after the encampments at Saint-Jean and Dundalk.

85   Maffei to unk., Camp before Belgrade, 30 Aug 1717 in BayHStA Kasten Schwartz 1308.
86   Maffei to unk., Semlin, 3 September 1717 in BayHStA Kasten Schwartz 1308.
87   *Daily Courant*, 24 December 1717.
88   Schuster *Studien zur Geschichte des Militärsanitätswesens*, p.21.
89   Maffei, Semlin, 2 October 1717 in BayHStA Kasten Schwartz 1308. J.W. Bekh, *Alexander von Maffei. Der bayerische Prinz Eugen* (Pfaffenhofen: Ludwig, 1982), p.392.
90   Maffei, Czaba, 26 October 1717, in BayHStA Kasten Schwartz 1308.
91   The two-battalion regiment of Maffei had originally 1600 men and only 429 men left. Given the tempting proximity to Bavaria, much of this loss could have been attributable to desertion. Bekh, *Alexander von Maffei*, p.410.

As late as 2 August, claimed a letter from camp, 'there is not yet talk of contagious diseases'.[92] The earliest mention of Eugene's, or anyone's, sickness relates to 6 August, not long before the battle, when a number of gentlemen were evacuated on account of the ravages of *rothe rühr* or 'bloody flux' and Charles Count de Charolais, a French volunteer, was prostrated by 'a kind of dysentery'.[93] There is some slight evidence that typhoid may also have been present with dysentery.[94] The almoner of one of the Bavarian regiments passed away on 16 August, the day after the battle, of a 'hot fever'.[95] The adjective 'hot' usually suggests what we would now call typhus and/ or typhoid. Another disease was an intermittent fever [*Mechselfieber*].[96] The intermittent fever that struck down Eugene was a 'tertian', where the intermittent period followed one day's fever and was in turn followed on the third day by renewed fever and paroxysm. One of Eugene's generals, the Count de Bonneval, took a tincture of quinine every morning of the siege as a preservative against fever.[97] The fever may have been malarial but one cannot be more definite than that. Nor, despite claims that 4,000 besiegers succumbed to *hitzigen Hautkrankheit* ['hot skin diseases'], is there any definite evidence of typhus breaking out.[98] Dysentery probably was the major component of this camp epidemic, as of most.

As to the putative determinants, of the six 'conditions' noted in Chapter 1, diet was conspicuously absent amongst the commonly cited culprits: provisions 'can be found in abundance and at a fair price', a newsletter assured readers. Whereas the earlier tendency had been to blame German soldiers for eating prodigious quantities of wrong foods like fish and fatty meats, and imbibing too much wine, the more recent tendency had been to decry their supposed dirtiness.[99] An English newsletter reporting on the Siege of Buda (1684) noted with distaste that the besiegers ' will not bury their dead horses or so much as the entrails of the beasts killed for food, which occasions such terrible stenches that it infects the air and causes the bloody flux, which rages very violently in the camp'.[100] German filth was often contrasted with the putative cleanliness of their Turkish enemies, who dug privies and rubbish pits but one must wonder why, if the Ottomans really were so much cleaner, did

92   Anon., 'Extract Schreiben aus dem Feld-Lager vor Belgrad', (Vienna: Publisher Unknown, 2 August 1717), p.6.

93   Anon., *Ausführliche Beschreibung des Ungarischen Feld-Zugs Anno 1717*. p.31; Jacques Bernard, *Lettres Historiques contenant ce qui se passe de plus important en Europe* (Amsterdam: Jacques Desbordes, July 1717) VOL LII, pp.434, 436.

94   B.M. Lersch, *Geschichte der Volksseuchen. nach und mit den Berichten der Zeitgenossen, mit Berücksichtigung der Thierseuchen* (Berlin: Karger, 1896), p.341.

95   Augustin et Alois de Backer, *Bibliothèque des écrivains de la Compagnie de Jésus* (Liege & Paris: C. Sommervogel, 1861), Vol.VI, p.127.

96   Ph. J. von Molo, *Über Epidemien im Allgemeinen und Wechselfieberepidemien insbesondere* (Regensburg: J. Manx, 1841), p.237.

97   H. Rey, 'Les Medecins navigateurs', *Archives de médecine navale* (Paris: J.B.Ballière, 1871), VOL XV, p.202.

98   Stefan Winkle, *Geisseln der Menschheit: Kulturgeschichte der Seuchen* (Munich: Artemis & Winkler, 2005), p.646.

99   Landersdorfer, 'Das Schicksal der bayerischen Soldaten im Türkenkrieg', pp.56-57.

100 Newsletter, London, 28 September 1684, *Calendar of State Papers, Domestic Series, Charles II, May 1684-Feb 1685*, p.157.

scavenging Imperials remark that their abandoned camp at Vienna (1683) was filthy and malodorous?[101] The filth of the Imperial camp (though some sources persisted in the fiction that the camp was 'entirely clean') in turn supposedly generated bad air.[102] Most physicians of the time blamed diarrhoea and dysentery on such bad air passing into the blood to mix with bile. The invisible exhalations and stench of dysenteric excrements were considered highly infectious and so when 'a great stench arose from unburied corpses and carcasses' it supposedly 'gave rise to much sickness…'.[103] Local peasants were press-ganged to bury the corpses and carcasses but the sickness got worse and on 1 September the Imperials moved camp to Semlin to escape the 'bad air' and 'great infection'.[104]

Bad air aside, where can the real source of the epidemic be found? A later report blamed 'dirt [which] caused much sickness and attracted terrible swarms of flies that furiously attacked man and beast'.[105] As to 'dirt', rules about what would later be called sanitation grew more frequent and stringent during the decades before and after Belgrade.

Marlborough's standing orders during his campaigns in Flanders specified that 'Houses of Office' should be built to keep the camp 'clean' and situated 'at least' one hundred paces beyond the quarter guard to the front of the camp.[106] De Quincy's 1728 *Art de La Guerre* recommended that every battalion should dig a pit for the sake of 'decency' [*proprieté*] some 200 paces in front of the lines, not just 100. A contemporaneous German equivalent stipulated that pits should be dug outside camps for animal manure and for all other 'stinking' things and, when half-full, the pits should be covered over and new ones dug.[107] Twenty years after De Quincy, Count Von Khevenhüller (whose ill-fated Danubian expedition will be discussed in Chapter 4) penned a military treatise which quickly disposed of the whole distasteful business in a paragraph. A latrine [*abtritt*] pit should be dug in woodland a few hundred yards from the camp. The pit should be deep and covered with earth several times a day. A private soldier who would not 'go' to the assigned latrine should be arrested. Carcasses and rubbish should also be dumped there.[108] The 1743 edition of Humphrey Bland's military treatise stipulated that such 'Necessary Houses' be made before the main body of an army arrived, that streets be swept clean every morning,

---

101 Landersdorfer, 'Das Schicksal der bayerischen Soldaten im Türkenkrieg', p.56.

102 Daniel Schneider and Gabriel Schweder, *Theatrum Europeum* (Frankfurt-am-Main: Merian, 1738), p.96.

103 Johann Storchens, *Theoretisch und practische Abhandlung von … Kranckheiten* (Eisenach and Nuremberg: Grießbach, 1735), pp.204-205.

104 Anon., *Ausführliche Beschreibung des Ungarischen Feld-Zugs*, p.60; Schneider and Schweder, *Theatrum Europeum*, p.104; Buda, 7 September 1717, *Gazette* (Paris, 1718), p.472; Eugene to the Emperor, Semlin, 3 September, Matuschka, *Feldzüge Des Prinzen Eugen*, p.154.

105 Remarques et Observations dans la campagne 1717 Kriegs-A, 'Turkenkrieg 1717', Fasc. XIII, 25.

106 'An Impartial Hand', *A system of camp-discipline, military honours garrison-duty, adjutants-duty, and other regulations for the land forces* (London: J. Millan, 1760), p.5.

107 H.F. von Flemming, *Der Vollkommene teutsche Soldat* (Leipzig: Johann Christian Martini, 1726), p.326.

108 Ludwig Andreas Graf von Khevenhüller, *Observations Puncten* (Vienna: J.P.Kraus, 1748), pp.108, 179.

that butchers and sutlers bury their 'filth' every day, and that dead horses be buried every day 'that the Air may be kept from Infection'.[109] Later military authors would demand more latrines, one for every company.[110] They would also stipulate that the privy or 'necessary' should comprise a long trench with a long pole resting on two forked stakes upon which men could sit over a pit. British standing orders from the 1740s demanded that 'old houses of office' should be 'filled up' (clearly the house of office was an enclosure or outhouse built over or around a pit) and new ones dug every six days. Standing orders for a British camp in October 1760 specified that 'new Necessarys be made very two days, and the Old ones fill'd up'.[111] It is unclear if these rules were aspirational or if they codified existing practice and, if the latter, to what extent were they enforced at Belgrade.

The medium in which infected ordure passed might have been water. A report of 1 August expressed concern that the well water was unhealthy and noted that water drawn from the Danube was the best available. It was even reported that Eugene had his personal drinking water and provisions for his own table brought all the way from Vienna.[112] This latter report is likely untrue, but hints at official anxiety over water supplies. While the Imperial army was at least able to draw water from the Danube, the Ottomans seem to have been driven to desperation and tried to draw water under fire from a well right in front of the Imperial lines.[113]

The 'terrible [entsetzlich] swarm of flies' were more likely carriers.[114] Flies can harbour pathogens in their mouths and digestive systems which can then be transmitted when they defecate or regurgitate. Moreover, the housefly's whole body is covered with bristles, and as it rubs its legs together to clean itself it discards scraps of material that has built up. Optimum temperatures for houseflies range from 10 to 26°C, and fly densities are highest at mean temperatures of 20 to 25°C. The climate around Belgrade today is continental, and is marked by hot summers with average temperatures of 23°C. Summers in the second decade of the 18th century were cooler than those of today as temperatures recovered slowly from the long-run minima of the 1690s, but contemporaries remarked that, for its time, the summer of 1717 felt 'unusually sultry' at Belgrade.[115] In other words, the temperature in July and August 1717 around Belgrade favoured dense swarms of flies. So, too, did the abundance of horse manure (the housefly's favourite site in which to deposit eggs) and open latrines, food waste, carrion and rubbish.[116]

109   Erica Charters, *Disease, War and the Imperial State: The Welfare of the British Armed Forces during the Seven Years' War* (Chicago: University of Chicago Press, 2014), p.92.
110   Johann H. Wirz, *Einrichtung und Disciplin eines Eidgenössischen Regiments,* (Zürich: Heidegger, 1759), pp.218-221.
111   'Impartial Hand', *A system of camp-discipline,* p.15.
112   James Lind, *An Essay on the Most Effectual Means of Preserving the Health of Seamen* (London: G. Wilson and D.Nicoll, 1774), pp.60-61.
113   Anon., *Glücks- und Unglücksfälle der Haupt-Vestung Belgrad oder Griechisch-Weissenburg* (Augsburg: Unknown Publisher, 1717), np.
114   Anon. *Extract-Schreiben auß dem Feld-Lager vor Belgrad,* unpag.
115   Lind, *Preserving the Health of Seamen,* p.60.
116   Vincent J. Cirillo, '"Winged Sponges": Houseflies as Carriers of Typhoid Fever in 19th- and Early 20th-Century Military Camps', *Perspectives in Biology and Medicine* no. 49 (1) (2006), p.53.

Nowadays, *Shigella dysenteriae* is mostly spread by person-to-person transmission but in army camps the main concern was (or should have been) with the movement of flies from manure or human faeces to food that would be eaten uncooked by humans. Hence the correlation between population density and diarrhoea/dysentery is weak as opposed to measles, to take one example.[117] *Shigella* is easily communicable because of its tiny infectious dose, tinier than that necessary for other bacterial-induced diarrhoeas. Yet *Shigella* is the least fatal of the main camp epidemic diseases under discussion: dysentery case fatality rates run no higher than 10 percent in refugee camps even among young children and the elderly.[118] Of course, dysentery brought indirect death in that, as we saw at Dundalk, soldiers laid low by dysentery were prey to other, more severe diseases, especially typhus.

Philippsburg 1734

Distemper or disease was not usually regarded as a specific condition but as part of a continuum, though there were exceptions like smallpox in which material contagion was thought to spread from person-to-person. The infamous *Morbus Hungaricus*, for example, went under different names: if it reached the head it was dubbed *die Hauptkrankheit* and if the throat, it was called *die Breune*.[119] Diarrhoeas subtly mutated into fevers and the latter assumed progressively darker gradations from bilious to putrid to malignant, according as the environment, specifically the qualities of the air, deteriorated. This view has its uses in trying to make sense of the late summer-autumn-winter seasonal rhythm described in the introduction and partially captured in many of the case studies, though Derry and the endgame at Riga happened in spring and early summer. The final example discussed in this chapter is exceptional in that is possible to trace the entire epidemiological arc that followed a French siege and capture of Philippsburg on the Rhine in high summer 1734, followed by forced marches up and down the left bank of that great river and, finally dispersal into winter quarters where the regiments suffered frightful losses through sickness. The case study includes all the places and operations that are presented separately elsewhere, camping, fortress warfare, marching, and hospitals and serve to remind us of the artificiality of the distinction.

The War of the Polish Succession (1733–35) began as a Polish civil war over the succession to Augustus II and which widened to draw in other European powers in pursuit of the perennial Bourbon-Habsburg rivalry which underpins most of the wars and campaigns under discussion in this work. War broke out in four theatres of war: Poland, the Rhine, Northern Italy and Sicily & Naples, all 'playgrounds

---

117 Robert Woods, *The Demography of Victorian England and Wales* (Cambridge: Cambridge University Press, 2007) p.327.

118 M. Toole, 'Complex Emergencies: Refugee and other Populations' in Eric K. Noji (ed.), *The Public Health Consequences of Disasters* (Oxford: Oxford University Press, 1997), 430.

119 Günther Christoph Schelhammer, *De Genuina Febres Curanda Methodo* (Jena: Bielcke, 1727), p.207.

for veterans of the War of the Spanish Succession'.[120] One such veteran was James Fitzjames, Duke of Berwick, who commanded a large army that crossed the Rhine at two points, above and below Philippsburg, in May 1734. A large detachment under *Lieutenant Général* d'Asfeld crossed upriver of the target and the main body, under Berwick himself, crossed downriver at Fort Louis. Having crossed to Kehl, Berwick's army faced the Ettlingen Lines which stretched from the Rhine near Karlsruhe up to the hills around Ettlingen. Maurice of Saxony won his reputation when he found a passage through the hills and on 4 May pushed through a thinly held part of the lines, thereby causing the whole of the Ettlingen defences to collapse. The collapse was helped by the fact that the Imperial commander, Prince Eugene of Savoy, had not enough men to hold to lines and was nervously looking over his shoulder at d'Asfeld's detachment which had already reached Philippsburg by 23 May.[121]

Berwick linked up with d'Asfeld and camped successively at Bruchsal (10-25 May) and nearby Kronau (25 May to 2 June). Rather than attack Eugene while he still enjoyed a numerical advantage, Berwick chose to immobilize his army by encamping at Bruchsal and the delay gave Eugene of Savoy the chance to slip away with his smaller Imperial army to the safety of a heavily fortified camp at Heilbronn: 'I really don't know how matters would have turned', admitted Eugene, if Berwick had attacked as 'he could have and should have done'.[122] It would seem that Berwick thought his troops, 'nearly all on their first campaign', needed to be blooded in a straightforward and choreographed operation like a siege in form. Moreover, they were poorly disciplined. Marauding by the troops encamped at Bruchsal was 'abominable', complained an officer of Dillon's Irish Regiment, and such was the scale of the problem that it drew a rebuke from Louis XV himself.[123]

Rather than push on against Heilbronn, Berwick next turned to Philippsburg which stood on the eastern bank of what was then a great bend in the Rhine surrounded by swamps and woods and formed a key defensive point of the Empire. He had 100-117,000 men and he split them three-ways leaving most of his cavalry on the west bank and dividing his infantry in two, with one part besieging the heavily fortified frontier outpost while another turned its back to the town and manned the lines of countervallation.[124] By 3 June 1734 governor Wuttgenau had been forced to evacuate the outlying Rhein-schanze on the western bank and on that same day the French began to dig the first parallel against the fortress proper. While inspecting

---

120 Michael Hochedlinger, *Austria's Wars of Emergence, War, State and Society in the Habsburg Monarchy* (New York and London: Longman, 2003), p.210.

121 Charles Pierre Victor comte de Pajol, *Les guerres sous Louis XV* (Paris: Firmin-Didot, 1881), Vol.I, p.210-211.

122 John, Sutton, *The King's Honor and the King's Cardinal: The War of the Polish Succession* (Lexington KY: The University Press of Kentucky, 1980), pp.144-150: Anon., *The Life and Military Actions of Prince Eugene* (London: T. Read, 1739), p.321.

123 L. Ó Briain (ed.), 'The Chevalier Gaydon's Memoir of the Regiment of Dillon, 1738' in *Irish Sword* no 22 (Summer, 1963), p.34 and no. 23 (Winter 1963), p.89.

124 Devillers to unk, 'Philisbourg' 13 July 1734 in M. Armand Bourgeois (ed.) *Lettres inédites de Jean Devillers d'Epernay* (Reims: Impr. de l'Académie, 1898), pp.17, 29; Jean Dumont, *The Military History of the late Prince Eugene of Savoy* (London: W. Rayner, 1737), Vol.II, pp.343-344; Pajol, *Les guerres sous Louis XV*, Vol.I, p.239.

the trenches on 11 June Berwick was killed by a cannon ball from the town and was replaced by d'Asfeld. All the while Eugene's strength grew with reinforcements from Hanover and Prussia so that by the first week in July his army was as large as the French, if not larger.[125] On 1 July the French seized a hornwork blocking their line of attack and on the same day Eugene marched his whole army through a wood and to within cannon shot of d'Asfeld who carried on, despite the proximity of that 'enterprizing Genius' Prince Eugene.[126] In fact, even more than Berwick, Villars, and the other veterans who commanded in this war, Eugene had quite lost his drive and daring. Rather than attack, he tried ineffectually to cross the Rhine down river.

Torrential downpours on 5 July flooded parts of the trenches which drove the besiegers to launch daylight attacks on a crownwork. Yet Eugene still failed to exploit d'Asfeld's difficulties and instead pulled his army back to Heilbronn. The young Frederick of Prussia, one of Eugene's entourage, was dismayed by his decline: 'he was still there in body but his spirit had fled'.[127] Or perhaps, like Berwick, Eugene distrusted his own troops. Complaints about indiscipline recur in the two armies and, worse, rumours of atrocities which exceeded the commonplace abuses attendant on levying contributions and foraging. These abuses reflected the poor quality of Eugene's troops in particular and he complained of 'unbelievable' atrocities reminiscent of the worst brutality of the Thirty Years War perpetrated by troops under his command in the districts around the Ettlingen Lines: 'The sacred Host thrown to the ground…children of four and five years slashed in the face and hands and, most horrible, women nailed to a cross with both hands and in such a cruel condition raped to death'.[128] 'It was better to see Philippsburg lost', asserted Eugene, 'than to risk an army in a dangerous attack and see it lost as well'.[129] On 17 July the French penetrated to the inner bastions of the main work and so threatened the heart of the fortress. Wuttgenau quickly capitulated at that point, as was habitual in fortress warfare in the Baroque Age. His resistance cost the French some 1,162 killed or dead, 4,956 wounded and sick and 2,734 deserters or, in all, about 10,000 all ranks.[130]

Like the other generals, d'Asfeld was old (he would be put out to pasture after this campaign), 'timid' and 'wavering in all things'.[131] Rather than push deeper into Germany, he crossed back over to the left bank of the Rhine, pressed north towards Worms and thence, on 6 August, to Oppenheim which he reached two days later.[132] Imperial forces marched on a parallel course to 'observe their motions', and forestall an assault on Mainz.[133] A showdown seemed 'unavoidable' as the armies tiptoed

125   Sutton, *The King's Honor*, pp.52-54; Anon., *Prince Eugene* p.325; Hochedlinger, *Austria's Wars of Emergence*, p.210.

126   Dumont, *Military History of the late Prince Eugene of Savoy* pp.343-344.

127   Cited in McKay, *Prince Eugene of Savoy*, p.239.

128   Sutton, *The King's Honor*, p.155.

129   Sutton, *The King's Honor*, p.159

130   Sutton, *The King's Honor*, p.158

131   Edmond-Jean-François Barbier, *Chronique de la régence et du règne de Louis XV (1718-1763), ou Journal de Barbier* (Paris: Charpentier, 1857-1866), Vol.II, pp.515, 520.

132   Pajol, *Les guerres sous Louis XV*, Vol.I, pp.243-247; *Daily Courant*, nos. 5723 and 5725 (London, 7 and 9 August 1734).

133   *Daily Courant* no. 5722 (London, 6 August 1734).

closer to Mainz between the 5 and 13 August.[134] But suddenly, on the night of 13 August d'Asfeld decamped from Oppenheim. Having split his army, leaving part in the hinterland of Speyer, he now grew fearful that Eugene might 'force battle on him' and so defeat him in detail.[135] Ordering his scattered army to concentrate immediately, d'Asfeld dashed south to evade pursuit. He need not have worried about pursuit because Eugene tamely withdrew to Heilbronn.

The latter part of the dash (between Lauterbourg on 19 August and Seltz on 21 August) turned into a gruelling forced march with the luckless troops forced to traverse six German leagues, or over 22 miles, a day for three days together. This was an unsustainable pace which left less than 50 men able to keep up with their battalion's colours and by far the largest part of the troops straggling behind.[136] After a halt near Fort Louis on 22-24 August, d'Asfeld's army crossed back to the right bank of the Rhine. The rest of the campaign was spun out camping at Kuppenheim and Offenburg and the accompanying map indicates the length of time spent at each encampment by the size of the triangular symbol. The sole purpose of the camps was logistical, to let troops live off the land and let the horses forage for as long as possible beyond French territory, before withdrawing into winter quarters. The War of the Polish Succession presents probably the most perfect example of 'war-as-process' with its slow tempo, modest aims framed by ongoing diplomacy, and the need to make war feed war. Above all, war as process was attritional.

D'Asfeld left 8,000 men in Worms and left 'large' garrisons in Speyer, Frankenthal, Neustadt, and Germersheim.[137] Strasbourg contained another major garrison of 9,000 men together with two smaller satellite garrisons of 3,000 men altogether at Hagenau and Lauterbourg.[138] Other regiments were quartered further afield: Dillon's Irish Regiment was unfortunate enough to have to trudge all the way to Arras, 'a very long march in abominable weather'.[139]

That summer, autumn, and winter three distinguishable cycles of disease afflicted the theatre of war which included the territories of the Rhenish Palatinate, Baden, Württemberg, and (though the region was not actually fought over) Alsace. The first cycle is the by now familiar flux. Conditions at the Siege of Philippsburg should have been optimal for the rapid spread of camp dysentery. A very large army lay constricted for six weeks within fortified lines, though the over-crowding was not as bad as that which Prince Eugene's army had endured at Belgrade some seventeen years earlier. However, the water supply was likely tainted: even in peacetime the well-water of the region was muddy and foul-tasting.[140] The only springs 'thereabouts', complained Gaydon, the chronicler of Dillon's Irish Regiment, lay behind the Imperial lines and so d'Asfeld's men had to drink 'thick and muddy' water drawn

134 Anon., *The Life and Military Actions of Prince Eugene*, p.333

135 'Strasbourg 12 August' in *Daily Journal* (London), Friday, August 16, 1734; Issue 4237.

136 The distance cited was six German Leagues. A German league measures 4,000 geometric paces, each such pace being 1.5 metres in length.

137 *London Evening Post*, no. 1078, 15 October 1734-October 17, 1734.

138 'Strasburg 12 December' in *Ordinarii Post-Zeitungen* (2 January 1735).

139 Ó Briain (ed.), 'Gaydon's Memoir', *Irish Sword* no. 23, p.93.

140 Richard de Hautesierck, *Recueil d'Observations de Médecine des Hôpitaux Militaires* (Paris: Imprimerie Royale, 1772), Vol.II, p.28.

3.4 French Manoeuvres: Rhineland 1734.

from wells or from the river. A physician pitied the soldiers when the Rhine burst its banks on 5 July and the wretched men were 'sent out every day to the toil of digging trenches while water and mud came up to their calves, nay, their knees'.[141] The water supply must have been further contaminated by flooded privies and cess pits. In a revealing exchange of the prescribed quixotic civilities, d'Asfeld begged a pitcher of spring water of Eugene who happily acceded to the request. To return the compliment, d'Asfeld sent him two mules laden with Burgundy wine.[142] Then there were the flies: less than a week before the capitulation an officer cursed the 'clouds of flies' that 'gave no rest, day or night'.[143]

Poor diet was still considered a cause of flux. Khevenhüller's military primer indicted condemned badly-baked bread, 'stagnant, swampy, smelly water' and rotten meat. However, he also implicated 'non-natural' or environmental causes, when he conjured up a picture of the soldier exerting himself in daytime heat and then sleeping outdoors in wet clothes on a chilly night.[144] A physician observing the epidemic at Philippsburg was less exercised about diet but connected the Rhine floods

141 Johann Simon Bauermüller, *Dissertatio. Medica inaugralis de febre castrensi* (Würzburg: Unknown Publisher, 1735) introduction np.
142 Anon., *Life and Military Actions of Prince Eugene*, p.329.
143 Devillers to unk, 'Philisbourg' 13 July 1734 in Armand Bourgeois, M. (ed.) *Lettres inédites de Jean Devillers d'Epernay* (Reims, Impr. de l'Académie,1898), pp.17, 29.
144 Khevenhüller, *Observations Puncten*, p.101.

with the 'humid and warm air' which at once caused, and spread the epidemic.[145] The same physician also admitted the possibility of contagion: 'the movement of morbid effluvia from a sick body to a healthy one is simple and frequent among soldiers because in their tents…they live in close quarters and lie down together'. Khevenhüller also posited airborne transmission of the putrid exhalations from dysenteric stools and so he emphasized the vital importance of segregating the privies of the sick from those of the healthy.[146]

'Many' besiegers fell sick during the leaguer due to 'fatigues and alarms'.[147] A report of 12 August had it that the Duke of Richelieu was ill at Speyer of a 'fever and violent head ache' while the elderly (he was almost eighty years old) *Maréchal de Bourg* lay 'very ill' at Strasbourg.[148] Both recovered. It is not until 24 August that one can hazard a guess at what 'many' sick might have meant. Writing from Kuppeheim, where the army dallied from 24 August to 3 September, *Maréchal de Camp* Jacques de Chabannes, Marquis de Curton, confessed that the number of sick in the hospitals 'scared' him, since they amounted to at least a quarter of the whole, and probably more.[149] The forced marches cannot have helped. Many sick soldiers must have been left behind and the countryside was anything but secure: a detachment of 50 foot soldiers of Dillon's Regiment which was scavenging only a league from the main camp near Worms was ambushed by enemy hussars and 'cut to pieces'.[150] Yet the army must have somehow dragged many of the sick, and dying, along. The burial records of the military hospital at Fort Louis show a pronounced jump on 24 August, the day the army straggled into the vicinity and peaked at fifteen a day on 3 September, the same day that d'Asfeld led a leisurely march to Offenburg where he tarried until 20 October, voraciously consuming the forage, before dispersing his army into winter quarters.[151]

Table 3.5 Burials at Fort Louis Hospital 1734-35

Jul	Aug	Sept	Oct	Nov	Dec	Jan	Feb
43	117	225	194	180	134	79	39

---

145 Christoph Ferdinand Hoelder, *De Morbo Castrensi Epidemico* (Württemberg and Stuttgart: Müller, 1736), pp.7-8.

146 Khevenhüller, *Observations Puncten*, p.108.

147 *Lettre historique et politique* no. 86 (Amsterdam, July 1734) p.117.

148 'Strasbourg 12 August' in *Daily Journal* (London, 16 August 1734), no. 4237.

149 De Chabannes to Intendant de Brou Kuppenheim Camp 24 August 1734, Pajol, d*Les guerres sous Louis XV*, Vol.I, pp.255, 270. He reckoned there could be 12-15 men a company in hospital and the infantry company at that juncture had an establishment of 48 other ranks: Chandler, *The Art of Warfare in the Age of Marlborough*, p.97; Victor Belhomme, *Histoire de l'infanterie en France* (Paris: Lavauzelle, 1893-1902), Vol.III, p.110.

150 Camp at Speyer 17 August *Daily Journal* (London) 22 August 1734; no. 4242.

151 Fort-Louis, Registres Paroissiaux (Avant 1793), Hôpital militaire Registre de sépultures, 1716-1734 – 3 E 141/19 pp.28-29; Registre de sépultures 1716-17343 E 141/20, pp.1-43; Claude Jordan (ed.), *Journal Historique* (Paris: Publisher, 1734) Vol.XXXVI, pp.276-277, 460; Pajol, *Les guerres sous Louis XV*, Vol.I, p.255; 'Camp at Spire 17 August' in *Daily Journal* (London) 22 August 1734; no. 424; *Mercure de France*, (Paris, October 1734) p.2316.

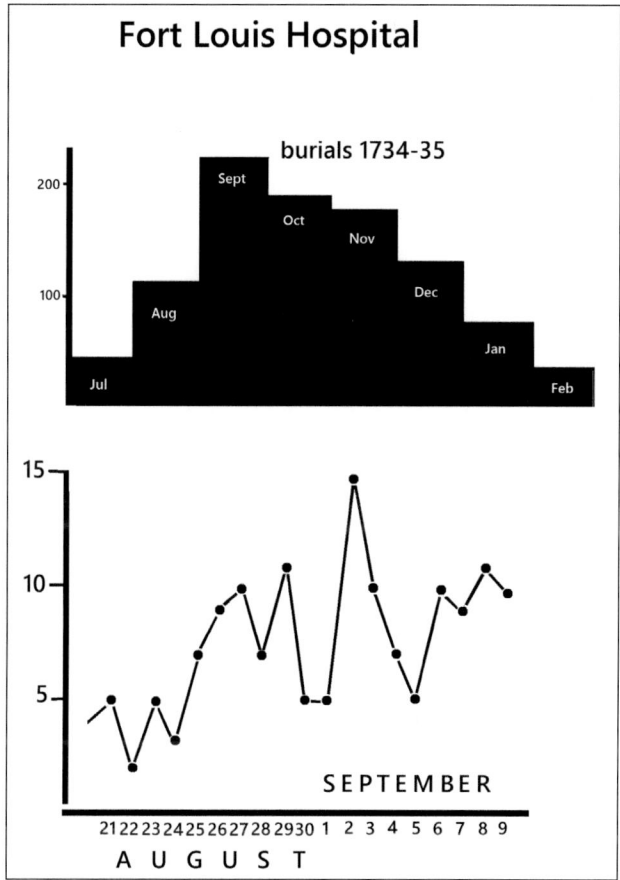

3.5 Burials at Fort Louis Hospital 1734-35.

As stated above, the first phase of the epidemic was a 'kind of dysentery' [*gattung ruhr*] which was exceptionally deadly and could carry off a susceptible individual quite suddenly.[152] An account from Lorraine almost certainly describes this sickness, doubtless spread by soldiers coming and going to the front:

> In September 1734., this species of dysentery showed itself in the village of Viterne in Lorrain; it came on with a breaking of wind upwards, and a very violent pain in the stomach and bowels; on this ensued a fever, and soon after frequent dysenteric stools, with a tenesmus and unquenchable thirst, and such an inflammation from the oesophagus downwards to the anus, that the patients thought their insides were on fire...Some who were seen

---

152 Rheinstrom/den 27. November in *Extra Ordinari Zeitungen* (Munich, 4 December 1734).

walking about the streets at five o'clock in the afternoon, were seized with it, and died at ten o'clock at night.[153]

A physician named Salzmann who lived in Speyer (on the French-held left bank of the Rhine) recounted how the contagion broke out 'among many, at one and the same time', in Speyer. Having begun in camps, it was carried by soldiers coming thence and 'by their women buying goods in the town' and from the citizens on whom the soldiers were quartered and amongst whom they wintered and passed to the country people. Likewise it spread to many of the townspeople who were employed about the camp and in the hospital.[154]

Other medical men discounted the importance of the first phase to focus on a second phase that began around the autumnal equinox, or 23 September.[155] According to Von Zinenau, who was apparently based in the Imperial headquarters of Heidelberg, both armies were afflicted by diarrhoeas and other sicknesses during and after the siege of Philippsburg, 'such as are bound to break out when so many men are gathered together'. However, from 'the beginning of autumn' a variety of fevers broke out and slowly spread; [these included] 'continued', 'benign', 'malign', and 'petechial' [fevers]. Salzmann noted that:

> In the months of August and September 1734 many sorts of diseases broke out in our district for reasons which I will set out below: diarrhoea, dysentery, various endemic fevers including tertians and continueds... among which was to be found a 'malign, miliary and exanthematic fever'.[156]

'Miliary' fever was so-called from the pustules or 'little blisters' that were its defining symptom but the name enjoyed only a brief vogue before being consigned a few decades later to the graveyard of archaic medical terminology along with other symptomatic categories of fever; 'nervous', 'putrid' and so on.[157] However, as Salzmann admitted; the miliary fever might also be equated with a specific disease, scarlet fever, that 'most commonly' broke out in late summer and was notable for patchy scarlet eruptions on the skin.[158] Miliary fever (*friesel* in his native German) was a disease that had only emerged (or been described) in the preceding 50 years and it sometimes presented with a rash that could be easily confused with the characteristic rash of 'purples' or typhoid. Salzmann was, however, careful to distinguish the miliary fever he described from smallpox [*morbis variolis*].[159] Another physician,

---

153 C.R. Hopson (transl. John George Zimmerman), *A Treatise on the Dysentery...* (London: John and Francis Rivington, 1771), pp.160-161.

154 G. Salzmann, *Historiam Purpurae Miliaris Albae* (Strasbourg: Unknown Publisher, 1736), p.8.

155 Molitor, Franz Joseph, *Dissertatio Inauguralis Medica De Febre Continua Maligna Et Intermittente Tertiana* (Heildeberg: Zinenau, 1736), p.2; Kramers, *Medicina Castrensis*, p.20.

156 Salzmann, *Historiam Purpurae Miliaris Albae*, p.3.

157 David Hamilton, *A Treatise of a Miliary Fever; with a collection of histories* (London: A. Bettesworth and C. Hitch, 1737), p.57.

158 Thomas Sydenham, *The Whole Works* (London: W. Feales, 1734), p.189.

159 Salzmann, *Historiam Purpurae Miliaris Albae*, p.3

from Germersheim, on the Imperial right bank, distinguished what he categorised as a malignant spotted fever [*bösartig fleck fieber*] from the 'child-pox' or smallpox that raged locally in the summer of 1734. He includes as the symptoms fever and *rote ruhr*.[160] Yet another noted the frequent occurrence of 'spots', not pustules, and insisted that the fever had 'a sudden onset [and] and abrupt and commonly fatal end'.[161]

We may leave the last word with J.G. Kramers, senior physician to the Imperial armies, who saw *flecken*, or spots, and *friesel*, or pustules, simply as interchangeable symptoms of malignant fever. He saw a single shape-shifting sickness that had its origins in the Rhine floods during the siege but mutated according to treatment and circumstances from, for example, an intermittent to a continued fever.[162] It is probable that typhoid was, yet again, the dominant component of the autumnal diseases and that any difference from earlier descriptions has to do with early eighteenth century fads which tended to confound 'purples' with 'miliary fever'.

It is abundantly clear from all the accounts that the point at which the opposing armies went into winter quarters represented a third, and even more lethal, phase. In Heidelberg the townspeople were forced by the sheer press of their unwelcome 'guests' to house them in 'tiny cells' [*angustis cancellis*] where the sickness lay in wait 'like a serpent hiding in the autumnal grass the better to spit out its venom in the end'.[163]

The sequence and timing of the various diseases (or the three phases of the same underlying one) is more prosaically laid out by Goddfried Baumler, municipal physician for Gemersheim. Baumler noted that a catarrhal fever had persisted 'in this country' for the past two years which afflicted the old in particular and, moreover, in 1734 smallpox had killed 'many children'. The outbreak of smallpox had 'barely passed' when bloody flux, 'often' mixed with fever took its place. The flux/fever attacked 'young and old' and persisted until October.[164] We are to take from this that the catarrhal fever and smallpox and outbreaks had died down, though not disappeared: on the left bank, the Salmbach parish register for 19 December 1734, for instance, contains an entry recording the 'sudden death' of a soldier of the Marcellin Regiment followed by a brief note bemoaning 'febris variolis'.[165]

Everyone hoped, Baumler recalled, that the severe cold that lasted all of November would usher in a 'healthy time' but at the beginning of that month 'a very special kind of hot fever' broke out. The onset was 'recognisable first of all by the headache' along with less distinctive symptoms including vertigo, and stomach aches. On the third or fourth day, 'all of a sudden' patients 'lost all their strength and the correct use

160 G.S. Baumler, *Kurze Beschreibung des im Wintermonat 1734 zu Germersheim und anderen Orten am Rheinstrom herumgegangenen hitzigen und bösartigen Fiebers* (Strasbourg: Dulßecker, 1743), p.5.

161 Bauermüller, *Dissertatio Medica inaugralis de febre castrensi*, p.2.

162 Kramer, *Medicina Castrensis*, pp.7, 73, 310.

163 Molitor, *De Febre Continua Maligna*, p.2.

164 Baumler, *Beschreibung des Wintermonat 1734*, pp.5-6.

165 Archives départementales du Bas-Rhin, Salmbach, Paroisse catholique (Avant 1793), Registre de baptêmes mariages sépultures 1727-1757, 3 E 432/2 fos. 4-6, http://archives.bas-rhin.fr/

of their wits from which it could be sufficiently concluded that this was no common hot fever but a quite malignant one'.[166] The patient would grow more confused over the days and their 'ravings' were most pronounced in the evening: 'sundowning' is common among cognitively impaired or demented patients and behaviours include confusion, disorientation, anxiety, agitation, aggression, and pacing, enlivened by visual and auditory hallucinations. Death would typically follow these symptoms by the sixteenth day. A few hours before one patient's death, Baumler observed that his 'throat swelled very heavily to the extent that he could barely breathe and could not swallow'. He observed the same swelling erupt at varying stages of the disease among other patients and from these observations he concluded that the sickness had its origins in an inflammation in the muscles of the throat and pharynx. Between the seventh and eleventh days, spots appeared. These spots did not always portend a fatal outcome and could even relieve the fever somewhat. The spots varied in size from pinhead upwards and the colour also varied from red, purple, brown, and black to blue. The prognosis was worst when the patches were two fingers wide and blue-coloured.[167]

Molitor's description of the disease at Heidelberg broadly corresponds to Baumler's.[168] The sickness began with lethargy and a splitting headache. Spots [petechiae] or 'white' pustules appeared rather later than in the cases described by Baumler, on or about the fourteenth day. Most of those showing such symptoms could be expected to recover, however most cases where the delirium deteriorated would end in death. Molitor also noted the confusing presence of worms [larva] in the stools. One account notes a catarrhal symptom, namely a swollen throat, while the other notes pustules or varioles. Neither identifies contagion, as we understand it, as the cause. Molitor, for instance, blames 'the ferment of 'invisible particles'.[169] Yet, for all the additional and unusual symptoms, this was typhus.

Ramon de Vermalle, the regimental surgeon in the French military hospital at Speyer, offered a confusing abundance of symptoms and signs, head ache, weakness, lassitude, loss of appetite, coughing, thirst, flux and, like Molitor, 'large worms'. Red spots erupted any time between the fourth and twelfth days to be followed by delirium.[170] One physician offered what he saw a clinching argument: 'Many take this catarrhal and malignant fever to be one and the same disease as the Morbus Hungaricus or Camp Fever, but they are wrong', he contended. 'The first symptom is a very severe and nigh unbearable headache, whence it is commonly called die hauptkranckheit. But we do not see such headaches in catarrhal fevers. Moreover, the delirium is far worse in Hungarian Fever than in Catarrhal fever'.[171] More convincing evidence is to be found in some of the news book reports. In mid-December it was reported from Strasbourg that 'most' of the French troops were

166 Baumler, *Beschreibung des Wintermonat 1734*, p.7.
167 Baumler, *Beschreibung des Wintermonat 1734*, pp.8-9.
168 Molitor, *De Febre Continua Maligna*, p.3.
169 Molitor, *De Febre Continua Maligna*, p.10.
170 Anon., *Commercium litterarium ad rei medicae et scientiae naturalis incrementum institutum* (Nürnberg: Sumptibus Societatis, 1735), pp.177-178.
171 Andreas Goelicke, *Disputatio Medica Inauguralis De Febre Catarrhali Maligna Petechizante* (Frankfurt: Philip Schwartz, 1741), p.17.

'dangerously sick' and that they were suffering from *kalte brand* in their feet which was likely to leave them crippled: *Kalte brand* or 'cold' gangrene sets typhus apart from other malignant fevers and happens, as discussed in Chapter 2, when the characteristic rash of typhus turns necrotic in the fingers and toes.[172] In Worms the *hitzige Krankheit* (a common synonym of typhus) and 'spotted fever' were raging in the hospital and killing nine out of every 10 patients. That the disease was deadly is also borne out by reports from Strasbourg that many of the barber-surgeons in attendance at Strasbourg hospital had died and 'almost no one dares be admitted to hospital'.[173] The report from Worms also tells of a recent macabre event: 'when a cart full of dead men was led out of Worms, a soldier lying on top of it sat up and asked where they were bringing him.[174]

This is not to assert that typhus was the only component of the wintertime disease cluster: a German newsbook report of 27 November claimed that most of the French soldiers had succumbed to common dysentery [*gattung ruhr*] from which they were but slowly cured.[175] However, typhus was the biggest, and deadliest, component: just how deadly is shockingly clear from the death toll.

Table 3.6 Deaths from Disease in Winter Quarters 1734-35[176]

Regiment	Battalions	Quarters	Numbers	Percent.
Richelieu	3	Sélestat/Schlestadt	900	60
Bourbonnais	3	Worm	800	53
Unknown	Unknown	Speyer	Unknown	50
Vivarais	1		233	47
La Couronne	2	Trier	303	30
Dillon	1	Arras	122	18

---

172 Neckarstrom 2 December, *Extra Ordinari Zeitungen* Munich 11 December 1734; Rheinstrom/den 27. November in *Extra Ordinari Zeitungen* Munich 4 December 1734. *Kalte Brand* in the present context denotes hospital gangrene. Charles White's *Observations on gangrenes and Mortifications* (Warrington: Unknown Publisher, 1790) was translated into German as *Bemerkungen über den kalten Brand* (Hanover: Helwingschen Hofbuchhandlung, 1793).

173 Rhinestrom, 10 December 1734, *Post und Ordinari Mittwochs-Zeitung*, No. 100, December 1734.Unk

174 Upper Rhinestrom., 20th December 1734, in *Mercurii Relation, oder wochentliche Ordinari Zeitungen von underschidlichen Orthen* (Munich, 1735) p.19.

175 'Rheinstrom 27 November 1734' in *Ordinari Post-Zeitungen* 23 January 1735.

176 Belhomme, *Histoire de l'infanterie en France*, Vol.III, p.111; 'Briefs aus Speyer vom 27 Jan.' in *Ordinari Post Zeitungen* no. vii (1735); André Corvisier, *L'Armée française de la fin du XVIF siècle au ministère de Choiseul: le soldat,* (Paris: Presses Universitaires de France, 1964), Vol. II, p.671.The figure of 233 deaths through sickness relates to December only! Oscar de Paoli, *Les regiments d'autrefois: Le regiment de la Couronne...*(Paris: Conseil Héraldique de France, 1891), pp.52-53;'French Army Theoretical Strengths in l735' in http://usacac.army.mil; Ó Briain (ed.), 'Gaydon's Memoir' *Irish Sword* no. 23, p.89.

The table's percentages are taken, for the purposes of comparison, with reference to the figure of 500, which is roughly the number of effectives to be found in a wartime battalion, and the number of battalions in each regiment is given in brackets.[177] The percentage of deaths attributable to disease would be even higher if one first discounted deserters and those killed in action and measured those dead of sickness as a proportion of the surviving effectives. For instance, La Couronne lost 53 deserters from its two battalions in addition to the 303 dead through sickness and Dillon's one-battalion regiment lost 118 men killed in action, on top of the 122 through sickness. If the latter's percentage were calculated by first discounting the number killed in action, one would take 122 as a percentage of 382 (rather than of 500) which would give almost 32 percent. The one-battalion Vivarais Regiment undoubtedly yields the most robust statistics because a run of *contrôles* has survived for that regiment and André Corvisier was thereby able to count the numbers who died through sickness in the appropriate column rather than rely on estimates. The general pattern in that regiments garrisoned in towns along the Rhine suffered a death toll of 50-60 percent while those further away (at Nancy and Arras) sustained much lighter mortality.

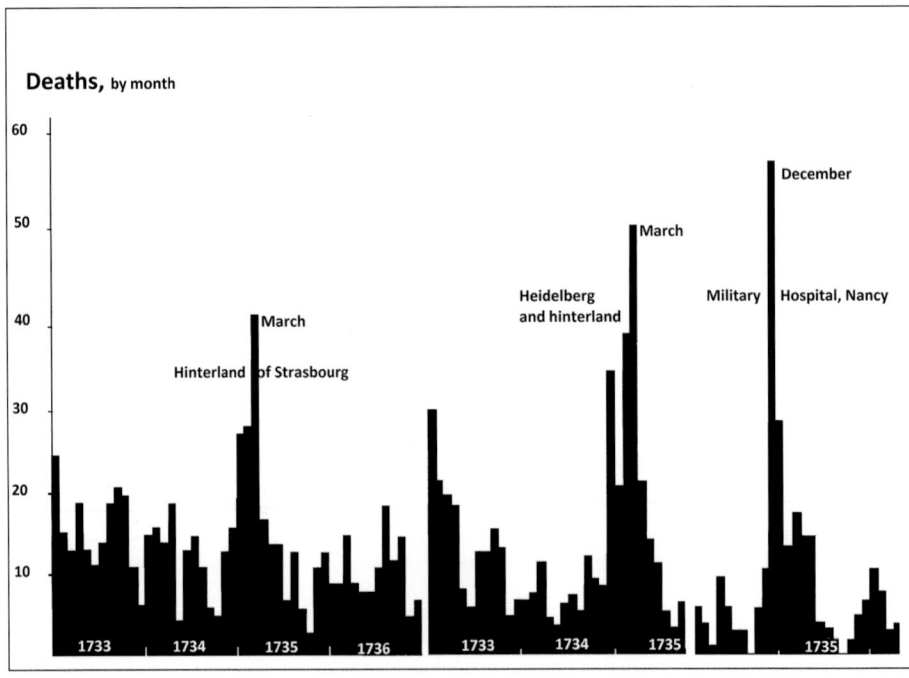

3.6 Burial registers: Strasbourg, Heidelberg and Nancy.

To extrapolate from the experience of the Vivarais Regiment, December was the cruellest month. This extrapolation is supported by other evidence. The burial

---

177 André Corvisier, *Les Contrôles de Troupes de l'Ancien Régime* (Paris: SHD, 1968) p.55.

register for the military hospital in Nancy, in the Duchy of Lorraine, shows a six-fold jump in entries for December 1734 followed by a sharp fall in January.[178] Moreover, of the 13 soldiers of the Royal Regiment of Alsace recorded in Lambsheim's burial registers, nine passed away in December.[179] There were about 3,600 men billeted in Speyer that winter, and sixty-one of them were buried on one day alone, 19 December.[180] One imagines this was the mortality peak. The typhus epidemic burned through the regiments on the Rhine in December but the number dying fell off in January and February: presumably the survivors acquired some degree of immunity to further attacks of the same disease. However, the 'numerous' youths recruited over the winter to fill the gaps in the ranks, themselves perished in 'vast numbers' from a 'malignant fever' though in some places (Speyer for instance in late January) the authorities held back the arrival of recruits for 'fear the diseases might attack them'.[181]

The hospitals were the source of the problem. Morbidity ran at over 90 percent in December: the battalions of the three regiments (La Couronne, Navarre, and Touraine) quartered at Trier each counted only 50 healthy men.[182] Such were the levels of morbidity that nearly every man must have been hospitalized at some point. And the conditions in those hospitals were grim. An officer soliciting the post of *commissaire de guerre* described grim harrowing conditions in the hospitals of Alsace:

> Horrific things are now happening at the hospital. The sick there are completely neglected. There are but two attendants [*infirmiers*] earning 2 sols a day to wash and attend 4 or 5 hundred men (rather than the prescribed ratio of 1:20) how can you get workers at such a wage? Six [attendants] are needed rather than two on 30 sols a day [5 sols each] to give the sick broth at the proper times. Sometimes the sick are left 24 hours without being seen for want of aid and help. They even want for food. As for cleanliness, how can two men look after 500? Moreover the sick are eaten by maggots [*verres*]; the frightful stench there gives rise to infection and pestilence [*la peste*].[183]

Like the letter-writer above, Baumler of Germersheim traced the cause of epidemic to bad air tainted by the exhalations from human ordure and described how, as he thought, the epidemic percolated to the civilian population:

---

178 Archives départementales de Meurthe-et-Moselle, Registres de l'état civil, Hôpital Militaire Nancy (1713-1714, 1733-1792), http://www.archives.meurthe-et-moselle.fr/fr/archives-en-ligne.html
179 Heinrich Rembe, *Lambsheim. Die Familien von 1547 bis 1800* (Kaiserlutern: Publisher, 1971), pp.82, 95, 102, 103, 104,112, 119, 153, 166, 178, 196, 204, 244, 248, 250.
180 Rheinstrom 29 December, 1734 *Mercurii Relation* (Munich, 1735) p.35; Jean de La Barre, *Continuation de l'histoire universelle* (Amsterdam: François l'Honore, 1738), Vol.IV, p.203.
181 *General Evening Post* (London) 10-12 April 1735, no. 239; *Ordonnance. portant règlement sur les décomptes*, 26 March 1735, p.1: Speyer, 27 January 1735 *Mercurii Relation*, p.110.
182 Lucenet, 'Les Epidemies dans l'Infantrie Francaise', p.210.
183 *Corvisier, L'Armée française*, Vol.II, p.685.

For I have observed that most of the citizens here became sick out of nausea at the sick soldiers that were billeted on them. And since these hot fevers in most cases were accompanied by severe diarrhoea, for which reason the sick soldiers were unable to get up, still less go outside, but let all run out beneath them; or if they did ever have a little strength, still did not leave the heated room at night time, but let their filth fall in the middle of it; so it is easy to believe that a nausea might have arisen from it and in consequence this poisonous hot fever have arisen in turn from that.

Now, I do not propose to deny completely that the air, with us in Germersheim and in the neighbouring places, may have contributed to this poisonous fever, especially since it is well known to all that during this past summer and autumn it was impossible to pass the soldier's camp without nausea because of the vile stench, unless one blocked one's mouth and nose and held one's breath.

Nor did we fare any better here, directly within the town of Germersheim; since the soldiers defiled the streets at night, especially the narrow laneways, so frequently with their excrement last summer and through the winter, that it was impossible to pass by without sensations of nausea because of the violent stench. And this unclean practice continues unfortunately up to the present hour. It is thus easy to guess that the air could have become corrupted by this stench, especially as it is commonly agreed that the air carries all exhalations away with it. In consideration of which it is easy to conjecture that they play a part in the current hot fevers.[184]

Without anticipating later discussion of hospital treatment, it is worth recalling that medical intervention was, at best, useless. Surgeon Vermalle of Speyer, for instance, recommended bloodletting, powerful emetics (he commended syrup made of Ipecacuanha) and purgatives.[185]

The hospitals, in particular, were seed beds of an epidemic that spread, sometimes after a longish time-lag. Burial registers show a civilian mortality spike in Strasbourg in January, immediately after the spike in mortality among hospitalized French soldiers. The town of course housed the biggest single military hospital in the theatre of war (with 5,000 patients as early as August 1734) and was very exposed to infection from the hospital. But the infection would not jump from town to hinterland until March 1735 when six contiguous parishes lying just to the north of Strasbourg show a mortality spike.[186] Mortality also spiked in Heidelberg in March 1735. Three parishes lying further north around Lauterbourg experienced

184   Baumler, *Beschreibung des Wintermonat 1734*, p.15.
185   Anon. *Commercium litterarium ad rei medicae et scientiae*, p.178.
186   Bischeim Paroisse catholique pp.11-26, Schiltigheim, pp.282-300, Wolissheim pp.16-24, Hoenheim, pp.137-156, Lampertheim, pp.78-107, Mittelhausbergen, pp.67-80.

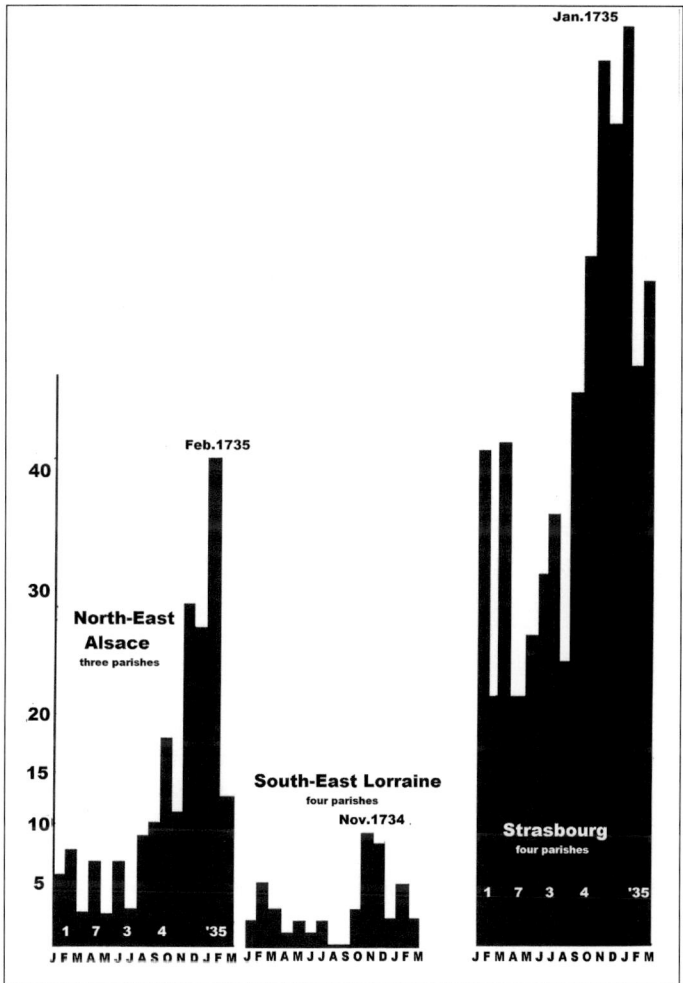

3-7 Burial registers: Alsace, Lorraine and Strasbourg.

a surge in mortality in February 1735.[187] Pforzheim, about twelve miles east of the Ettlingen Lines, was badly hit as early as January.[188]

Working backwards from the various spikes, where did the epidemic begin? One theory has it beginning in Metz and spreading thence to Alsace and to French troops in the Palatinate.[189] Another points the finger at Polish troops who marched through Silesia and Prussia for carrying typhus which was then spread,

187 Archives Départementales du Bas-Rhin; Paroisse catholique Registre de sépultures 1684-1765 pp.4-6; Salmbach, Paroisse Catholique, Registre de baptêmes mariages sépultures 1727-1757, 3 E 432/2 fos. 4-6; Lauterbourg, Paroisse Catholique, Registre de baptêmes mariages sépultures 1720-1738 pp.142-144.
188 Upper Rhinestrom, 18 January 1735, *Mercurii Relation*, p.82.
189 Corvisier, *L'Armée française*, p.671.

firstly, to German and thence to their enemy across the Rhine.[190] A third theory, favoured by the present writer, is that in autumn 1734, when troops were stationed along both sides of the Rhine, a virulent typhus probably began in Strasburg and later broke out among civilians in Heidelberg, Heilbronn, Germersheim, and 'in other places along the Rhine and Moselle'.[191] The epidemic was next carried to Lorraine by French troops returning from the siege of Philippsburg.[192] A report from Strasbourg on 3 November highlights the strategic importance of that town and describes 'most' of our 'great and powerful' army passing through the streets before dispersing in all directions, 'to France, Italy, Brabant and the upper Alsace'. The troops were 'in a pretty bad condition and many are sick, because all of the hospitals are full, some are also dying'. Some 700 men had been admitted to hospitals in the town and hinterland of whom 500 had died, 131 recovered, and the rest were still abed.[193] Reports reaching the enemy a month later claimed that 11,000 men had perished in the hospitals of Strasburg.[194] The spread from an epicentre in Strasbourg east into the enemy cantonments is corroborated by reports from Heidelberg on 18 and 20 November that notes a dangerous [gefährlich] illness among the French soldiers in Strasbourg which is daily increasing among the townsfolk [burgerschaft] and carries off 'abundance' of them.[195] By January there was still 'a big number' of patients in Strasburg hospitals but 'not as many' were dying 'compared to a few weeks ago'.[196]

Rapid diffusion up and down the Rhine, to Sélestat/Schlestadt and Speyer respectively, is corroborated by the French regimental mortality statistics. That the French troops were hit first and hardest by the outbreak is the tenor of most newspaper reports, though one claims that in early January Imperial and French troops on the Rhine both suffered 'great mortality' from 'malignant fevers'.[197] The spread to troops quartered along the Moselle was only slightly delayed: at the end of January we are told that the French garrison at Trarbach, on the Moselle about 37 miles downriver of Trier, had been 'severely weakened' by sickness, but was being reinforced by 'many' recruits to take the places of the dead.[198]

190 George C. Kohn, *Encyclopedia of Plague and Pestilence: From Ancient Times to the Present* (New York: Infobase Publishing, 2008), p.144.

191 Rhinestrom, 10 December 1734, *Post und Ordinari Mittwochs-Zeitung*, No. 100, December 1734.

192 Harald Westergaard, (ed.) Friedrich Prinzing, *Epidemics Resulting from Wars* (Oxford: Clarendon Press, 1916), p.842.

193 'Extract of a letter from Strasbourg', 3 November 1734, *Ordinari post Zeitungen* anno 1734, p.742

194 Neckarstrom, 2 December 1734, *Ordinari post Zeitungen anno 1734 den 2. Januarij*, p.789.

195 *Ordinarii Post Zeitung* (4 December); *Daily Journal* (London) Friday, November 22, 1734; Issue 4324.

196 Strasbourg 2 January *1735 Mercurii Relation, oder wochentliche Ordinari Zeitungen von underschidlichen Orthen* (Munich, 1735) p.51.

197 The Hague, 11 Jan. 1735, *General Evening Post* (London, England),7-9 January 1735, no. 199; Bauermüller, *De Febre Castrensi*, p.2.

198 Moselstrom 28 Jan. 1735 *Mercurii Relation*, p.109.

Burial records from both sides of the Rhine broadly confirm that a severe epidemic spread to the civilian population by March 1735.[199] It was equally severe in the vicinity of Strasbourg and in selected parishes in Baden-Württemberg.[200] Yet, further afield, Dattenfeld in the Prussian Rhineland shows no sign of this pattern.[201] Likewise, four parishes situated just outside Alsace and west of the Vosges show no mortality surge whatsoever.[202]

To sum up, the epidemic raced along the Rhine and the Moselle between December 1734 and March 1735 amongst both civilians and soldiers. Baumler and others were correct to surmise that it began amongst the soldiery in their camps and later their winter cantonments and spread by contagion to civilians who came into contact with them but, of course, Baumler was wrong about the nature of that contagion. It was carried by 'bad air' in the sense that the victim breathed in air contaminated by louse faeces while in the vicinity of an infected patient or while handling their clothes or bedding. It was also a classic war epidemic in that it does not seem to have spread far beyond the war zone, with one odd exception. A 'contagious fever' began amongst the English 'lower class' in February (brought, one witness surmised, by sailors) was 'spreading vastly' by March and by April was prevalent 'more than ever'. The descriptions of this fever exactly coincide with those of the Rhenish epidemic though as the epidemic progressed the pustules were entirely replaced by are 'brown, black, purple spots' which 'always denote danger'.[203]

It has been possible to superimpose modern diagnostic categories on the summer, autumn and winter diseases but contemporary perceptions of these as a single phenomenon retain their usefulness. That a critical number of soldiers should be hospitalized, or at least bedridden, was a necessary and almost sufficient condition of the typhus epidemic. One quarter of the soldiers in the camp at Kuppenheim in August evidently was not enough to trigger an epidemic in that the nearest hospital

199 Archives Départementales Bas-Rhin Registres Paroissiaux, Ostwald, Registre de sépultures 1685-1741, 3 E 365/4 pp.64-76; Schiltigheim, Registre de sépultures 1637-1738, pp.282-300; Illkirch-Graffenstaden, 3 E 217/36, Registre de sépultures 1715-1774, pp.11-24; Bischheim, Registre de sépultures 1725-1792, pp.11-26; Mittelhausbergen, Registre de sépultures 1686-1742, 3 E 296/3 pp.67-80; Lampertheim, Registre de sépultures 1712-1744, 3 E 256/15, pp.78-107; Wolfisheim, Registre de mariages sépultures 1724-1787, 3 E 551/4, pp.16-24; Hoenheim, Registre de sépultures 1685-1758, 3 E 203/9 pp.137-156.

200 Heidelberg and Leimen: Deutschland Tote und Beerdigungen, 1582-1958. Database. FamilySearch. http://FamilySearch.org: 14 June 2016. Index based upon data collected by the Genealogical Society of Utah, Salt Lake City. Stuttgart (Vaihingen), Heilbronn (Brackenheim) and Ochsenburg. Notizen u Tote 1609-1827, Ancestry.com. *Württemberg, Germany, Lutheran Baptisms, Marriages, and Burials, 1500-1985* database on-line]. Provo, UT, USA: Ancestry.com Operations, Inc., 2016.

201 Deutschland Tote und Beerdigungen, 1582-1958, https://familysearch.org/ark.

202 *Archives départementales de Meurthe-et-Moselle*, Bourscheid Baptêmes, mariages, sépultures.1714-1746 pp.60-69; Vescheim Sépultures (1725-1783), 9NUM/712ED1E1 fos 12r-13r; Danne-et-Quatre-Vents, Sépultures, 9NUM/171ED1E4 1726-1770, fos 34-38; Hommarting, Baptêmes, mariages, sépultures, 1701-1741, 9NUM/338ED1E1 pp.173-176/195.

203 Thomas Short, *A General Chronological History of the Air, Weather, Seasons ...* (London: T. Longman, 1749), Vol.II, p.55; M. Huxham, *Observations on the Air and Epidemic Diseases* (London: J. Hinton and Henry Whitfeld,1759), pp.124, 125, 128.

at Fort Louis evidently coped and mortality was kept low, relative, that is, the frightful death toll to come.

But by late November the 'greater part' of the French army has succumbed to a 'dangerous sickness' which was said to have begun at the Siege of Philippsburg.[204] Inevitably, the hospitals (most of them buildings hastily converted, like the Bishop's Palace at Speyer) were overcrowded and understaffed as the attendants sickened and died. The epidemic was 'continuing' among the French troops on the Rhine and Moselle in mid-December and indeed the squalor and congestion did not ease until March. These improvements were attributed to the efforts of Jean Claude Adrien Helvétius, first physician to the Queen and Inspector-General of the military hospitals in Flanders, who visited the hospitals in Alsace, had 2,000 blankets issued and lodged convalescent officers in burghers' homes.[205] More likely, conditions improved because they could not have gotten worse: for one thing, the sheer scale of mortality resolved the problem of congestion.

Conclusion

As discussed when comparing Derry and Riga, gauging the severity of an epidemic from before and after unit or garrison strengths will only tell so much. More sensitive metrics must be found elsewhere. The commander of beleaguered Vienna complained on 7 August 1683, about half way through the siege, that he was losing more of his men, sixty a day, to *die Ruhr* than to Turkish fire.[206] Such estimates of a day's loss are fairly common in reports of siege operations, and are more likely to be based on an actual tally than on more global estimates. Alternatively, where muster totals are given within two or three days of each other then it is a simple matter to compute a daily rate of loss.

Table 3.7 Deaths Per Day of Sickness as a percentage of garrison strength[207]

	Garrison	Day	Percent
Swedes	Riga	5 June 1710	0.43
Protestant Association	Derry	25 July 1689	0.4
Imperials	Vienna	9 August 1683	0.375
Imperials	Belgrade	16 August 1717	0.24

---

204 'Neckarstrom 2 December' in *Extraordinarii Zeitungen* (Munich, 11 December 1734). *Kalte Brand* in the present context denotes hospital gangrene.

205 Monique Lucenet, *Médecine, chirurgie et armée en France au siècle des Lumières* (Paris: Editions I&D, 2006), p.114.

206 Landersdorfer, 'Das Schicksal der bayerischen Soldaten im Türkenkrieg', p.56.

207 Stoye, *Siege of Vienna*, p.104 cites a garrison strength of 11,000 together with 5,000 men raised from the townspeople.

By that criterion, Riga and Derry, of the three case studies, appear as neck and neck in terms of deaths per day, though the death rate in Riga may be understated, since the rate is that of early June when the siege had another month to run (and the sick rate to increase), whereas the Derry figure represents a point just days before the relief fleet broke through. However, applying the morbidity metric, the Swedes in Riga emerge as worst-hit of all. Morbidity is comparable to that prevailing in the French army in northern Italy, a case study to be discussed in the final chapter. Derry is relegated to second tier alongside the French encampment at Kuppenheim.

Table 3.8 Morbidity as percent of total strength

	Garrison	Date	Morbidity
Swedes	Riga	10 July 1710	56
French	Milanese	January 1735	50
Protestant Association	Derry	30 July 1689	25
French	Kuppenheim	25 August 1734	25
Imperials	Belgrade (Semlin)	5 August 1717	22

The most overcrowded place came off worst of all, but one. That one was Riga, which though nowhere near as congested as Derry, endured a much longer siege. A tentative equation 'congestion plus duration equals epidemic severity' does not work for the reason that the scale of morbidity and mortality at Riga has much more to do with a contingency (the outbreak of plague) that the duration of the siege. The only way to beat the plague was to outrun it, and that choice was not open to the soldiers and burghers of Riga in May 1710. Plague defies attempts at generalization.

4

Marches

Napoleon's retreat from Moscow in 1812, though it took place after the period of this study, confronts us as the inescapable example of just how catastrophically a march could go wrong. Napoleon's *Grande Armée* left Moscow in mid-October and the last of some 22,000 survivors straggled across the Niemen into Prussian-occupied Poland on 14 December 1812. They were all that remained of about 150,000 men; the 95,000 men who marched from Moscow together with lines of communication units that they swept up as they retired. The rest had perished, been taken prisoner, or been killed, in that order of magnitude.

Napoleon's claim that the Russian winter defeated him should not distract attention from his strategic overreach, careless logistics, and tactical blunders. For instance, he let himself be nudged into retreating along his axis of advance, which had already been picked clean, and so horses quickly died for want of fodder and quite soon the columns could not cart their loot, their provisions, and their sick and wounded.[1] All that said, Napoleon's excuse has some factual basis and exceptionally frigid temperatures enveloped the latter nightmarish stages of the retreat. December night-time lows in Smolensk and Vilnius do not normally drop below minus eight.[2] But on the night of 14 November, after the French evacuated Smolensk, readings fell as low as -23.75°C. Loison's division, containing many German and Italian recruits, lost all but 2,000 men while deployed to guard the road between Oshmiana and Vilnius, most of them meeting an 'icy death' through hypothermia on the night of 6 December when the barometer dropped to -37.5°C. Humans, even ragged and poorly shod ones, can work in such temperatures: at forced labour camps in Kolmya during the Great Patriotic War, the 'zeks' or inmates were excused work outside the camp only when the temperature fell below -50°C.[3] However they, at least, passed their nights indoors, unlike Napoleon's wretched soldiers. Armand de Caulaincourt, a close personal aide of Napoleon, memorably described the effects of cold on those debilitated by hunger or hobbled by frostbite:

> …in this condition the drowsiness engendered by cold is irresistibly strong. Sleep comes inevitably, and to sleep is to die. I tried in vain to save a number

1   Adam Zamoyski, *1812: Napoleon's Fatal March on Moscow* (London: Harper Perennial, 2005), pp.391-392, 415.
2   'World Weather', www.worldweatheronline.com.
3   Anne Applebaum, *Gulag: A History of the Soviet Camps* (London: Allen Lane, 2003), p.126.

of these unfortunates. The only words they uttered were to beg me, for the love of God, to go away and let them sleep. To hear them, one would have thought sleep was their salvation. Unhappily, it was a poor wretch's last wish. But at least he ceased to suffer, without pain or agony. Gratitude, and even a smile, was imprinted on his discoloured lips. What I have related about the effects of extreme cold, and of this kind of death by freezing, is based on what I saw happen to thousands of individuals. The road was covered with their corpses.[4]

A road strewn with frozen corpses: such is the image of the retreat from Moscow that is burned in historical memory. Yet most men succumbed to the indirect, rather than the direct (hypothermia and frostbite) consequences of extreme cold. The sub-title of Stephen Talty's *How Typhus Killed Napoleon's Greatest Army* leaves the reader in no doubt as to that indirect cause. Talty makes a convincing case in powerful and engaging prose, except that he blames typhus for losses during the march to, as well as the retreat from Moscow. Talty boldly asserts that 'unmistakable' signs of typhus appeared as early as June when, as discussed in chapter one, the symptoms produced by *Rickettsia* are easily confused and, crucially, typhus was ever a winter rather than a summer sickness.[5]

It is clear, however, that disease was 'the lead killer on the campaign, and typhus the most lethal disease present'.[6] Typhus, directly and indirectly, brought about one of the worst single increments in the ongoing catastrophe after the retreating army reached the apparent safety of Vilnius and finally sourced food and shelter. However, Napoleon had pushed ahead, putting his brother-in-law Prince Murat in charge in his absence. Murat had been ordered to wait a week but, unnerved by Cossack raids, he ordered the army to resume its flight, leaving behind an estimated 20,000 wounded, disabled and sick in the makeshift hospitals and houses of Vilnius.[7] As soon as organized units pulled out, Cossack irregulars poured in, plundering strag-glers and the sick. That typhus had broken out was credible given the season and the situation: eyewitnesses confirm that those who had escaped Vilnius carried typhus with them to Königsberg [Kaliningrad].[8] The sick in the hospitals were thrown out the windows or piled up on the floor:[9] Sir Robert Wilson, a liaison officer attached to the Russian general staff, described the scene:

The hospital at St Bazile presented the most awful and hideous sight: seven thousand five hundred bodies were piled up like pigs of lead over

4   Armand-Augustin-Louis Caulaincourt (ed. Jean Hanoteau), *With Napoleon in Russia* (New York: Mineola, 2005), p.259.

5   Stephan Talty, *The Illustrious Dead: The Terrifying Story of How Typhus Killed Napoleon's Greatest Army* (New York: Crown, 2009), p.49.

6   Talty, *The illustrious Dead*, p.258.

7   Zamoyski, *1812*, pp.504-5.

8   Olivier Datour, and Alexandra Buzhilova, 'Palaeological Study of Napoleonic Mass Graves Discovered in Russia' in Christopher Knüsel and Martin Smith (eds.), *The Routledge Handbook of the Bioarchaeology of Human Conflict* (London: Routledge, 2013), p.523.

9   Zamoyski, *1812*, pp.525.

one another in the corridors…. and all the broken windows and walls were stuffed with feet, legs, arms, hands, trunks and heads to fit the apertures, and keep out the air from the yet living.[10]

The 'pigs of lead' simile is apt: molten lead flowed from the smelting furnace and was cast in oblong 'pigs' or blocks which were laid across each other in high stacks.

Worried about epidemics, the Russian authorities hastily collected corpses from streets, squares, and houses and buried them in the ready-made trenches of a French redoubt covering a road outside the city. Archaeological investigators in 2002 found the jumbled remains of at least 3,266 soldiers (together with three *cantinières*), noted that nitrogen enrichment found in the bones was most likely the result of prolonged nutritional stress, and so concluded that 'cold was, with exhaustion and starvation, the main cause of the death'.[11] A later search for the DNA of infectious agents in dental pulp of 35 soldiers found that three had evidence of infection with *Rickettsia prowazekii* and seven with *Bartonella quintana* which was associated with 'trench fever', a relapsing fever.[12] The proportion infected with hospital fever, at less than 10 percent, seems improbably small and the investigation lays bare the present limitations of scientific investigation. Absence of evidence is not evidence of absence: the fact that DNA *Rickettsia prowazekii* is not detectible in many more of the soldiers does not prove that they did not, or could not have, suffered from typhus. Trench fever was much more prevalent and is, of itself, rarely lethal. However, it would have been deadly, as would privation, if it left the victim too weak to walk. In other words, hunger, disease and cold are inextricably linked in a tangled chain of causation. The sick soldier stripped by Cossacks perished from hypothermia, but the ultimate or 'real' cause was the trench fever that so weakened him he lagged behind or strayed from the herd.

This brief account of the retreat from Moscow has been included because the story is unavoidable in a chapter about, so to speak, death marches. Yet the retreat from Moscow is just too singularly catastrophic to be representative of the three case studies to follow. More than 85 percent of the soldiers died, compared to the Russian army that invaded the Crimea in 1737 and lost 'only' half its strength in twice the time. Too many things went wrong on the retreat from Moscow. These include (in no particular order) gross strategic miscalculation, logistical ineptitude, extreme weather, the anomie to be expected in a vast multi-national army, exacerbated by distant and uninspiring leadership. The three case studies exhibit some, but never all, of those problems.

10   Martin R. Howard, *Napoleon's Doctors: The Medical Services of the Grande Armée* (Staplehurst: Spellmount, 2006), p.168.
11   M. Signoli, *et al.*, 'Discovery of a mass grave of Napoleonic period in Lithuania (1812, Vilnius)', *Comptes Rendus Palevol*, 3:3 (May 2004), p.227.
12   D. Raoult, *et.al.*, 'Evidence for louse-transmitted diseases in soldiers of Napoleon's Grand Army in Vilnius'. *J Infect Dis.*, 193:1 (January 2006), pp.116, 120.

Crimea (1736)

For hundreds of years the Crimean Khanate had raided northwards into the heart of Muscovy (Moscow itself had been burnt down in 1571) to carry off huge preys of cattle and slaves: the very word 'slave' derives from 'Slav' and emanates from these raids.[13] Not until the Belgorod Line was built between 1635 and 1638 across the high feather-grass country between the basins of the Dnieper and the Don would the Tatars begin to be contained. A vast and uninhabitable no man's land lay between the Belgorod Line and the outer boundary of the Khanate proper. Between 1679 and 1681 Muscovy added the Izium line to enclose a V-shaped area whose salient pointed towards Crimea, foreshadowing attacks to finally bottle up the Tatars within the peninsula.[14] The attacks came in 1687 and 1689, after Russia was awarded Kiev and the territory east of the Dnieper by the Poles in return for joining the anti-Turkish 'Holy League' alongside the Habsburg Empire, Venice, and Poland. These two offensives were led by Prince Vasily Golitsyn, chief adviser and lover of the regent Sophia Alekseyevna. His 1687 offensive will be described in order to illustrate the 'enormous logistical challenge' it presented.[15] Golitsyn set out from Akhtyrka [*Okhtyrka*] rather late, on 2 May, with some 132,000 men. Gambling that the 100,000 horses would graze green forage on the way, his army carried little or no fodder. On 30 May Golitsyn rendezvoused on the Samara with 50,000 Cossack irregulars and trudged on, dragging his 20,000 carts in a ponderous *wagenburg*, 1.5 km across and 5 km long, screened by horsemen. The column managed to cover only six miles a day, about half the normal day's march, until halting on 13 June at the Konskie Vody [*Konka*] river to replenish hay and water. The weather was hot, the steppe dry, and the Tatars set the grass ablaze in a literal 'scorched earth' tactic to deny the invaders forage.[16] By the time the Russians approached the Karachakra River on 16 June the cavalry mounts and cart horses were too sick and exhausted to press on to Perekop [*Or Kapi*] which sat athwart the narrow isthmus leading to Crimea and was another 130 miles away off, or six weeks' march, at the current snail's pace.[17] Golitsyn had to turn back and lost one third of his army, for little or no apparent benefit. He tried again in 1689, setting out earlier, marching faster, and making better use of riverine transport. He had also built a fortress at Novobogoroditskoe at the junction of the Dnieper and the Samara to use as a forward magazine, storing 6,300 tons of grain. This time Golitsyn actually reached Perekop, but could not afford to wait long enough to attack the fortifications. The many obstacles besides steppe fires included

13   Michael Khodarkovsky, *Russia's Steppe Frontier: The Making of a Colonial Empire, 1500–1800* (Bloomington: Indiana University Press, 2002), pp.18-19. 21.

14   Carol B. Stevens, *Russia's wars of emergence, 1460-1730. Modern wars in perspective* (Harlow: Pearson Longman, 2007), p.193.

15   Brian Davies, *Warfare, State and Society on the Black Sea Steppe, 1500–1700* (Oxford: Routledge, 2007), p.179.

16   Carol B Stevens, 'Food and Supply: Logistics and the Early Modern Russian Army' in Brian L. Davies, (ed.), *Warfare in Eastern Europe, 1500-1800* (Leiden: Brill Academic Publishers, 2012), p.142-3.

17   Davies, *Warfare, State and Society on the Black Sea Steppe*, p.180.

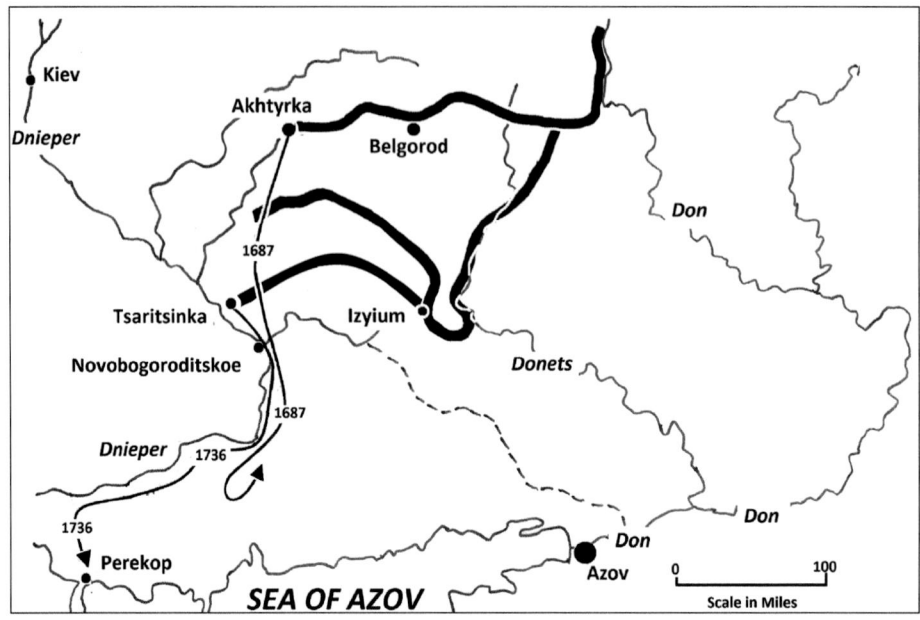

4.1 Russian lines on the Pontic Steppe.

spring thaws and autumn rains that made rivers impassable and turned tracks into mud and, above all, distance.[18]

The distance, at least, had shortened by 1735, by which time the Russians had extended the Izyum Line further south.[19] Czarina Anna Ivanovna's war with Turkey was in large part an outgrowth of the War of the Polish Succession, since France had long encouraged Turkey to attack Russia in an effort to disrupt an alliance between Romanov and Habsburg.[20] On 1 October 1735 General Mihail Ivanovich Leont'ev set out south with 28,000 men to ravage the Crimea and, in his own words, 'exterminate' the Nogai Tatars who inhabited the Pontic steppes north of Crimea. On 6 October he began crossing the dry grasslands, but just a week later the rains began and brought the *Rasputitsa* or 'mud season' when roads turned into quagmires. Leont'ev turned back, having lost 9,000 men through hardship and sickness.[21]

The following year a much larger expedition was led by Field Marshal Burkhard Christoph von Münnich/Minikh. He was a German military engineer who had

---

18   Willard Sunderland, *Taming the Wild Field: Colonization and Empire on the Russian Steppe* (Ithaca, N.Y.: Cornell University Press, 2004), p.32.

19   Russisch-Türkischer Krieg: Karte der Kriegsoperationen der russischen Armeen an Don und Dnjepr, 1736, Archivaliensignatur: Hessisches Staatsarchiv Marburg, HStAM\WHK\WHK 20/03.

20   Bruce W. Menning, 'The Imperial Russian Army, 1725-96' in F. Kagan and R. Higham (eds.), *The Military History of Tsarist Russia* (Basingstoke: Palgrave, 2008), p.56.

21   A. Stoyanov, 'Russia marches South: army reform and battlefield performance in Russia's Southern campaigns, 1695-1739' (Ph.D Thesis, Leiden University, 2017) at http://hdl.handle. net/1887/48241, p.206. (accessed 20 February 2018)

risen to be president of the Military College, thanks to powerful patrons, and now wished to seal his reputation by a field command. The strategic objective of the Crimean expedition was to break into the peninsula and establish a naval base on the Black Sea. Meanwhile, the Don army commanded by Field Marshal Peter Lacy, an Irishman, laid siege to Azov, the most easterly of a chain of forts built by the Ottomans to guard the estuaries of the Don, Dnieper, and Bug.[22]

Münnich had made impressive logistical preparations at Tsaritzinka, which lay over 100 miles closer to Crimea than had Golitsyn's base. Münnich's 54,000-strong army brought 8,000 wagons, carrying enough flour to give every man a daily ration of one and a half pounds of bread for two whole months and barrels of beer to 'cheer' him. Münnich gambled that his horses would find grazing on the steppe and drinking water in the tributary creeks of the Dnieper if he set out in April, just after the snows melted. Moreover, his men would batten onto last autumn's harvest in the Crimea.

Between 11 and 19 April Münnich's army duly embarked on the trek across the 'vast expanse of nothing except grass and sky'.[23] The army trundled forward in five vast hollow squares bristling with pikemen to guard the supply wagons within. After rendezvousing with Cossack detachments on 5 May, Münnich's army numbered 58,000 men. Fourteen days later Münnich reached the Perekop Line which stretched for seven *versts*, or almost five miles, across the isthmus 'from sea to sea'.[24] The line comprised a rampart fronted by a dry ditch, interspersed with six stone towers bristling with guns and was backed by the citadel of Perekop itself. Though the Tatars considered them 'impregnable', the fortifications quickly collapsed when the Russians stormed one of the towers.[25] Not content with his 'resounding' victory in taking the line and the fortress with light casualties Münnich believed he could subjugate Crimea before the end of July, that is, before Ottoman reinforcements could debark at Kaffa [*Feodosia*] in the south-east of the peninsula and reinforce the Tatars. From the beginning, Münich had dared to hope that he could conquer Crimea and was reluctant to give up on this grandiose plan: 'In 1736 Azov will be ours. We will become masters of the Don, Donets, Perekop, the Nogai domains between the Don and the Dnepr along the Black Sea and perhaps even Crimea will belong to us'.[26] Münnich disregarded the advice of his council-of-war, which pointed out that only eight days' rations remained and favoured waiting on supply wagons from Ukraine. Fearing that he would forfeit forward momentum, Münnich pressed on. He took the precaution of detaching Leont'ev with 10,000 Russian regulars and

---

22   Jean-François de Bourgoing (transl. Gerhard Anton von Halem), *Vie du comte de Munnich...* (Paris: Nicolle 1807), p.66.

23   Lavender Cassels, *The Struggle for the Ottoman Empire 1717-1740* (London: John Murray, 1966), p.10: *Russisch-Türkischer Krieg: Karte der Kriegsoperationen der russischen Armeen an Don und Dnjepr, 1736*, Hessisches Staatsarchiv Marburg, HStAM\WHK\WHK 20/03; Stoyanov, 'Russia marches South', p.214.

24   *The Gentleman's Magazine*, (London, 1736), Vol.VI, p.490.

25   Brian Davies, *Empire and Military Revolution in Eastern Europe Russia's Turkish Wars in the Eighteenth Century* (London: Continuum, 2011), pp.192-196; Bourgoing, *Vie du comte de Munnich*, p.68.

26   Davies, *Empire and Military Revolution in Eastern Europe*, p.191.

3,000 Cossacks to take the Ottoman fortress of Kinburn and so block the Bucak Horde from raiding his lines of supply and communication. Münnich set off down the isthmus from Or-Kapi on 26 May but perforce had to march even more ponderously than before, the great squares grinding to a halt every few hundred paces as wagons broke down and oxen collapsed in their yokes. Tatar horsemen picked off stragglers and pounced on any gaps that opened in the formations.[27] It took the Russians all of 10 days to cover the 62 miles to the port town of Kezlev [*Yevpatoriya*] by which time rations had run out and the men were parched from thirst. Along the whole 90-mile route from Perekop to Kezlev there flowed only three fresh water streams, the rest being salt-water inlets, and the retreating Tatars had not neglected to poison wells and springs. Major General Biron's adjutant, who penned memoirs of this campaign, recalled scouring deserted villages for buried grain, beating sun, unrelenting heat, and agonies of thirst, especially on the last three days of the march. 'In vain' did the rearguard keep a barrel of wine to revive those struck down by heat, thirst, and exhaustion and, but for a downpour a few miles from Kezlev, the army would, thought Biron's adjutant, have been destroyed.[28]

The invariable advice for a column marching in summertime was to set out well before dawn and take shelter from the midday sun.[29] A well-documented example of what happened when this advice was ignored is provided by the British expeditionary force in Portugal in 1762, discussed in the final chapter. From Porto de Muge on the lower Tagus to Santarem was about nine miles, hardly an excessive day's march. However, the 3rd Foot, or 'Buffs', did not set off until six and so endured the 'extreme' midday heat of high summer. The surgeon and the officer in charge of the march offered excuses for what happened next: reading between the lines it seems that the troops, 'choked with heat and dust', were not allowed rest until after they had covered seven miles. Until then men who 'dropt' were left resting in shade, 'under the Care of Proper persons' while the column pressed on. However, when the march resumed, 'the men fell down sick so fast that there were not sufficient well men left to attend them'. By the time the column trudged into Santarem, fully half the soldiers had fallen out and eleven men had died, three of the bodies never to be recovered.[30] Another report counted 10 men, one woman and three children dead and another 18 persons missing.[31]

Biron's adjutant was surely right. Short of water, enduring a far longer march than the Buffs on the road to Santarem, and harried by enemy horsemen, the Russians could not have pushed on much further, even to Kezlev, but for the opportune deluge.

27 Jeremy Black, *European Warfare in a Global Context, 1660–1815* (New York: Taylor & Francis, 2007), p.84.

28 Anon. 'Zapiska o tom, skol'ko ia pamiatuiu o krymskich i tureckikh pokhodakh' at http://www.runivers.ru/doc/d2. (accessed 11 December 2017).

29 Friedrich Wilhelm von Bessel, *Entwurf eines Militair-Feld-Reglements* (Hanover: H. E. C. Schlüter, 1778), p.309.

30 Peter Bernard to Loudoun, Asinhage, 31 July 1762 and Major Biddulph to unk., 31 July 1762, RSC Loudoun Manuscripts (medical) MS0192/1, fos. 55r, 56.

31 Patrick J. Speelman, 'Strategic Illusions and the Iberian War of 1762' in Patrick J. Speelman and Mark H. Danley (eds.), *The Seven Years' War: Global Views* (Leiden: Brill Academic Publishers, 2012), p.449.

At Kezlev the Russians found abundant stores of wheat and rice to feed themselves for three weeks, vindicating Münnich's contested decision to travel fast and light. Münnich had considered resting at Kezlev and baking bread for the march, but the Tatars had wrecked nearly all the windmills and so 'what was ground in one day was consumed the same day'. After resting for only four days and with epidemic disease spreading, the field marshal slipped out of town on the evening of 9 June to advance on Bakhchysarai, the capital of the Crimea and site of the Khan's palace.[32] It would prove a march too far.

A horse that is deprived of water for a prolonged period of time will drink too much when finally let drink. Moreover, a horse's stomach is relatively small and a horse can quickly eat more grain than the stomach can handle. If the grain stays in the stomach for an extended period, fermentation may occur, producing gas that contributes to distension and pain. Many of the Russian horses had been allowed gorge on water and grain at Kezlev. Consequently, stomach colic or distension would disable one third of the cart horses and force the Russians to dump much of their grain. Deftly evading a blocking force, Münnich entered Bakhchysarai on 16 June and set it aflame. He wanted to press on to Kaffa (indeed, the Tatars assumed he would and ravaged the countryside in that direction) but since he found no supplies in Bakhchysarai or Aqmescit [Simferopol] his army was again running dangerously short of food, the heat was 'unbearable' and a truculent cabal of senior officers were plotting against him.[33]

> ...the army was visibly shrinking, a third sick and the rest [of the soldiers] so weak, that they could hardly drag their legs after them. I have above mentioned some of the reasons of this, to which may be added the heat, which is extreme in Crimea during this season of the year, so that it was decided to return to Perekop, to rest the troops during the hottest of the hot weather.[34]

Glumly, Münnich started back for Perekop, which he reached on 17 July.[35] Evidently this was a forced march in the heat of high summer by men tortured with thirst (though not as severely as they had on the road to Kezlev) who were now also suffering pangs of hunger. Even when foragers uncovered hidden stocks of grain in the villages, there were no mills to grind the grain.[36] Münnich hoped to revictual

---

32   Ernst Herrmann, *Beiträgezur Geschichte des Russischen Reiches* (Leipzig: J. C. Hinrichsen, 1843), p.205.
33   Stoyanov, 'Russia marches South', p.215; Christoph Hermann von Manstein, *Mémoires historiques, politiques et militaires sur la Russie* (Lyon: Jean-Marie Bruyset, 1772), Vol.I, p.198.
34   Bourgoing, *Vie du comte de Munnich*, p.78.
35   Charles W. Ingrao, Nikola Samardžić, Jovan Pesaljeds, *The Peace of Passarowitz, 1718* (Bloomington: Purdue University Press, 2011), p.136; Virginia Aksan, *Ottoman Wars, 1700-1870: An Empire Besieged* (Harlow: Longman, 2014), p.103; Davics, *Russia's Turkish Wars*, p.199; *Mercure de France* (September 1736) p.2119.
36   Christian Friedrich Hempel, *Leben, Thaten, Und Betrübter Fall, Des Weltberufenen, Russischen, Grafens, Burchards Christophs von Münnich...* (Bremen: Nathanael Saurmann, 1742), p.265.

at Perekop and then turn back right away. Von Manstein, a protégé of Münnich, claimed that the returning army found 15 days' supply of biscuit that had been brought from the Ukraine and so, with sutlers bringing other provisions, the camp enjoyed an 'abundance' of supplies.[37] However, Biron's adjutant claimed otherwise and recalled paying exorbitant prices, albeit for luxuries like bread and ham. This latter source was hostile in that Biron was a brother of Ernst, Duke of Courland, who was Münnich's bitter factional rival at court.

Even if initially available, as Von Manstein claimed, provisions and forage quickly ran short. Tatar horsemen might be unable to break a battle square but they were adept raiders, slipping across the Sivash or 'Rotten Sea' (a shallow lagoon separated from the Sea of Azov by the Arabat Spit) by hidden fords to intercept supply trains, pick off foraging parties forced to venture far out onto the steppe, and steal horses. The Russian position was hopeless. Most of the Cossacks were quickly sent home to spare forage and provisions but the main army remained encamped for almost six weeks, until late August, when Münnich at last secured permission from the court to withdraw from the camp and its 'stench-generated diseases'.[38] He first sent off the sick with a guard of dragoons and 2, 000 Don Cossacks. Next, between 25 and 27 August, he razed and slighted the lines and forts and on 28 August marched his sadly depleted army north.[39] On the way he joined up with Leont'ev who was retreating from Kinburn and brought with him a flock of 20,000 sheep to feed the army. After a month's march, the survivors reached the Samara River.[40]

When Münnich mustered his army at the original jump-off point he found, we are told by Biron's adjutant, that it was 'almost entirely ruined' [*razorennoyu*].[41] Various global estimates corroborate the claim that Münnich lost around 30,000 men or just over half his starting strength of 58,000. Since fewer than 2,000 of men had been killed or taken prisoner, the loss was attributed to 'unending hardships'.[42] Even Münnich's hagiographer accepted that however 'brilliant' the campaign, it had been 'costly'. Losses are even heavier when calculated on the basis of the 11 regiments of dragoons and 15 of infantry that made up most of the regular component of Münnich's army and who probably had less chance to desert during the long treks over the steppe than had the Cossack irregulars. At the outset of the campaign each regiment counted 1,500 men but in the final review there were on average only 600 left 'fit to serve'. Conceivably, the missing soldiers could have included the bedridden sick but from the context it is clear, as even one of the general's admirers confessed,

---

37   Von Manstein, *Mémoires historiques*, pp.199-200.
38   Herrmann, *Geschichte des Russischen Reiches*, pp.225-226, 228-229.
39   Von Manstein, *Mémoires historiques* p.202.
40   *Mercure de France* (October 1736), p.2352.
41   Anon., Zapiska o tom, skol'ko ya pamyatuyu o krymskikh i turetskikh pokhodakh. http://www.runivers.ru/doc/d2 (accessed 11 December 2017).
42   Pietro Paolo Trompeo (ed.), Franceso Algarotti, *Viaggi di Russia* (Turin: Garzanti, 1961), p.71; *Le Courier*, XC, (9 November 1736).

that one half of the army had 'perished' [*péri*] of 'hunger and privation'.[43] Only the Kinburn detachment 'was in any state of preservation'.[44]

Table 4.1 Before and After: Münnich's 1736 Crimean Expedition

Opening Strength	35,802
Losses in Action	2,000
Losses through sickness	19,602 [56 percent]
Survivors	16,200

Münnich could certainly have done more to conserve captured stores and provisions. In addition, he can be faulted for pushing too hard, by force-marching his hapless soldiers. Even an unbiased outsider like the Italian traveller Algarotti criticized Münnich for harshness in contrast to Peter Lacy who was fondly called 'father' [*baska*] by his troops.[45] The following two summers Lacy would bypass the Or-Kapi line by crossing along the Arabat Spit in 1737 and by wading across the Sivash in 1738. Shortages of fodder and water forced him to turn back from both incursions, on 16 and 6 July respectively. He had lasted somewhat longer in Crimea than Münnich, and at much less cost.[46] It was 'climate and geography' that thwarted them both.[47] The difference was that Lacy recognised, and worked within, the logistical constraints imposed by steppe warfare whereas Münnich did not and so his army suffered a frightful loss of life, even by the standards of the Russo-Ottoman wars.

An ominous silence falls over the six-week encampment near Perekop where the epidemic must have been at its worse, following the nightmare march from Bakhchysarai. None of the sources even mention disease as such (they speak of privation and hardships) except for Biron's adjutant who talked of 'all sorts of diseases' including, fevers [*likhoradka*], agues [*Goryachka*] and 'bloody flux' [*krovavymi ponosami*]. *Goryachka* denotes a more acute fever than *likhoradka* and might be translated as an 'ague' or acute fever marked by paroxysms of chills and sweats recurring at regular intervals. This fever was not malarial: *anopheles* far prefers to lay eggs in pools of fresh water rather than in the brackish water pools that surrounded Perekop. In addition to blaming long watches and lack of rest, the adjutant offered the by now old-fashioned dietary explanation that the soldiers, raised on sourdough rye bread, were not used to eating wheaten bread. Moreover, many

43   Von Manstein, *Mémoires historiques*, p.205; Bourgoing, *Vie du comte de Munnich*, p.81.
44   Louis-Félix Guynement De Keralio, *Histoire de la guerre des Russes et des impériaux, contre les Turcs* (Paris: Debure, 1780), Vol.I, pp.26, 60; David Hume (ed.), C.H. von Manstein, *Memoirs of Russia, Historical, Political, and Military* (London: T. Becket and P. A. Hondt, 1770), p.121.
45   Robert Bufalini, 'The Czarina's Russia through Mediterranean Eyes: Francesco Algarotti's Journey to Saint Petersburg' in *Modern Language Notes*, 121:1, (2006), pp.154-166.
46   Davies, *Russia's Turkish Wars*, pp.211-214, 232-233.
47   Cassels, *The Struggle for the Ottoman Empire*, p.110.

soldiers cooked the cereals or ate them raw rather than trouble themselves after a day's hard marching to laboriously grind the grains on hand mills.[48]

More to the point, the adjutant also blamed dirty water. On the march, the soldiers certainly had to drink water drawn from wells which the Tatars had deliberately contaminated with filth and doubtless the soldiers filtered the water as best they could by straining it through a handkerchief in the manner recommended by Porzio in *De Militis in Castris*. However, filtering would not have prevented bacterial infection. Perekop lay within a maze of salt water lagoons and the nearest wells, to judge from a campaign map, lay twelve miles, or a long day's march, to the north-west, near the source of the Kalanchak River.[49] Crimea was, and is, chronically short of water. Prior to annexation by Russia in 2014, 85 percent of Crimea's fresh water needs were met by the North Crimean Canal which runs through the isthmus from the Dnieper River. Münnich and his chief surgeon Paul Condoidi took the problem of sickness seriously: they segregated the sick in each regiment, sent the worst cases in convoy all the way over the steppe to the bend of the Dnepr at Kazykermen, and had the sick plied with a concoction of boiled Kvas (beer made from rye bread) and vinegar. Every fourth day was devoted to cleaning camp, digging deep latrines, and building bath houses.[50] Most of these steps probably helped, but dehydration is a potentially fatal complication of dysentery which could hardly be remedied if water supplies were tight.

We have encountered dysentery at Dundalk and Philippsburg as a gateway disease that decanted patients into squalid and overcrowded hospitals where they would likely contract 'malignant fever' and perish. However, a dysentery epidemic could be nasty in its own right. The Derry and Belgrade case studies are examples of 'stand-alone' dysentery where the besieged and the besiegers, respectively, suffered 22 and 25 percent mortality. Münnich's army suffered double that proportion, albeit over a period twice as long, in what was, to all appearances, another dysenteric epidemic.

With Azov captured, the Russian effort would shift west in 1737. While Lacy was ravaging the Crimea, Münnich marched south west from the Dnieper across the steppe to the Bug and captured Ochakov, a key Turkish fortress on the Black Sea.[51] He left General Stoffeln behind with a garrison of 8,000 men who, when besieged in September, were ailing from dysentery. Even after the siege was lifted, the men of the garrison were falling ill and dying by the hundreds during the autumn and winter of 1737–38. More than 1,000 soldiers died in January 1738 alone, and the Tsarist authorities initially accepted Münnich's explanation that the sickness was 'scurvy' due mainly to bad quarters, hunger, and tainted water. Severe winter epidemics masked the outbreak of plague but by mid-June Stoffeln was admitting to having lost 1,722 men (almost one quarter of his force) over the preceding six weeks

48 De Keralio, *Histoire de la guerre des Russes et des impériaux,* pp.47-48; Herrmann, *Geschichte des Russischen Reiches,* p.205; 'Zapiska o tom, skol'ko ia pamiatuiu. http://www.runivers.ru/doc/d2 (accessed 14 December 2017).

49 Charte derer von der Russisch-Keyser, armee im Jahr, BNF, département Cartes et plans, GE DD-2987 (3055 B).

50 Davies, *Empire and Military Revolution in Eastern Europe,* p.199.

51 David R. Stone, *A Military History of Russia: From Ivan the Terrible to the War in Chechnya* (Westport: Praeger, 2006), p.66.

4.2 The Balkans, Crimea and the Pontic Steppe showing the Russian march to Crimea (1736) and the Habsburg march on Niš and Vidin (1737).

and spoke of scurvy [*tsinga*], 'fever with spots', and the dreaded plague, wreaking 'terrible havoc' on the troops who 'died like rotten sheep'. The outbreak of plague was entirely predictable once the huge Russian irruption into the old plague foci of the Pontic Steppe multiplied the number of targets and vectors.[52] Plague lethality fell on a different scale of deadliness than any of the other diseases discussed: Ochakov together with Kinburn had to be evacuated and, when Stoffeln returned to the Ukraine in September 1738, fewer than one-third of his soldiers survived to accompany him.[53]

Serbia (1737)

Habsburg emperor Charles VI needed to maintain Russian support for the Pragmatic Sanction (designed to ensure the succession of his daughter Maria Theresa) and in 1737 he joined in Russia's war against the Ottomans. The plan was that the emperor would raise an auxiliary corps to assist the main effort by the Russians along the Black Sea coast of what is now Romania. As it happened, the Russians chose to fight in Ukraine and Crimea, leaving Charles VI to shoulder the main burden of the

---

52 John T. Alexander, *Bubonic Plague in Early Modern Russia: Public Health and Urban Disaster* (Baltimore: Johns Hopkins University Press, 2003), p.25.

53 Davies, *Empire and Military Revolution*, p.225; Stoyanov, 'Russia marches South', p.222.

war in the Balkan theatre.[54] The Habsburg operational plan, such as it was, envisioned one army marching westward from Belgrade on Bosnia, a second eastward towards Wallachia, and a third moving south-eastward over 120 miles downriver to Widdin [*Vidin*] which was an important Turkish garrison below the Iron Gate lying close to where Bulgaria, Wallachia and Serbia met. The Vidin corps under Field Marshal Seckendorff was the biggest of the three, and comprised about 26,000 infantry, 15,000 cavalry, and 3,000 irregulars. It would be riven by quarrels between the field marshals Count Schmettau and Count Andreas Ludwig von Khevenhüller, who commanded the infantry and cavalry contingents, respectively.[55] Seckendorrf had left magazines along the Danube and made careful plans to ferry supplies for this force by boat to Vidin but to his consternation, he was ordered at the last minute to make for Nish [*Niš*]. This was about the same distance away as Vidin, but it necessitated a gruelling overland march south along the Morava Valley.[56] Schmettau's *Mémoires Secrets* describe officers driving their heatstricken men onward with 'orders, curses, and even blows from their batons'.[57] The strategic thinking behind the march on Niš was sound given that Bosnia formed a salient and reinforcements from Bulgaria or Romania could be cut off by occupying Niš and Vidin, respectively. However, the Habsburg armies were too scattered and, all too soon, would be too small for this ambitious scheme.

At the beginning of August Khevenhüller was sent towards Vidin with a detachment of some 9,000 troops from the main army which had just taken Niš. He tramped laboriously down the Timok valley, threading through the aptly named 'Passo Angusto' or 'narrow pass' on 10 August before halting at Bregovo and Rakitnitza or 'Raconitz'.[58] One flank of his camp was anchored on a patch of slightly higher ground beside the Danube (most likely on the site of modern Kudelin) and the rest of the camp lines stretched in a southerly direction uncomfortably close to a 'great swamp' formed by the delta of the Timok.[59]

On 14 August Austrian cavalry reconnoitred the defences but took such heavy losses that Khevenhüller began to lose faith in the feasibility of a siege.[60] Warned of this pessimistic assessment, Seckendorff reinforced Khevenhüller's detachment

54   Erik Lund, *War for the Every Day: Generals, Knowledge, and Warfare in Early Modern Europe, 1680-1740* (Westport: Praeger, 1999), p.169.

55   Lund, *War for the Every Day*, p.168; J. Hellert (tranl. J. Hammer), *Histoire de l'Empire ottoman, depuis son origine jusqu'à nos jours* (Paris: Bellizard et al., 1835-43), Vol.XIV, p.391.

56   A. Z. Hertz, 'The Ottoman Conquest of Ada Kale 1738', *AO*, 6, (1980): p.154; Comte de Schmettau, *Mémoires secrets de la guerre d'Hongrie durant les campagnes de 1737, 1738 et 1739* (Frankfurt, 1771), p.4.

57   Lund, *War for the Every Day*, p.176.

58   Schmettau, *Mémoires secrets*, pp.33-35; *Der orientalische Mercurius* (Frankfurt and Leipzig, 1737), pp.149, 151.

59   Étienne Briffaut, 'Théâtre de la guerre sur la Timock, 1737' (Vienna, 1738), BNF, département Cartes et plans, GE D-16599; Marsili, Luigi Ferdinando, *La Hongrie et le Danube* (The Hague, 1726-1741), BNF, département Cartes et plans, GE BB 565 (13, 15-42), Sectio, XV. Tab. 17; Schmettau, *Mémoires*, p.48; Lund, *War for the Every Day*, p.176; *Der orientalische Mercurius* p.171.

60   Anon., *Geschichte und Thaten des jüngstverstorbenen grossen Kriegs-Helden, Ludwig Andreas Grafen Khevenhüller* (Breslau and Leipzig: Publisher Unknown, 1744), p.106; Jean Nouzille,

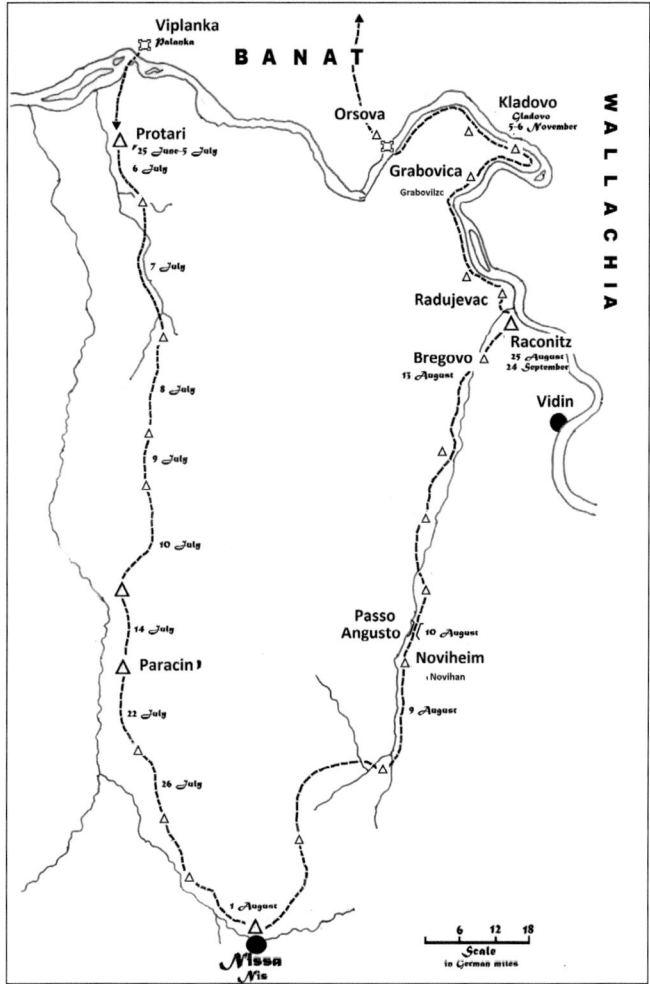

4.3 Seckendorff's march across Serbia, 1737.

and, toward the end of the month, joined him at Raconitz.[61] At this juncture came disquieting reports that the campaign in Bosnia had gone awry and that Seckendorff's corps was now threatened by resurgent Bosnians. Seckendorff promptly cut Khevenhüller's detachment to about 5,000 men, too few to besiege Vidin. Khevenhüller then withdrew across the Timok to Radujevac which, like

Le Prince Eugene de Savoie et le Sud-Est Europeen 1683-1736 (Paris: Honoré Champion, 2012), pp.377-78.

61   A.Z. Hertz, 'The Ottoman Conquest of Ada Kale 1738', *AO*, 6 (1980), p.155; Étienne Briffaut, *Theatre de la guerre en Hongrie, Bosnie, Servie, et Tartarie, Crimee…avec toutes les marches et contre marches de la campagne de 1737…* (Vienna: Publisher Unknown, 1738); Otto Elster, *Geschichte der stehenden Truppen im Herzogtum Braunschweig-Wolfenbüttel von 1600-1714* (Leipzig: Heinsius, 1899-1901), Vol.II, pp.97-105.

Rakitnitza, lay on the banks of the Danube. A contemporary plan depicts an unfortified camp delineated by the regimental lines, the eponymous village of Radujevac, and the Danube. Within the perimeter was a substantial two-storey 'Contumaz Haus' or quarantine station (sited to check the spread of Bubonic plague into the Habsburg domains) which was used, one imagines, as a hospital.[62] Khevenhüller hoped to hold the line of the Timok as far upstream as the 'Passo Angusto'. However, the Ottomans laid a pontoon bridge across the Timok on 28 September and, after hard fighting, their Janissaries clawed out a foothold on the Habsburg side. Imperial troops pinned the Turks to the river bank but could not drive them back across the Timok.[63] Consequently, the Turks appeared to threaten a narrow defile at Kusjak along the Danube which offered Khevenhüller his only avenue of retreat: he raced his men to the gorge leaving them 'dispirited and exhausted'.[64]

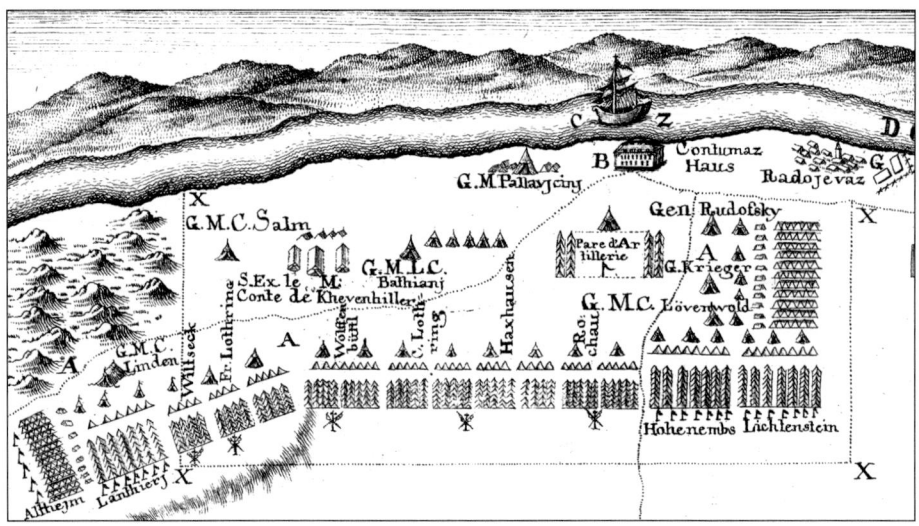

4.4 Radujevac Camp 1737. Detail from: Johann Jacob Lidl, *Plan von der Attaque deren Türcken unter den 28. Septembris 1737, alwo das unter commando des Herrn Feld-Marschallen Grafen von Khevenhüller Excellenz stehende Corpo…* (Vienna, 1737)

Khevenhüller next followed the river to the Ključ or 'key', that salient formed by the Danube as it winds from Kladovo to Brza Palanka, and spent October encamped there. He, and many other officers, fell sick and he was replaced at the end of October by Major General Count Leopold Salm who was ordered to hold the stockade of Brza Palanka.[65] Salm had too few men to do so and when threatened by a land force of 15,000 Turks backed by a flotilla, he hastened along the south bank of the Danube

---

62   Marsigli, Luigi Ferdinando, *La Hongrie Et Le Danube en XXXI. Cartes très fidelément gravées d'après les Desseins originaux & les Plans levez sur les lieux par l'Auteur même. Sectio XV., Tab. 17 Orsawa – Widdni* at http://www.oldmapsonline.org (accessed 18 January 2018).
63   Anon., *Grafen Khevenhüller*, p.116.
64   Hertz, 'Ada Kale', p.156.
65   Schmettau, *Mémoires secrets*, pp.123, 125, 128, 131; Anon., *Grafen Khevenhüller* p.118

towards Orşova, harried by the Ottoman vanguard.[66] To escape beyond reach of their pursuers, Salm's troops marched for thirty miles to Teregova throughout the day and night of 11 November. That same day the Turks simultaneously assaulted the island by boats and Fort St Elizabeth by land.[67]

What caused the troops to sicken? The mouths of the various tributaries of the Danube, the Timok included, were hotbeds of malaria and the camps of Rakidnitza and Radujevac were pitched right beside a swamp in what was, until the early 20th century, one of the dozen worst affected regions in all of Bulgaria.[68] Khevenhüller's anonymous biographer attributed the epidemic to wet ground and bad air and lauded Khevenhüller for heeding the advice of physicians to decamp from Rakitnitza. Hungary 'has ever been a graveyard of Germans', the biographer asserted, but the air this year was 'especially fatal' to foreigners because of the 'wet and rainy weather'.[69] The Danube's seasonal flooding ran late that year, the river was swollen well into the campaigning season and the water meadows sodden and glistening with shallow pools of water.[70] The alteration of hot days and occasional downpours provided ideal conditions for *Anopheles Sacharovi*, the species widely distributed in the Balkans at that time, which lighted on humans in preference to other sources of a blood meal.[71] The reported symptoms of Schmettau's 'hot fever' sound very like those of malaria.[72] The latter was certainly a component of the epidemic, but how big a component?

The Habsburg army had been reinforced by contingents from the states of the Empire hired out by their princes and two such auxiliary units kept good records. The Sommerlatte Regiment of the Brunswick contingent had set out on their long march in early May: comparison with Münnich's line of march as delineated in Image 4.2 shows that the Brunswickers had the longer journey. The regiment covered the latter stages of their journey by river boats from Linz as far as Belgrade. The troops then disembarked at Wischniz [*Višnjička*] about four miles downriver of Belgrade on low ground within an alluvial ox-bow cut by the Danube. Until then, the regiment had 'scarcely any' sick.[73] The regiment rested at Wischniz for 15 days before setting out downriver for Orsova on 12 August. By now the Brunswickers were 'suffering severely' from sickness and 200 of their number had to be left behind, hospitalized in Belgrade. The near vertical line on Image 4.5 shows that the numbers of sick increased sharply between 12 and 21 August, that is, between leaving Wischniz and shortly after arriving at the Contumaz Haus. The incubation period for *P. Vivax* runs from 12 to 18 days, which tallies perfectly with malaria contracted at Wischniz and well-established before the regiment reached Radujevac.

66   Schmettau, *Mémoires secrets*, pp.132, 136.
67   A.Z Hertz, 'Ada Kale: Key to the Danube', *AO*, 3 (1971) pp.151, 153-158.
68   Konstantin Markov, L'Etude du Paludisme en Bulgarie (1923) in 'Hostilities Against Malaria', http://berberian11.tripod.com/markov_malaria.htm.
69   Anon., *Grafen Khevenhüller*, p.111.
70   Umar Būsnavı (transl. and ed. C. Fraser), *History of the War in Bosnia During the Years 1737-1739* (London: Oriental Translation Fund, 1830), p.4.
71   Lund, *War for the Every Day*, p.176.
72   Schmettau, *Mémoires Secrets*, pp.54, 114.
73   Elster, *Braunschweig-Wolfenbüttel*, Vol.I, p.99.

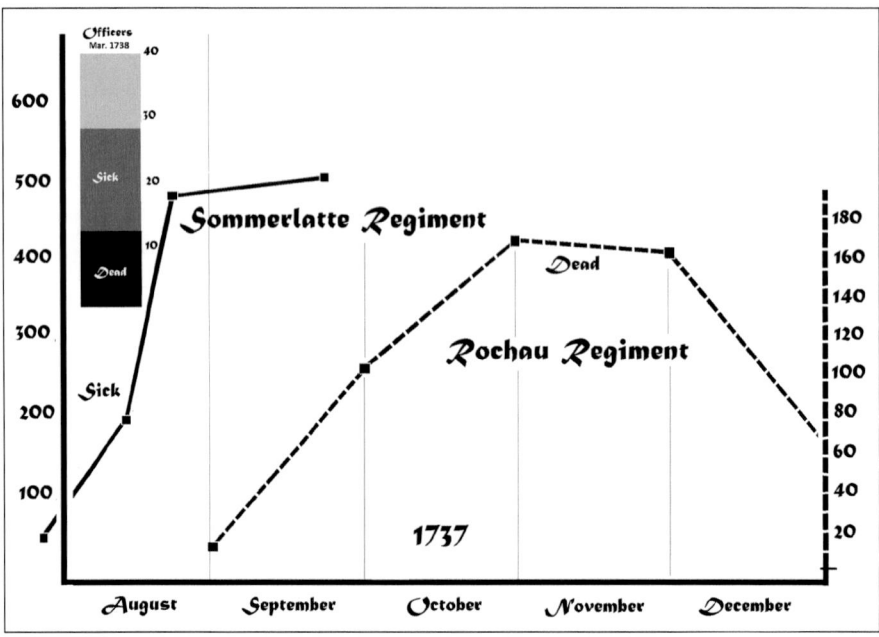

4.5 Sick and dead: Sommerlatte and Rochau Regiments.

Comparison with a known malaria outbreak among troops stationed near freshwater marshes elsewhere suggests that the Sommerlatte regiment was indeed afflicted by malaria. Towards the close of the War of the Austrian Succession British troops went into cantonments in Zeeland in July 1748. Pringle's clinical observations on the sickness that afflicted them are useful, even though he laid the blame on 'moisture and corruption of the air'. The epidemic began a fortnight or three weeks after the troops went into their cantonments. The Royal Scots Greys, a dragoon regiment, were cantoned near Den Bosch 'surrounded with meadows either then under water or but lately drained' and were one of the worst hit units which, by the time the epidemic began to abate in mid-September, 'had in all but 30 men who had never been ill'. Another regiment quartered one and a half miles further from the Greys, and further from the marshes, suffered very little.[74] Disease incidence falls with increasing distance from the breeding site: though mosquitos can fly over seven miles in a night, they prefer to travel as short a distance as possible. Finally, Pringle noted that '…the mortality was not in proportion to the number of the sick nor to the alarming nature of their symptoms' and indeed there were only 31 fatal cases in two (admittedly understrength) dragoon regiments.[75] Yet the disease disabled the patient for quite a long time: Schmettau, author of our main source the *Mémoires Secrets*, was struck down by what he calls 'the hot fever' in late September and remained hors de combat for six whole weeks. For present purposes, malaria was significant not primarily as a killer in itself but as a gateway sickness that prostrated troops for

---

74 Pringle, *Diseases of Armies*, pp.62, 65, 174.
75 Pringle, *Diseases of Armies*, pp.65, 181.

lengthy periods and left them vulnerable to the diseases and accidents of neglect, dirt, exposure and overcrowding in the forced marches and hasty retreats to come. Malaria cannot account for the headline statistic, namely that the Sommerlatte Regiment lost 57.6 percent of its strength through sickness (losses in action, namely the 35 killed and wounded at the Battle of Radujevac, were light) between July and January (see image 4.5). This is rather greater than what we know to have been the death toll among officers: a dozen of the 40 officers in the regiment perished, while almost three-quarters of them fell sick at one time or another.[76]

Table 4.2 Sommerlatte Regiment 1737-38[77]

	mid-August	late September	mid November	late January
Healthy	780	631	402	271
Sick	499	604	*564*	350
Dead	187	231	*500*	845

On 15 August the regiment set out for Niš, waited there for what must have been a short time, and then marched back again with Seckendorff to the mouth of the Timok, reaching it by 22 September at the latest. By now the fortunes of Sommerlatte's Brunswickers were intertwined with those of the Saxon auxiliary regiments of Von Rochau and Haxtenhausen which also formed part of the reserve. The Saxons had marched all the way from Cracow and had been late arriving at the first rendezvous but had followed the path of the main army and caught up with it at Nis. A run of *tabellen* enumerating the Rochau Regiment has survived from which it is possible to infer that losses through sickness ran at 36 percent, a figure significantly lower than the Sommerlatte Regiment's.[78]

One explanation that springs to mind is that the Saxon sick were embarked on 27 September and evacuated on the *St Elizabeth* before Turkish horsemen slipped in to the camp during the six-hour battle at Radujevac and slaughtered some 230 of the sick who had been left unguarded.[79] However, 'fortunate' is not an adjective that

---

76   'Notizen zur Geschichte des Braunschweiger Infanterie Regiments von Sommerlatte, nachher von Both während des Feldzugs nach Ungarn 1737-38', Stadtarchiv Braunschweig, H VI 6: 4., fos., 2-4.

77   Elster, *Braunschweig-Wolfenbüttel*, Vol.I, pp.98-104. Elster cites the many returns in a way that conflates 'effective', 'serviceable', [*dienst.*] 'strong' and 'state' [*stende*] interchangeably. I took the opening strength of 1,466 and traced the trajectory from that base line. While the total number of sick and dead in November was 1,064, the apportionment of that figure between sick and dead is an extrapolation from the relative proportions amongst the officer body of the regiment: these two extrapolations are italicised.

78   Elster, *Braunschweig-Wolfenbüttel*, Vol.II, pp.97-105: 'General Tabella', Neustadt 15 June 173; 'Tabella', Gradovica 8 October 1737, 'Monaths Tabella', 31 August, 31 October, 30 November, 30 December; 'Tabella' 8 October, SachsHStA, Loc. 3281/6 unpag: Luh, *Kriegskunst in Europa 1650-1800*, p.59.

79   *Mercure Historique et Politique* (The Hague, 1737), pp.555-556; Luh, *Kriegskunst*, p.60; De Kéralio, *Histoire de la guerre des Russes et des impériaux*, Vol.II, p.275; p.275; Jean De La Barre, *Continuation de l'histoire universelle de…Jacques-Bénigne Bossuet* (Amsterdam: Etienne Roger, 1738), pp.606-608; Schmettau, *Mémoires Secrets*, p.115.

springs to mind when following the evacuation of the Saxon sick. A Lieutenant von Gablentz wrote a piteous plea to his captain on 6 October:[80]

> ...no one could believe the preposterous suffering we officers have to endure here in Orsava, since no one will help us move along and most of our Serbs [*Raitzen*] are sick and many have run off. We cannot travel unless our ship is towed for a quarter of a mile so it must wait. This quill cannot adequately describe our misery. We already have 48 dead [and] today is the 8th day without bread; this night, not counting the aforementioned 48 men, 7 more men have died.

Three quarters of the sick from Rochau's and Haxtenhausen's Regiments, who were eventually ferried from Orsova to Belgrade, perished on the way. Most of the survivors who made it to the hospital in Belgrade died in turn and were doing so in late October at the rate of three score a day which was equivalent to 10 percent of the sick roll every day.[81] Major General Von Jasmund chose colloquial and apparently callous terms like 'bite the grass' [*inß graß beißen wird*], 'snuff it' or 'croak' to describe death, though once he waxed poetic in predicting that a clerk 'will never again hear the cuckoo's call'. Von Jasmund identified the diseases as 'hot fever' [*hitzigen fieber*] and dysentery [*dissenterie*] and lacerated the physicians at the hospital as 'fitter for stealing than healing'. He also castigated profiteers who had 'bought up all the cheese, butter and wine and left the common soldier only munition bread [*kommisbrodt*]'.[82] All in all, the Saxon contingent was unlucky. The troops had been forced to leave blankets and tents behind in Cracow at the beginning of their epic march. What was left of the baggage had been pillaged (by Habsburg troops) during the Battle of Radujevac. Clean water had been hard to get. The surgeons did not isolate the contagious sick in time and could not cure their distempers. There was not enough transport to bring the sick to hospitals, which were in any case, squalid, overcrowded and poorly supplied.[83] Whatever advantage the Saxon sick enjoyed from escaping the massacre at Radujevac, it was a slight one. A more plausible explanation for heavier mortality in the Sommerlatte Regiment, as compared to the Rochau Regiment, is that the former had a month's head start. Sommerlatte's had 499 troops laid low with sickness by 21 August whereas it was a month later (around the time Khevenhüller's corps moved camp across the Timok from Rakitnitza to Radujevac) that comparably heavy sickness began to afflict the Saxons.[84]

---

80   Stefan Kroll, *Soldaten im 18. Jahrhundert zwischen Friedensalltag und Kriegserfahrung. Lebenswelten und Kultur in der kursächsischen Armee*. (Paderborn: Ferdinand Schöningh. 2006), p.465.

81   Letter from Major General Von Jasmund to Count Sulkowski, Belgrade, 22 October 1737, SachsHStA, Loc. 3281 [unpag.]; Elster, *Braunschweig-Wolfenbüttel*, p.99.

82   Letter from Major General Von Jasmund to Count Sulkowski, Belgrade, 22 October 1737, SachsHStA, ; Loc. 3281 [unpag.]; Luh, *Kriegskunst*, p.60.

83   Luh, *Kriegskunst in Europa*, p.59; Kroll, *Soldaten im 18. Jahrhundert zwischen*, pp.464-465.

84   Monats-Listen und Tabellen vom Rochauischen Infanterie Regiment, Sächsisches Hauptstaatarchiv Dresden 11237, Loc. 10863/1; Schmettau, *Mémoires secrets*, p.114.

To answer the questions posed earlier: 'hot fever' or malaria was the biggest component of the epidemic as a direct cause of mortality: the mortality rates observed among British troops in Zeeland may have been atypically low due to good medical care and the end of the war being in sight. More importantly, malaria was an indirect cause by creating the vulnerabilities whereby soldiers would fall victim to the more common, and often fatal, diseases such as dysentery. The overall mortality rate was 36 and 56 percent, respectively, in the two regiments under review and this may represent the range of outcomes in the army as a whole. Sommerlate's soldiery certainly contracted malaria during their ill-advised stopover at Višnjička and Rochau's took ill of malaria while encamped beside the malarial swamp where the Timok debouched into the Danube.

The Imperial armies were consistently outmanoeuvred in the campaigning season of 1737 and in the subsequent two campaigns, to the extent that the Habsburgs were forced to cede their conquests south of the Danube and the Sava. This would mark the limits of Habsburg expansion until the ill-omened annexation of Bosnia and Herzegovina in 1908. Strategically, the 1737 campaign, then, was a greater matter than capturing a fortress on the Rhine and ceding it in the peace negotiations. In nearly all of the case studies to date it would have been difficult to pin-point strategic consequences of epidemic disease, since both sides typically proved equally vulnerable. The outcome of the 1737 campaign and, indeed the whole war, can largely be explained by the Habsburgs trying to do too much with too little. Yes, their armies were debilitated by epidemics but there is no evidence that the Ottomans were any better off, except for the fact that their armies approached Vidin later than Khevenhüller's detachment when *Anopheles* was feeding less frentically. Although the Danubian wetlands were reputed to be the 'graveyard of Germans', deaths through sickness did not necessarily run much higher in the Balkan theatres than on the Rhine frontier: we have only to recall the heavy losses on both sides of the Rhine in the autumn and winter of 1734-5. Lüh correctly notes, however, that death rates through sickness were 'not significantly less' in the Balkans in the 1730s than they had been sixty years before.[85] The sample in Table 4.3 corroborates the claim but also reminds us of the bewildering variability and particularity of the impact of disease, dependent as it is on time, place and contingency.

---

85   Those killed and wounded in action at the Battle of Slankamen on 19 August amounted to just 154.

Table 4.3 Deaths Through Sickness[86]

Troops	Place	Campaign	Percent
Hanoverians	Morea	1685	30
Württemberg	Morea	1688	62
Zacco (Bavarian)	Hungary	1691	73
Bavarians	Belgrade	1717	15
Rochau (Saxon)	Serbia	1737	36
Sommerlatte (Brunswick)	Serbia	1737	56

Bohemia 1742

Whereas France had been diplomatically isolated in the War of the Polish Succession, she secured the support of two major German states, Prussia and Bavaria, before the next Bourbon-Habsburg conflict. In the War of the Austrian Succession (1740-48) the French did not content themselves with ravaging the Palatinate and tentatively probing across the Rhine but projected their power further east than ever before. Frederick the Great of Prussia, with his trademark duplicity, concluded a separate peace with the Habsburgs in June 1742, leaving a large French army stranded in Bohemia and cut off from its remaining ally in Bavaria.[87] Army commander *Maréchal de Broglie* was forced to withdraw to Prague. Most of his men camped within the oxbow on the Moldau [Vltava] just north of the city and dug a continuous covered way enclosing the mouth of the oxbow and the Kleinseite [Malá Strana] suburb on the western bank of the Moldau.[88] There never was any danger of the Austrians storming the city, since the garrison was simply too strong, though 742 of them were killed outright by shot and shell and another 1,325 were wounded. It is not possible at this stage of the operation to disaggregate losses through action, desertions, or sickness. Writing to Louis XIV's chief minister Cardinal Fleury, Broglie claimed that he was losing 50-60 men a day through bomb and shot in mid-September, but this is almost

---

86   Luh, *Kriegskunst* pp.55-57, 59. In the Hungarian campaign of 1691 the Bavarian regiment of Zacco mustered 2,100 soldiers on 12 July, but by 20 October the regiment's strength stood at 425 healthy and 130 sick men, with 1,545 victims of 'white' and 'red' flux [*rühr*] and spotted fever or typhus [*flecktyphus*] because of hard marching, inclement weather and befouled water. The Hanoverian contingent of 2,452 lost 736 men to disease in the period from April 1685 to January 1686, as opposed to 256 in action. Alexander Schwenke, *Geschichte der Hannoverschen truppen in Griechenland 1685–89* (Hanover: Hahnsch Buchhandlung, 1854), p.57; George Finlay, A *History of Greece* (Oxford: Clarendon Press, 1877), Vol.V, pp.176-78. Kroll, *Soldaten im 18. Jahrhundert zwischen*, p.464; R. Andler, 'Diewürttembergischen Regimenter in Griechenland 1687–89', *Württembergische Vierteljahrshelfte für Landesgeschichte*, 31 (1922/4), pp.250, 252.

87   Rohan Butler, *Choiseul. Vol. 1: Father and Son 1719-1754* (Oxford: Oxford University Press, 1981), pp.320-324.

88   'Guérineau De Boisvillette (ed.) 'Lettre inédite sur le siège de Prague en 1742, par le fils du comte d'Entraignes, seigneur de Saint-Prest', *Procès-verbaux de la Société archéologique d'Eure-et-Loir, 1861-1863* (Chartres: Petrot-Garnier, 1864), pp.210, 217.

certainly an exaggeration to mask heavy losses through desertion and disease.[89] Charles Louis Auguste Fouquet, duc de Belle-Isle, Broglie's resentful subordinate, warned his patron, war minister De Breteuil, not to be taken in by Broglie's mendacious optimism: 20 men were dying in the hospitals every day through 'our own fault', and had been since June.[90] Desertion was also 'very high', insisted Belle-Isle and, indeed, an Austrian source noted that on 28 August about 30 French deserters came to the Austrian camp, having slipped away from their posts during the night. More would have followed, the deserters said, if they 'could find a way to escape'.[91] A common-sense conjecture would be that desertion and disease were both indices of misery and both, at least when it was at all possible to slip away, tended to track each other. The assumption was shared by Wellington who in 1809 saw a link between 'hardship and distress' on the one hand and desertion on the other.[92] It is likely, then, that strategic consumption in Broglie's army was due in roughly equal parts to combat, runaways and sickness.

Sick soldiers were distributed among five large makeshift hospitals and also scattered in private houses. All but one of the hospitals were churches, the biggest being the Jesuit Klementium which was an enormous complex of dormitories and cloisters in the Altstadt [Staré Mestoor] on the east bank. The prevailing distemper was 'no ordinary camp fever', and inflicted 'great mortality'. Belle-Isle complained of fever and 'the headache that accompanies it' and at the onset local physicians noted nausea, fever, headache, and delirium:

...in a word, the symptoms resembled those of the malign petechial fevers [typhus] which we have all witnessed in these regions of Germany. One [symptom] above all was noticeable and almost universal, namely diarrhoea. I will not say which of the symptoms pointed towards recovery or deterioration [and] among the symptoms that physicians claim normally accompany a malign fever there is one, I say, which deserves special notice: even though the French were in our atmosphere where commonly our men exhibit petechiae, rashes or pustules [miliaria alba] when struck by malign fevers. Not a single one of the descriptions by French physicians (or by ours, indeed) notes a patient suffering from rash.[93]

89 Broglie to Cardinal Fleury, Prague, 15 September, Charles Louis Auguste Fouquet duc de Belle-Isle, *Campagne de messieurs les maréchaux De Broglie et De Belle-Isle, en Boheme...* (Amsterdam: Marc Michel Rey, 1772), Vol.VI, p.29.

90 Belle-Isle to Marquis de Breteuil, Prague, 15 July 1742, Belle-Isle, *Campagne en Boheme*, Vol. VI, p.265; Voltaire, *Histoire de la guerre de mil sept cent quarante & un* (London: Jean Nourse, 1756), p.151.

91 Henry Cornet, (ed.) *Siége de Prague: Journal Critique d'un Lieutenant-Ingénieur dans l'armée Autrichienne devant Prague* (Vienna: Tendler, 1867), p.55.

92 Bamford, *Sickness, Suffering and the Sword*, pp.252, 253: Bamford himself found 'no obvious connection' at regimental level.

93 Belle-Isle to Marquis de Breteuil, Egra, 29 December 1742, Belle-Isle, *Campagne en Boheme*, Vol.VI, p.296; Johann Scrinci and William Bache, *Diss. De febri maligna castrensi Gallorum* (Prague: Publisher Unknown, 1743), pp.387, 389.

The local medical fraternity attacked their French counterparts for indiscriminately letting blood in all cases of fevers, 'once, twice, thrice a day and even oftener until the patient breathed his last'. Clysters were administered more than once a day and so too were emetics and laxatives, even when the patient suffered from non-stop diarrhoea.[94] Emetics were considered appropriate for the early stage of typhus while venesection (specifically cutting the vein at the forehead) was recommended as a means to ameliorate delirium and headaches so it would seem that the French medics believed, rightly or wrongly, that they were dealing with an epidemic of typhus or hospital fever.[95] They may have been wrong in their diagnosis given the apparent absence of *petechiae* on their patients. Nor, by the same token (or want of token) was this the middle phase in the seasonal continuum of dysentery, typhoid/malaria, and typhus because typhoid spots or 'purples' had not erupted. Moreover, one would expect typhoid to give a sharper September-October spike in the numbers of men hospitalized, comparable to that at Saint-Jean for instance (see Chapter 2), whereas the numbers gently fluctuated, from 3,000 in early July, to 2,500 on 20 September, 4,000 on 30 October and just over 2,000 in mid-December.[96]

On balance, it is likely that severe flux formed the background noise of the epidemic. Food and, especially, forage were running low and by July the cart horses, 'half starved [and] staggering about', were being slaughtered for food. Broglie, with his usual glib dishonesty, maintained that the 'troops are eating a pound of horse-meat a day as easily as it were beef and so far it has caused no sickness'.[97] The Prague physicians offered the standard causes: privation, cold, bad diet (specifically gorging on horseflesh) and long watches. Above all, they blamed the filth of the hospitals where patients suffering from severe diarrhoea were packed into crowded little chambers and 'very often' relieved themselves beside their beds, thereby polluting the air 'with putrid effluvia'.[98] Indeed, it would be surprising if troops hospitalized in such squalor escaped typhus or hospital fever altogether: a senior officer of the Navarre Regiment, for instance, was 'gravely ill of a malign fever' in mid-September.[99]

Maréchal Jean-Baptiste Desmarets, Marquis de Maillebois, led a relief column from the Rhine, reaching Amberg, in the upper Palatinate, on 14 September. Thence, with no fewer than 60,000 men, he marched towards Eger [Cheb], just over the border in Bohemia. The Habsburg commander Charles of Lorraine interposed his army between those of Broglie and Maillebois. The latter flinched from committing to battle and was shortly afterwards dismissed. Broglie, who stole out of Prague, took over as commander-in-chief of the armies in Germany and left Belle-Isle in command of Prague, with effect from 27 October 1742. Belle-Isle, as envoy to the

---

94   Scrinci and Bache, *De febri maligna castrensi Gallorum*, pp.388-389.
95   Theodor Zwinger, *Epitome totius medicinae* (Lyon: Boudet, 1712), p.544-545.
96   Anon., *Relation Von der Belagerung Prag* (Prague: Publisher Unknown, 1742), p.14.
97   Eleazar Mauvillon, *Histoire de la derniére guerre de Boheme* (Amsterdam: D. Mortier,1750), Vol.II, p.223; De Séchelles to Marquis de Breteuil, Prague, 1 August 1742, Belle-Isle to Marquis de Breteuil Prague, 12 August 1742, Broglie to Cardinal Fleury, Prague 15 September, Belle-Isle, *Campagne en Boheme*, Vol.VI, pp.306, 308, 344, 347.
98   Scrinci and Bache, *Diss. De febri maligna castrensi Gallorum*, p.391.
99   Belle-Isle to Marquis de Breteuil, Prague, 13 September 1742, Belle-Isle, *Campagne en Boheme*, Vol.VI, p.20.

Imperial Diet, had been the driving force behind the forward policy to wage war on Austria in support of Charles Albert of Bavaria and the latter's claim to the imperial title.[100] It was fitting that he should now have to struggle with the dire consequences of his warmongering; and they were dire, as he never ceased to remind de Breteuil.

Belle-Isle had to break out and make for the closest French garrison at Eger, over 100 miles away. Otherwise his army would be trapped and lost, which would be 'shameful and humbling'. He had until mid-December before provisions ran out, a doomsday which Belle-Isle later put back to early February 1743. The Austrians turned back to Prague with just 18,000 men, too few for a tight blockade.[101] Prince von Lobkowitz, who had been left behind to command this force, stripped bare the countryside for a radius of six miles around the city and quartered his main army some 20 miles away, on the eastern side of the Moldau, leaving only a detachment of hussars to observe the French.[102]

Belle-Isle managed the retreat with stealth, speed, and no little skill, winning the deathbed plaudits of Cardinal de Fleury, who expressed 'great pleasure' at Belle Isle's sortie from Prague and his 'assured' handling of the operation.[103] Belle Isle did not take with him the bedridden, the sick, and the many servants accompanying the army and left *Brigadier* François de Chevert behind with a skeleton force of about 900 healthy soldiers from all the regiments 'to amuse the Austrians with the Appearance of a Garrison, and take Care of the Sick'.[104] Chevert was able to hold out until 26 December, the same day that Belle-Isle reached Eger, which was long enough to capitulate on favourable terms: two-thirds of his men set out to join their comrades in Bavaria (1,600 deserted on the way, as it happened) and the Austrians even supplied carts for the sick.[105] Some 2,000 men who 'could stir neither leg nor foot' were left behind as prisoners-of-war.[106]

100 Peter Campbell, *Power and Politics in Old Regime France, 1720-1745* (London: Routledge, 1996), p.170.

101 Belle-Isle to Breteuil Prague, 13 September, 25 and 31 October and 2 December 1742, Pierre François Dumoulin, *Campagnes de Messieurs les maréchaux de Maillebois, de Broglie, de Belle-Isle, de Noailles, et de Coigny: l'an 1741-1744* (Amsterdam: M.M. Rey, 1760), Vol.VI, pp.15, 136, 161, 229.

102 William Coxe, *History of the House of Austria* (London: Bohn, 1807), Vol.II, p.285.

103 Cardinal de Fleury to Belleisle 7 January 1743, SHD A¹ 3006, no., 38.

104 William Biggs, *The Military History of Europe...* (London: R. Baldwin, 1755), p.95.

105 *Mercure de France* (January, 1743) p.171.

106 Lobkowitz to Chevert, Prague 2 January 1743, Chevert to Belle Isle, Orkelt, 2 Jan 1743, Belle Isle to Chevert, Amberg, 5 Jan. 1743, SHD A¹ 3006, nos. 21, 24, 33; Belle-Isle to Marquis de Breteuil, Eger, 31 December 1742, Anon., *Campagne de messieurs les maréchaux De Broglie et De Belle-Isle,* Vol.VI, p.311, 313.

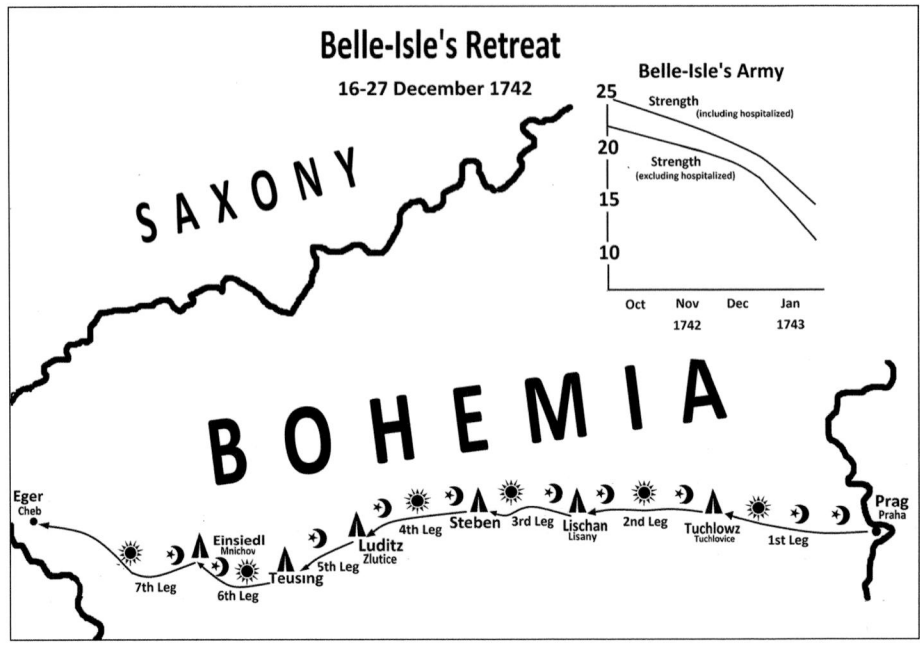

4.6 French march from Prague to Eger, December 1742.

Belle-Isle spread false intelligence and sent decoys to convince von Lobkowitz that a French *grand fourage* would shortly sweep to the south-west of the city and so lull von Lobkowitz into ignoring first reports of enemy troop movements. Meanwhile, Belle-Isle's army marched along the Pilsen road throughout the night and the next day, all 26 miles to Tuchlowz [Tuchlovice] in a single bound where enemy cavalry at last raised the alarm. On the march he sacrificed mobility to all-round strength by creating five compact self-contained divisions, each having its own elements of foot, horse, cannon, and baggage train. Belle Isle's army rested up on the 18th until the moon was high when the first of his five columns set off, to be followed at intervals by the others until the last left at dawn.[107] The second leg of the march was a running fight in which hussars and Croat light horsemen assailed the van, middle, and rearguard but the French managed to swivel field guns into action and punish the attackers for their presumption. Thereafter, the chastened horsemen hung on the rear and flanks of the retreating army but did not close. Two highways ran to Eger, one by Pilsen [Plzeň] to the south and one by Karlsbad [Karlovy Vary] to the north. Lobkowitz ordered all available troops to concentrate on cutting these arterial routes. After moonrise, or between eleven and one o'clock, on the night of 21-22 December the French marched from Steben, the half-way point of his journey, on the high road towards Karlsbad but three miles out of Steben, Belle-Isle's columns wheeled left to strike out between the roads across the frozen hill-country.[108]

---

107   Butler, *Choiseul*, pp.362-363, 365.

108   Thomas Carlyle, *History of Friedrich II of Prussia: Called Frederick the Great* (London: Chapman and Hall, 1871), Vol.V, pp.258-259; *Mercure de France* (December, 1742) p.1945.

Contemporaneous authorities reiterated the platitude that an army should withdraw like a 'wounded lion', but the more thoughtful accepted that retreat while in contact with a pursuing enemy was the severest test of a general. They were at one on the importance of the columns marching slowly and steadily, never stopping but never letting the pace pick up to a 'headlong rush', keeping good order, sacrificing rearguard troops, burning baggage if necessary but never abandoning the guns as trophies for the enemy.[109] Frederick the Great, who advanced and retreated so often across Bohemia during his wars against Maria Theresa, dictated specific orders for troops retreating while being harassed by irregular cavalry in article XVI of his 'Military Instructions'. These began by bombastically declaiming that 'hussars and pandours are dreadful only to those who do not know them', while implicitly admitting that 'where we have to pass woods, defiles, and mountains, the loss of some men is almost inevitable'.[110]

Belle-Isle's retreat followed most of the precepts, but for his decision to go off-road. He clearly had no illusions about the ordeal ahead when he wrote from Steben that 'now we are in the mountains it will be much worse'.[111] The fourth, fifth, and sixth legs of the march do not look longer on the map than the earlier legs but, given the rugged terrain, they took more time and exhausting effort to complete. For example, the column set out on the fourth leg well before dawn broke and did not reach Luzitz until midnight that same day where they snatched a few hours of rest.[112] The column set out on the seventh leg at midnight and at dawn on Christmas Day faced the rugged gorges and steep pine-clad slopes of the Königswart [Kynžvart] in the eastern foothills of the Tepler Mountains, the most daunting challenge of all.[113]

Belle-Isle was too sick to mount a horse but, carried on a litter, he was everywhere, admonishing and chivvying the troops to keep moving because he dreaded the 'unbearable cold' that killed many soldiers when they were forced to halt, 'above all at night'.[114] The Marquis de Vauvenargues, a *capitaine* in the Régiment du Roi evidently thought that Belle-Isle pushed them too hard:

> The army hastened its flight through forest and snow. It marched without halting. Sickness, hunger and exhaustion overwhelmed our young soldiers. Poor fellows! One could see them cruelly abandoned and stretched out on the snow. Fires burning on the ice lit up their final moments [and] the ground is their bed for ever.[115]

109 Carl Von Clausewitz (ed. Anatol Rapaport) *On War* (London: Penguin, 1982), p.360; Charles Sevin, Marquis de Quincy, *L'Art de La Guerre* (The Hague: Unknown Publisher, 1741), Vol.I, p.188.
110 T. Foster (ed.), Frederick II (King of Prussia), *Military Instruction from the Late King of Prussia to His Generals* (London: Cruttwell, 1818), pp.80-81.
111 Duc de Broglie (ed.) *Frédéric II et Louis XV: d'après des documents nouveaux; 1742-1744* (Paris: Calmann-Lévy, 1887), p.143.
112 De Broglie (ed.), *Frédéric II et Louis XV*, p.144, 148.
113 Butler, *Choiseul*, p.338.
114 Butler, *Choiseul*, p.363.
115 De Broglie (ed.) *Frédéric II et Louis XV,* p.146.

Vauvenargues may himself have been a victim because he died five years later of a lingering '*maladie de poitrine*' (a consumption or pleurisy) that he had contracted on the retreat from Prague.[116] It would, however, have been a grave mistake to halt more frequently because those who straggled or were left behind to beg quarter of the hussars were generally finished off on the spot or stripped naked and left to perish in the snow.[117] Habsburg apologists discreetly ignore such atrocities, but gloat over the carnage: 'The ways were strewn with corpses, heaps of one and two hundred men and officers were found frozen rigid.'[118] French sources, on the other hand, dismissed tales of horrendous losses as Habsburg propaganda.

How well did Belle-Isle's columns actually weather the retreat? Reduced to sleeping on snow and ice, gnawing on a meagre ration of frozen bread and harassed by pitiless light cavalry: 'no European army ever experienced more dreadful sufferings', opined a writer, just eight years before Napoleon's retreat from Moscow.[119] Nowadays, average December temperatures near Kynžvart run to minus 1.7°C, which is almost as cold as Vilnius, and wind chill factor was probably more severe. Even before reaching the Tepler Mountains, Belle-Isle complained of an 'unbearable' north wind.[120] He had to leave 800 men in hospital at Eger, 'most of whom have lost their feet to frostbite', which indicates that the temperature fell below minus four degrees for prolonged periods: ice crystals which constrict the blood vessels in the extremities (fingers, toes, nose and ears) do not form at higher temperatures.[121] As discussed above, just a few hours of exposure to a cold wind can precipitate hypothermia. After the convulsive shivering, mental confusion, slurred speech, and numbness, a victim of late stage hypothermia will also grow very drowsy which gives us that common trope in survival narratives of the mountaineer or polar explorer who wants to lie down and rest but is sternly warned by his companions that if he sleeps he will never wake up. A 19th century author of a purported memoir knits this trope into a dramatically fictionalized narrative of Belle-Isle's retreat:

> He had to cross the highest mountains in Europe at 1,000 toises over sea level which produced a 'mortal' cold. Seven thousand men perished in crossing the mountains near Eger experiencing a cold that neither exercise nor food could combat. Hands, feet, noses and ears were frostbitten. The cold induced sleep and their comrades prodded them with bayonets to keep

116 Wallas May, *Luc de Clapiers, marquis de Vauvenargues* (Cambridge: Cambridge University Press,1928), pp.66, 93.

117 Carlyle, *History of Friedrich II*, Vol.V,. pp.258-259; Louis-François-Armand de Vignerot Du Plessis Richelieu *Mémoires du Maréchal duc de Richelieu* (Paris: Publisher, 1858), Vol.II, p.20.

118 F.M. Pelzel, *Geschichte der Böhmen* (Prague and Vienna: Hagen, 1782), Vol.I, p.882; De Homann, Héritiers,'Kriegs-Expeditions-Carte von Bohmen: Carte des expéditions de la guerre en Boheme', (Nuremberg, 1743).

119 Coxe, *History of the House of Austria*, Vol.II, p.286.

120 Butler, *Choiseul*, p.363.

121 Belleisle to Marquis de Breteuil, Egra 2 January 1743, Anon., *Campagne de messieurs les maréchaux De Broglie et De Belle-Isle*, p.16.

them awake. Those left behind in Prague recovered while those who were sent on the march died for the most part.[122]

The memorialist was making the case that ministers who sat snug and warm in Versailles had no idea of the challenges facing Belle-Isle, who would have been better off remaining in Prague and seeking terms from the Austrians that allowed him to retreat, so his claim that nearly half of those who set out perished on the way is an exaggeration. In fact, the first reports speak of much lighter casualties. Days after reaching safety at Eger, Belle Isle admitted to the war minister that he had lost up to 1,500 foot soldiers and horsemen. He was in gloomy mood and was certainly not covering up his problems because elsewhere in the letter he admitted to an 'infinite number' of sick and confessed that his army was 'finished'[au bout].[123] Maurice of Saxony, no friend of Belle-Isle's, wrote to Broglie stating that the enemy captured about 4-500 men and massacred a 'greater number'.[124] Missing from these accounts were the many men (1,165 by one count, 1,309 by another) who quietly dropped out on the march to die and were neither captured nor killed by the hussars.[125] Consequently a later report that more than 3,000 men overall had been lost in the retreat is quite credible.[126]

'A thing well done': Belle-Isle had led over four-fifths of the evacuees to safety for 11 days over rugged terrain in bitterly cold weather.[127] However, they arrived in truly wretched shape. Quite apart from the fact that so many troops were sick, Belle-Isle also lost 800 men to frostbite. They would, likely, have their feet amputated and their soldiering days cut short with equally abrupt finality. By now, too, typhus had finally broken out. We are told that the French troops retreating from Prague brought a 'little epidemic' with them to their quarters at Amberg in the Oberpfalz or Upper Palatinate and to neighbouring Weiden. This was 'in all probability' *kriegstyphus*. In both places up to seven percent of the civilian population perished that year, double the normal civilian death rate in early modern Europe. A long run of burial records survives for Weiden and it is apparent that seven percent mortality represents the sharpest spike in the entire period from 1671 to 1745.[128]

---

122 Du Plessis Richelieu, *Mémoires du Maréchal duc de Richelie*, Vol.II, p.19.
123 *Campagne de messieurs les maréchaux De Broglie et De Belle*-Isle, Vol.VII, pp.17-18.
124 De Saxe to Broglie, 4 Jan 1743, SHD A¹ 3006, no. 29.
125 Georges-Louis, Le Rouge, 'Retraite de Monsieur le Marechal Duc de Belleisle de Prag a Egra' in *Recueil contenant des cartes nouvelles dressees sur des morceaux leves sur les lieux et les memoires les plus nouveaux*. (Paris: Le Rouge, 1742); 'Return of Infantry Regiments at Eger', 3 Jan 1743, SHD A¹ 3006, no. 25.
126 De Saxe to Folard, 30 Jan 1743, SHD A¹ 3006, no. 234; Biggs, *Military History of Europe*, p.96.
127 Carlyle, *History of Friedrich II of Prussia*, Vol.V, pp.258-259
128 Georg Bäumler, 'Medizinalstatistische Untersuchungen über Weiden/Opf: Von 1551 bis 1800'. *Archiv fur Hygiene und Bakteriologie*.no. 120 (1938) pp.218, 225-226: Post, *Food Shortage and Epidemic Disease* p.252; Tallett, *War and Society in Early Modern Europe*, p.105.

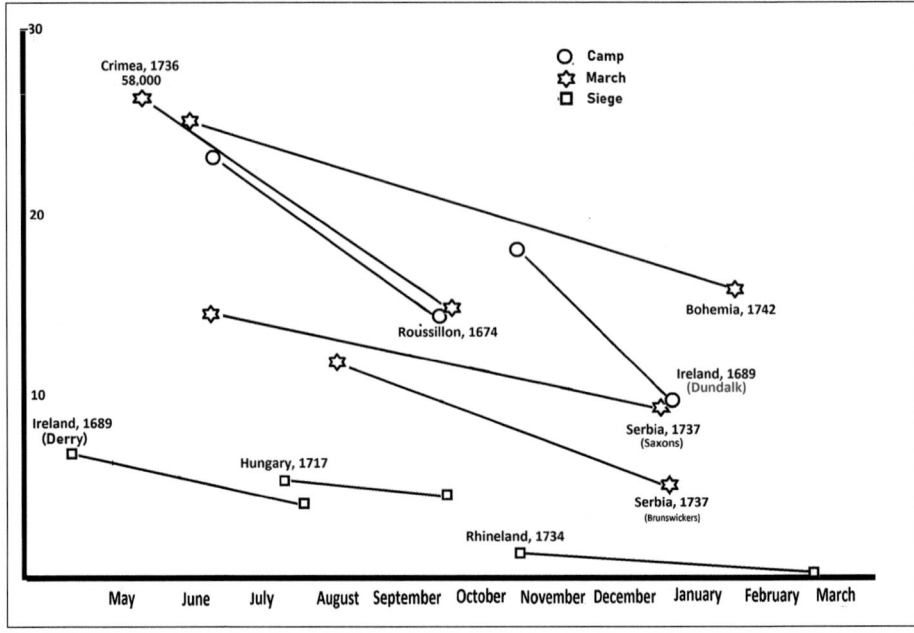

4.7 Mortality trajectories in camp, march, and siege.

Table 4.4 Belle-Isle's Army[129]

	20 September	31 October	16 December	2 January	23 January
Strength	25,000	24,000	20,000	17,200	14,600
Hospitalized	2,500	4,000	2,230	2,600	4,000

Taken together, losses from sickness before, during and after the retreat were heavy: not counting the 1,600 deserters from Chevert's evacuees, Belle-Isle lost 35 percent of his men through sickness between September 1742 and late January 1743. This was only one phase, albeit the direst one, in a longer mortality trend evident from the *contrôles* of the first battalion of the Navarre Regiment. It is possible to extract from the *contrôles* 479 soldiers who were serving in the battalion at the beginning of 1742 or who joined up that year. Only 198, or 41 percent, of those men were still alive and serving by year's end. A handful were killed in action and these can be subsumed within the 78 men in an indeterminate category. Almost 38 percent had

129 Mauvillon, *Histoire de la dernière guerre de Boheme*, p.222; Anon., *Relation Von der Belagerung Prag* p.14; Voltaire, *Histoire de la guerre de mil sept cent quarante & un*, p.154; Broglie to Marshal Maillebois, Prague 3 October, Belle-Isle to Marquis de Breteuil Prague, 14 October 1742, ibid, Prague, 31 October 1742, Anon., *Campagne de messieurs les maréchaux De Broglie et De Belle-Isle*, Vol.VI, pp.96, 119, 15; Chevert to Belle Isle, Orkelt, 2 Jan 1743, De Saxe to Broglie, 4 Jan 1743, De Vaudreuil Return of Infantry Regiments Amberg 26 Jan 1743 SHD A¹ 3006, nos. 24, 29, 209.

'died' and another 16 percent were accounted 'prisoner'.[130] The latter category almost certainly includes the 1,800 'moribund' men left behind in Prague when Chevert set off to Amberg and the laggards who fell into the hands of the pursuing hussars. Up to 54 percent of the battalion's soldiers perished, directly or indirectly, of sickness in just one year.

Conclusion

We have examined case studies illustrating three distinguishable tactical scenarios presented by encampments, sieges, and marches. On the face of it, the latter two contexts presented particular challenges of prolonged immobility and rapid movement, respectively. Sure enough, the accompanying graph plotting various mortality trajectories reveals that Münnich's trek to, through, and from Crimea exhibits one of the sharper falls. However, that is an outlier compared to the relatively much lower mortality rates that characterized the Serbian and Bohemian case studies. Admittedly, the Navarre Regiment lost more than half its strength but that wastage was spread over a whole year, whereas Münnich lost the same proportion of his army in half that time. To return to Image 4.7, the other really deadly outbreaks arose from encampments, at Saint-Jean (Roussillon) and Dundalk (Ireland) respectively. To this might be added the experience of French regiments quartered in the Rhineland during the winter of 1734-35 who lost between 30 and 60 percent of their strength: the Vivarais Regiment lost 47 percent in the month of December alone (see Chapter 3). What really mattered is what happened to the sick once they were segregated from the healthy and the whole. Tactical context has surprisingly little influence on epidemic mortality.

---

130 Contrôle (1743), Regiment de Navarre 2nd Battalion, Companies of Louboye, Candau, Chateauroux, Musy, Grannod, Dargil and Bichot, SHD GR 1 Yc 602.

5

Hospitals

Introduction

In *Madness and Civilization*, Michel Foucault traced continuity from the medieval lazarettos to the many new types of houses of enclosure and confinement of the seventeenth century including prisons, lunatic asylums, and hospitals. The *Hôpital Général* in Paris for instance, was a *cité* of over 30 walled-in acres serving as a poor house and place of enclosure, segregation and redemption for beggars, vagabonds, and convicts.[1] The *Invalides* of Paris was a military hospital for that most deserving category of the poor, the decrepit veteran. Military hospitals partook of the same impulse to segregate and enclose a source of 'disorder' so surgeons and physicians recommended keeping the sick in a separate tent away from their healthy comrades, lest the latter be 'infected' and 'contagious destruction' spread.[2]

Physicians and surgeons traced the underlying cause of sickness to sudden alterations in one or more of the six 'non-naturals', those conditions external to the body. Surgeon Donald Monro's advice after the Seven Years War captures most of these non-naturals: 'Take care that the soldiers be well cloathed; that they lie dry, and be well provided with straw and blankets, and with wood and to avoid exposing them to sudden changes from heat to cold'.[3] At the outset of the period under review, food and drink was treated as the most important of the non-natural categories. Before Pringle and Lind, Luca Porzio's *De Militis in Castris Sanitate Tuenda* was probably the most authoritative treatise on military medicine: it was first published at Vienna in 1685 and reprinted at Naples in 1701 and 1728, the Hague in 1739, Leiden in 1741, Paris in 1744, and London in 1747. Porzio was conscious of the dangers posed by 'effluvia' from 'putrid Waters, Ponds and Marshes', 'exhalations' of living men and animals and the 'emanations' of dead ones, but still gave greatest weight to diet.[4] Johann Valentin Wille's 1674 *De Morbis Castrensibus Internis* devoted most of his attention to 'bad diet' though he admitted 'it is easier to prescribe wholesome

---

1   Richard Mowery Andrews, *Law, Magistracy, and Crime in Old Regime Paris, 1735-1789* (Cambridge: Publisher, 1994), Vol.I, p.346.

2   Von Flemming, *Der Vollkommene teutsche Soldat*, p.322.

3   Donald Monro, *An account of the diseases which were most frequent in the British military hospitals in Germany: from January 1761 to the return of the troops to England in March 1763* (London: A. Millar et al., 1764), pp.314-315.

4   Porzio, *The soldier's Vade Mecum*, p.199.

food than to get it'. He considered other non-naturals and warned, for example, of corrupted air blocking the pores and preventing evacuation by transpiration.

Preoccupation with diet was even stronger outside the medical professions, as evidenced by reports of a 1710 catastrophe. In June of that year Philip V, the Bourbon contender for the throne of Spain, having failed to cut a path from central Spain through Catalonia to his French backers, encamped to the north of the Estany d'Ivars, the then largest lake in Catalonia. Here he remained from 10 June to 25 or 26 July while sickness 'ruined' his army.[5] The causes cited included the soldiers eating raisins and unripe melons because they had been short of bread for 'many' days, bad drinking water, and as an afterthought, the bad air of 'a marshy region'.[6]

While the root of the word 'contagion' is to be found in the Latin verb to 'touch' [tego], medical men usually conceived of contagion operating at a (short) distance via 'putrid effluvia'. Contagion loomed as a more serious problem according as medical authorities laid greater weight on 'little Particles floating in the Air' operating 'at distance' which 'miasma' (as it came to be called) caused 'epidemical, catching, and highly malignant' diseases.[7] 'Hence the first most important health rule for an army was to maintain the purity of air, water and place', insisted Ernst Gottfried Baldinger (superintendent of the military hospitals supporting the Prussian encampment near Torgau in 1761), 'as we already know from the immortal writings of Hippocrates'.[8] News book reports from Belgrade in 1717 which bemoaned 'a great stench that came from unburied corpses and carcasses and which gave rise to much sickness...' reveal that the emphasis on air was now well established in lay discourse.[9]

The Spanish built the first permanent military hospital in Europe at Mechlen, in 1585, during their Eighty Years War against the Dutch rebels. Armies were expanding and manpower growing scarcer, which prompted Cardinal Mazarin, chief minister to the King of France from 1642 until his death in 1661, to assert that 'money is nowhere better spent than on hospitals to treat the sick soldiers, for one of these men cured is worth ten new recruits'.[10] Louis XIV's 1708 edict created a *Service de Santé* comprising 50 permanent hospitals along the frontiers, notably at Lille, Ypres, Dunkirk, Metz, Strasbourg, and Perpignan. If the stated ambition of these hospitals was to cure, not just to care, then it is appropriate to consider the medical treatment they supplied.

5   Francesc Castellví, *Narraciones Históricas,* (Madrid: Erásmo Percopo, 1999), Vol.III, pp.47-53, Vol.I, pp.166-167; *Gazette de France* (Lyon, 1710) p.150; Jules-Alexis-Bernard, Chevalier de Bellerive, *Histoire des Campagnes de Monsieur le Duc De Vendosme* (Paris: Saugrain l'aîné, 1715), p.240.

6   *Gazette* (Lyon, 1710) p.150: Bellerive, *Histoire des Campagnes de Monsieur le Duc De Vendosme,* p.240.

7   Nedham Marchamont, *Medela medicinae a plea for the free prosestion and renovation of the art of physic* (London: R.Lownds, 1665), p.116; Michael Ettmüller, *Etmullerus abridg'd: or, A compleat system of the theory and practice of physic* (London: E. Harris, 1699), p.115; Georges Vigarello, *Histoire des pratiques de santé* (Paris: Seuil, 1993), p.111.

8   Ernst Gottfried Baldinger, *Von den Krankheiten einer Armee: aus eignen Wahrnehmungen in dem letztern preußischen Feldzuge,* (Langensalza: Johann Christian Martini, 1765), p.84.

9   Anon., *Ausführliche Beschreibung des Ungarischen Feld-Zugs,* p.60.

10   Tallett, *War and Society in Early Modern Europe: 1495-1715,* p.111.

Fevers were, by far and away, the biggest category of sickness. The potions most commonly administered in hospitals comprised three or four varieties of the same basic febrifuge. Jean Claude Adrien Helvétius, first physician to the Queen of France, criticized such 'uniform prescriptions' [*formules*] which allowed for no variation between hospitals in hot and cold climates, marshy and dry regions. Indeed, he claimed that most of the prescriptions were 'defective and even dangerous'.[11] Despite such learned objections, these exact *formules* continued to be prescribed for military hospitals.[12]

Quinine was the nearest thing to a new wonder drug in the period under review and was known variously as Peruvian Bark, 'Kinkina', Jesuit's Powder, Cinchona, and Quinquina.[13] A 1705 French publication on 'campaign diseases' promised that 'Quinquina' dissolved in wine would 'infallibly' cure intermittent fevers and especially tertian fever or, as we know it, malaria.[14] Quinine lived up to its promise when targeted at malarial fevers, and Pringle recounts proudly how virtually all the men in a dragoon regiment in his care succumbed to malaria in 1748 but, thanks to 'proper evacuations', followed by 'bark', only 15 actually died.[15] However, quinine was not often administered as a specific but as the major ingredient in all febrifuges. Emetics or, more often, purgatives were considered necessary before quinine could usefully be administered. Pringle's preference was for Ipecac or 'Ipechuana' which was a root crop native to the Brazilian forests which had been first administered (unsuccessfully) in a syrup by the *médecin* of the Army of Roussillon in 1692.[16] Ipecac was a powerful fast-acting emetic which was expected to reduce a continuous fever to an intermittent and thereby admit the use of Quinine. As to laxatives, the 'simple' febrifuge contained two ounces of Quinine, a quarter-ounce of Lesser Centaury [*Centaurium pulchellum*], a quarter ounce of Epsom Salts, a saline laxative, and so on. The 'purgative' febrifuge was differentiated from the 'simple' only by the addition of a quarter-ounce of Séné [*Cassia acutifolia*], which was a herbal laxative, together with two ounces of Epsom Salts.

The feverish or 'full-blooded' patient should be bled from the 'median vein', near the bend of the arm, by the surgeon's lancet. The surgeon should next encourage the patient to sweat in order to expel malignant humours and prescribe him a healthy and digestible diet.[17] Venesection was universally accepted, with more or less enthusiasm. Paracelsians remained resolutely critical of the reigning Galenic

---

11   Jean Claude Adrien Helvetius, *Lettre de M. Helvetius, Conseiller d'état, premier médecin de la reine* (Paris: Quillau, 1748), pp.4,11,12, 28.

12   A.J. Delaye, *Formules de médicamens rédigées par ordre du roi, à l'usage des hôpitaux* (Marseilles: Jean Mossy, 1781), p.93.

13   Robert Boyle, *Of the reconcileableness of specifick medicines...* (London: Sam.Smith, 1685), p.17; David, Abercromby, *A moral discourse of the power of interest* (London: Thomas Hodgkin, 1690), p.189.

14   Jean Claude Adrien Helvetius, *Memoires instructifs sur l'usage de differents remèdes specifiques pour les armées du roy, & les malades de la champagne* (Paris: Pierre Le Mercier, 1705), p.61.

15   Pringle, *Diseases of the Army*, p.189.

16   Pringle, *Diseases of the Army*, pp.207, 210; Bernard Le Bovier de Fontenelle, 'Eloge de Monsieur Chirac', *Œuvres de Monsieur Bernard Le Bovier de Fontenelle* (London: Publisher Unknown, 1785), Vol.IV, p.207.

17   Von Flemming, *Der Vollkommene teutsche Soldat*, p.322.

paradigm, denied that disease arose from an imbalance of the four humours, and sternly warned that great and frequent bleeding 'corrupts the blood'. Yet even such critics accepted the supposed need for moderate bleeding.[18] Richard Brocklesby, Physician-General of the British Army, who looked down on surgeons, nonetheless confessed that 'I made no scruple to use the lancet freely' during the Seven Years War.[19] In any event, patients clamoured for venesection whether the medical men wanted to or not. A British regimental surgeon serving in the War of the Austrian Succession confirmed that officers and men called out to be bled straightaway before any other treatment and that this 'common custom' was 'without rhyme or reason'.[20] Notoriously, when George Washington caught a throat infection in 1799, doctors drained nearly half his blood and, likely as not, killed him. Less well known is the fact that it was the illustrious patient who demanded to be bled so heavily.

After fever, bloody flux was the most common of the deadly camp diseases. The four main features of the condition each demanded separate treatment. Counter-intuitively, the haemorrhage required 'frequent bleeding' because intestinal inflam-mation indicated a 'plethora' of blood. The intestines had to be scoured by an emetic. The flux itself required a strong astringent: French army physicians used acacia gum which was the hardened sap of various species of the acacia and Armenian bole, a reddish clay.[21] The fourth feature, painful bowel cramps, could be ameliorated by opiates. When all this was done, Pringle recommended what he considered a 'small dose' of the purgative calomel (five grains mixed with 25 grains of rhubarb) to 'keep the body open'.[22] Paracelsians had left a legacy of chemicals like calomel, a toxic mercury chloride mineral, which were quietly incorporated into the orthodox *materia medica*.

Physicians and surgeons cannot be accused of sloth or hidebound conserva-tism just because they continued to work within the classical framework system-atized by Hippocrates and Galen. This tradition was 'rich, inclusive and flexible' and so capable of incorporating various and complex regimens and remedies which included natural products from the New World and chemicals from the Paracelsians.[23] Moreover, from the learned doctor to beardless surgeon's mate, they carried, to a greater or lesser extent, a millennium's weight of authority which must have had significant placebo effect. One hopes so, because their remedies, with the partial exception of quinine, possessed no medical efficacy.

Broadly speaking, two categories of hospital emerged. The first was the 'fixed' (also denoted as 'standing' or 'general') hospital. The first permanent French mili-tary hospitals were set up first in newly conquered frontier towns like Lille (1673)

---

18   Thiers de, Marconnay, *Nouvelles découvertes*, pp.7-8, 12-13, 24, 63, 125.
19   Richard Brocklesby, *Oeconomical and Medical Observations* (London: T. Becket, and P. A. De Hondt, 1764), p.139.
20   Paul Kopperman, (ed.), *'Regimental Practice' by John Buchanan MD* (Farnham: Ashgate, 2012), pp.26, 165, 185.
21   Delaye, *Formules de médicamens rédigées par ordre du roi*, p.93-94.
22   Pringle, *Diseases of the Army*, pp.268, 271-73, 277.
23   Roy Porter, *Flesh in the Age of Reason* (London: Allen Lane, 2001), p.50.

and Perpignan (1675).[24] At this time, the French launched most of their campaigns just over their frontiers, so it made sense to site their fixed hospitals contiguously and permanently. However, for other states, and for the French for much of the 18th century, fixed hospitals were wartime expedients sited in the campaign theatre, some 12-13 miles back from the front.[25] The French, for instance, maintained nineteen fixed hospitals in north-west and central Germany during the Seven Years War. The first purpose-built British army hospital was not built until 1745: this was at Berwick-upon-Tweed, as part of a large new barracks there. As late as the reign of Frederick the Great, the Prussians had not built a single permanent hospital.[26] The buildings were commonly 'barns, granaries, stables and churches' but the single type of building considered most suitable was the monastery, as we saw in the case of Perpignan. Even monasteries, however, were less than ideal. For instance, in 1694 the Franciscan Convento de Jesús, outside Barcelona's walls, was made available as a military hospital. A report written by the Inspector General of Hospitals in February 1696 yields an insight into what was considered the ideal building. A hospital should be roomy enough for beds to be laid out in rows, thus letting staff move freely. In addition, each ward should have sufficient windows in order to ventilate bad air and let in fresh air. As it happened, the Convento de Jesús had been built for a small community of monks, and comprised poky and airless cells, relieved only by narrow cloisters.[27]

The fixed hospital was dominated by physicians rather than surgeons and the tendency was for the numbers of medical staff, especially in British general hospitals, to grow over succeeding wars, as all but the most trivial cases were increasingly evacuated from the front. While the British hospital was directly administered by the state, the French fixed hospital was usually run by an entrepreneur who looked after all supplies, provisions, and medicines, all of which outgoings were refundable according to an agreed daily rate for each hospitalised soldier. A 1747 ordinance consolidated various piecemeal instructions and concentrated authority over the controller or the entrepreneur (of public and privately-run military hospitals respectively) unequivocally in the hands of the *commissaire des guerres* and reflected a preference for uniformity, centralization, and tight control by the Secretary of State for War. Helvétius, discussed above, reflected a later successful reaction by medical 'experts' [*gens habiles*] against this authoritarianism. The 1747 ordinance stipulated a system of tickets-of-entry, tickets-of-leave, and nominal rolls to prevent the director or contractor from padding out his numbers by claiming ration allowances for non-existent, dead, or discharged soldiers. Such bureaucratic checks were necessary. One Monsieur Montlys, contractor for the fixed hospitals of the French army in Germany in 1757, was 'the most honest man in the world' but his subordinates

---

24   Comité d'histoire du service de santé, *Histoire de la médecine aux armées* (Paris-Limoges: Charles Lavauzelle, 1982), Vol.I, pp.373, 400.

25   Monro, *An Account of the Diseases*, p.329.

26   Von Bessel, *Entwurf eines Militair-Feld-Reglement*, p.317; Joan Lane, *A Social History of Medicine: Health, Healing and Disease* in England, 1750–1950 (London: Routledge, 2001), p.172.

27   Christopher Storrs, 'Health, Sickness and Medical Services in Spain's Armed Forces c.1665–1700', *Medical History*, 50:3 (July 2006), pp.325-350.

were either men of 'probity without intelligence' or 'intelligence without probity'. Montlys exercised little control over his assistants and when it became apparent that the hospitals were little better than 'slaughterhouses', his *compagnie* lost the contract.[28]

The second category was the 'flying' [*fliegendes*] or marching [*ambulants*] hospital. This followed the regiments closely enough that the journey would not kill the patient but was still removed a safe distance from the fighting.[29] Typically the men were put in 'sick tents' behind the regimental lines or in a house close by.[30] By the time of the Seven Years War the French army provided one such hospital for 20,000 men on paper, though in practice the hospital was usually broken up and scattered to follow detached corps. For their part, the British preferred smaller regimental hospitals. Like the British, the Habsburgs demanded that a 'well-ordered' regimental field hospital be set up.[31]

Surgeons, rather than physicians, provided the primary care at the flying hospital. The French mobile hospital of the Seven Years War, for instance, had an establishment of 37 surgeons and assistant surgeons, but no physicians whatsoever. The surgeon should know enough to recognise the 'common diseases' of soldiers, like dysentery, and perform 'triage' by separating the living from the dead and dying: the specific meaning of dividing into three parts came later. The surgeon should carry out daily inspections to ensure patients were clean, well-fed, and warm and that orderlies and 'women for cooking and washing' were in attendance.[32] However, treatment was basic: Colombier describes how the sick soldier was 'laid on straw amongst the dead and dying. He is bled, pansed [wounds dressed], plied with emetics, fed broth and eventually loaded onto a cart' to be sent to the fixed hospital.[33] In 1764 Richard Brocklesby, later Physician-General to the Army, decried the 'narrowness of thinking' and 'incapacity' of surgeons and decried the typical regimental hospital as

> A small old house, with low ceilings; a large kitchen or common room below stairs; and no other apartment in the house half so big as that kitchen; small lozenge windows without apertures, designed to keep the miserable inhabitants warm, in lieu of fire. Most commonly, the habitation hired for an infirmary has for some time been altogether unoccupied, with the walls still damp, the boarded floors half rotten, and the roof, in several parts, open above...[34]

---

28   Lee Kennett, *The French Armies in the Seven Years' War* (Durham: Duke University Press, 1967), p.131; F. Olier,'Les Hopitaux Sedentaires francais aux Armées d'Allegmagne durant la guerre de Sept ans (1757-1763)' in 'Service De Santé' at http://vial.jean.free.fr/new_npi/revues_npi/22_2001/npi_2201/22_fra_sante4.htm (accessed 04/04/2019).

29   Von Bessel, *Entwurf eines Militair-Feld-Reglement*, p.317.

30   Monro, *An Account of the Diseases*, p.330.

31   Von Khevenhüller, *Observations Puncten*, p.161.

32   Khevenhüller, *Observations Puncten*, pp.159, 161, 179; G.A. Brambilla, *Discours sur la Prééminence et l'utilitité de la Chirurgie* (Brussels: Emmanuel Flon, 1786), p.21.

33   Jean Colombier, *Code de médecine militaire pour le service de terre* (Paris: Costard, 1772), Vol.II, pp.293-294.

34   Brocklesby, *Oeconomical and Medical Observations*, pp.37, 49.

'I have seen', he recalled, 'such cottages stuffed with forty, fifty, sixty, nay, with seventy or eighty poor sick soldiers, all lying heel to head, so closely confined together within their own stinking cloaths, foul linen, &c. that it was enough to suffocate the patients, as well as others, who were obliged to approach them'.[35]

Perpignan 1674

As discussed in Chapter 2, between the camp at Saint-Jean and the hospital at Perpignan, at least a third of Schomberg's army perished of dysentery and (probably) typhoid between June and November 1674. Flux, in this case, was more than just the sickness that laid the conditions for typhus but was a killer disease in its own right. However, the fact that the relative mortality rate in Notre-Dame-de-la-Réal parish in Perpignan peaked in December suggests that typhus was also present. The correspondingly high mortality in the hospital that same month, with three deaths for every discharge, further suggests that the hospital was the font and origin of the typhus epidemic.[36]

Secretary of State for War Louvois was bombarded with complaints that the patients subsisted on a thin soup and that 'many' tens of patients went 'whole days' without a bite to eat.[37] Someone, Schomberg hinted darkly, was pocketing most of the generous daily allowance towards the patient's diet. On 16 September Schomberg confronted Intendant Carlier about thefts from the patients and the latter, affronted, replied: 'I am an honest man...'.[38] Historians seem to take it at face value that Carlier was crooked or incompetent but since he was an old client of Minister for Finances Jean-Baptiste Colbert, he was naturally an object of suspicion to Louvois, Colbert's factional rival.[39] The struggle between Colbert, proponent of the navy and colonial expansion, and Louvois, the advocate of land war, had already swung decisively in the latter's favour when the French attacked the United Provinces in 1672.[40] Consequently, Carlier was vulnerable to scapegoating and trumped-up charges. He was duly sacked as Intendant de l'Armée in 1675, and as Intendant of Roussillon in January of the following year, ostensibly on the grounds of age and ill-health. He died just a few days later.

In addition to complaints of embezzlement, came better-founded allegations of neglect. Carlier's successor boasted in 1675 that he established 'good order' and

35   Brocklesby, *Oeconomical and Medical Observations,* p.54.
36   Memorial dels soldats son eixits del ospital general de Perpignan en la mois de Decembre 1674' ADPO, C131. December 1674 is the only month for which the hospital register has survived.
37   Ayats, *Armées et Santé,* p.129.
38   Louis André, *Michel Le Tellier et Louvois* (Paris: Armand Colin, 1942), p.381.
39   Guy Rowlands, *The Dynastic State and the Army Under Louis XIV: Royal Service and Private Interest 1661–1701* (Cambridge: Cambridge University Press, 2002), p.147; Alain Ayats, 'Les Premieres Années de l'Intendance du Roussillon, *Histoire, économie et société* 15:1 (1996), p.119.
40   Sharon Kettering, *Patrons, Brokers, and Clients in Seventeenth-Century France* (Oxford: Oxford University Press,1986), p.203.

cleanliness [*propreté*] which may imply these had been lacking.[41] Indeed we are told that 300 patients were left lying 'almost abandoned' in the cloister. Other patients had to endure being 'in the midst of the dead' for days at a time before corpses were taken away for burial. Moreover, the patients had no sheets or blankets and the attendants sold the clothing of the deceased. Some of these complaints, such as the lack of bedclothes, were so commonplace as to be unremarkable and others were attributable to a shortage of attendants: as early as 8 July, Carlier was grumbling that most of them had died or fallen sick.[42] It cannot have been easy to attract replacement attendants, especially if they were to be denied customary perquisites like purloining the clothes of dead patients. Over a century later, medical reformers were still condemning the 'barbarous practice' of 'putting several sick men in the one bed, and often to leave the dead, dying and living together, because it is not yet time for triage of the dead and half-dead'.[43]

In short, there were too few attendants and too little space. A report on the hospital almost a century later indicates that summertime conditions in the crowded hospital must have been dire:

> The hospital comprises just one very large and fine chamber whose windows face west and here all the sick must be admitted and often the feverish and wounded will be left lying beside those suffering from dysentery. The latrines abutting the hall are almost as great a nuisance because, however carefully maintained, they release an often unbearable smell into the chamber, especially in summer when there is no water flowing by.[44]

The hospital at Perpignan, in 1674, was a temporarily rented edifice and it would be the following year before a permanent hospital was built on the same site, capable of accommodating 1,200 sick.[45] Schomberg advised that the new hospital should be located without the walls because the existing location was unhealthy and it would be a source of infection to the townspeople but Louvois rejected his argument, stating that the priority was to ensure the physical security of the sick from enemy attack which, in a frontier zone, demanded they be behind walls.

Lombardy 1734-1735

The Italian theatre of the War of the Polish Succession (1734-35), discussed in Chapter 3, saw France send an army of 40,000 troops to fight alongside the forces of Charles Emmanuel III of Sardinia-Piedmont and of Bourbon Spain. The allies succeeded in driving the Austrians out of Naples and the Duchy of Milan but the Austrians launched vigorous counter-attacks from their logistical base in the

---

41   Ayats, *Armées et Santé*, p.132.
42   Carlier to Louvois, Camp at Saint-Jean de Pages, 8 July 1674, *SHD* A¹ 415, no. 68.
43   Brambilla, *Discours sur la Prééminence et l'utilitité de la Chirurgie* p.21.
44   De Hautesierck, *Recueil d'observations de medecine des hôpitaux militaries*, p.61.
45   Ayats, *Armées et Santé*, p.131.

Seraglio culminating in a 'bloody draw' at the battle of Parma or Crocetta on 29 June 1734.[46] Strategically, the French won in the sense that the Imperial army retreated, to the confluence of the Po and Secchia where it was reinforced and placed under the command of Count Lothar Josef Königsegg. For the next two months the armies faced-off across the Secchia River. Meanwhile, the French forced the surrender of Modena, whose Duke had made the mistake of trusting the Austrians for protection. On 15-19 September Königsegg pushed the allies back to Guastalla before being hurled back in a bloody encounter. Losses were even heavier than at Parma but the encounter 'decided nothing'.[47]

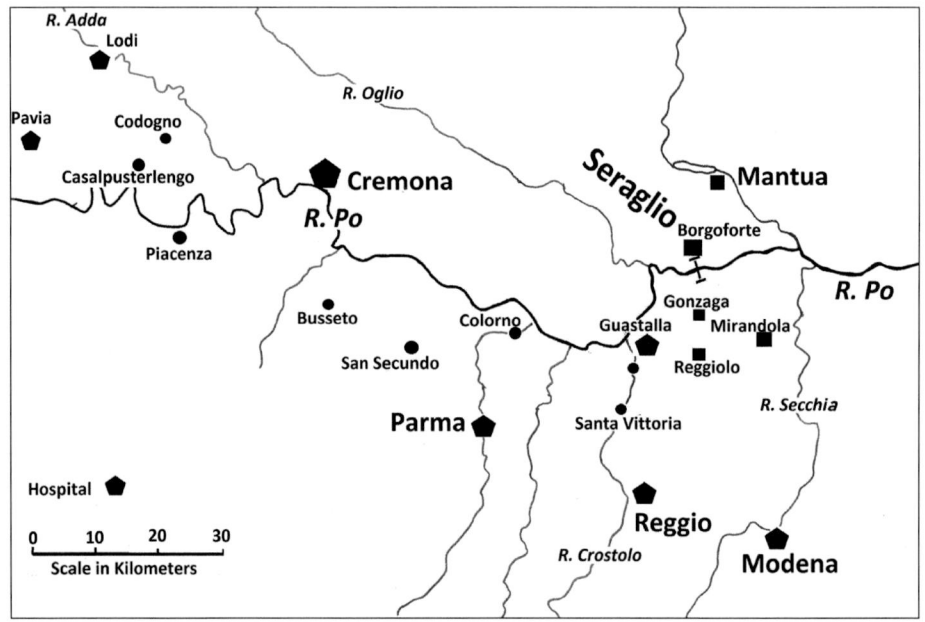

5.1 Lombardy 1734-35.

Marches and counter-marches would drag on well into the winter without any more battles to punctuate the dance. The Imperials were forced to life a siege of Modena in late October while a French army concentrated at Reggio to attack Mirandola. The expected clash never happened because the armies bogged down in 'heavy rain' and waterlogged country.[48] Later that month, the allied army crossed the Oglio, whereupon the Imperials broke the dams and flooded a 'vast width' of

---

46 Sutton, *The King's Honor& the King's Cardinal*, pp.166-168; Hochedlinger, *Austria's Wars of Emergence*, p.210.

47 P. Massuet, *Histoire de la guerre présente, contenant tout ce qui s'est passé de plus important en Italie, sur le Rhin, en Pologne et dans la plupart des cours de l'Europe* (The Hague: chez l'Honoré, 1735), p.332.

48 Modena, 24 October 1734, *OPD*, p.722.

low-lying countryside.[49] In late November the French were pressed even further back towards the line of the rivers Adda and Po and were forced to evacuate their flying hospitals from Cremona, Guastalla, and Gualtieri (close to Guastalla) back behind the Adda, to Codogno, Lodi, and Casalpusterlengo.[50] In mid-December the Imperials crossed the Po by a pontoon bridge at Borgoforte and advanced towards Gonzaga and Reggiolo with the apparent intention of snipping off the Guastalla salient. *Maréchal* de Broglie (father of the de Broglie who would command so ineptly in Bohemia in 1742) raced from Cremona with a large detachment but, as luck would have it, 'snow and continuing rain' had bogged down any further Austrian advance. The French troops had been 'constantly on the march' and were now 'completely worn out'.[51] Nonetheless, they were driven to another effort and in the days before Christmas they pressed over the Crostolo on pontoon bridges, only to be pushed back.[52] At last, the armies broke off contact and slipped away into winter quarters: the line of the rivers Adda, Po and Crostolo roughly delineated the wintertime boundary between Allied and Austrian territory.

The reason for the preceding march-by-march account of French movements in the latter months of 1734 is to emphasize that, however lacking in the sanguinary glamour of battle, the campaign was gruelling and the 'fatigue and marches in terrible weather' of November and December reduced the French, especially de Broglie's detachment, to a 'very bad state' with half of the army disabled by sickness.[53]

The sickness(es) that afflicted the army of Italy can best be seen as a single epidemic with three successive phases of the kind dissected in the introduction. First, a 'serious' outbreak of dysentery caused 'great mortality' and lasted from July to October. The common soldiers were blamed for greedily consuming 'fruits and new wines'.[54] Dysentery overlapped with an epidemic of 'malign' fever in August and September. Two physicians (in Cremona and Gualtieri, respectively) noted that the symptoms of this malign fever were loss of appetite, stomach pain, high fever, headaches, and rash. All of these symptoms pointed to typhoid. The fact that the months from April to July were exceptionally dry and the rivers 'did not flow freely' suggests that dirty water may have been a cause.

In addition to directly killing many, these diseases supplied the requisite number of sick to generate a 'malign' and 'burning' fever epidemic which took off in October. The disease usually culminated in delirium and those afflicted sometimes suffered from 'gangrene of the tip of the nose and toes, not unlike what happens with

---

49 Cremona, 25 October 1734, *OPD*, p.724.

50 Mantua, 16 November 1734, *OPD*, p.766; Savoy, 22 November *OPD*, p.777; Milan, 20 November, *OPD*, p.786; Cremona, 23 November 1734, *Gazette*, no. 55, p.639; Parma, 8 December 1734, *OPD*, p.818.

51 Félix François d'Espié, *Mémoires de la guerre d'Italie* (Paris: veuve Duchesne, 1777), p.254; Cremona 29 November 1734, *Gazette*, no. 55, p.651; Cremona 13 December 1734, *Gazette*, no. 57, p.675; Parma, 13 December, *MR*, 1735 (8/9, No. 1); Edmond-Jean-François Barbier, *Chronique de la régence et du règne de Louis XV (1718-1763), ou Journal de Barbier* (Paris: Charpentier, 1857-1866), Vol.II, pp.529-530.

52 Cremona, 23 December 1734, in *MR* (1735), p.35.

53 Comte de Bueil to d'Angervilliers, 3 January 1735, SHD, A¹ 2810, p.14.

54 Quingentalo 27 August 1734, *Daily Courant* (London), 4 September 1734; no. 5747.

frostbite'. This was, of course, typhus the classic 'famine fever' that struck those who were hungry, uprooted, cold, wet and, above all, demoralized and so was in a very real sense 'brought about' by the abrupt change to wet weather which persisted throughout November.[55] Quite apart from the foul weather, the long counter-clock-wise march of the French was demoralizing because it involved a hurried retreat followed by an ultimately pointless advance into the Guastalla salient. An officer who went on home leave later claimed that 'nothing much happened' that winter but, though were no major troop movements, incessant and exhausting probes, reliefs, raids and rallies went on. Nowhere was this little war busier than around Guastalla, and nowhere was the epidemic worse.[56]

At the height of the epidemic in January 1735 about half of all troops were sick in hospital, not to mention the 'many more' sick in quarters who could not be taken to hospital through lack of carts or bad roads. By March, some battalions were worn down to hardly more than 100 men, including convalescents.[57]

Table 5.1 Soldiers in Hospital: Army of Italy[58]

October 1734	3,000
November 1734	5,600
December 1734	10,000
January 1735	11,000
February 1735	8,000
March 1735	5,073

The graph depicts an epidemic that peaked in January (slightly later than the Army of the Rhine's typhus epidemic) when half of the army lay sick. The esti-mate of army strength used to compute losses must be approximate. The autumn strength of about 24,000 was reinforced by another 10,000 men in November and December, yielding a cumulative strength of 34,000 of whom 14,000, or 41 percent, died between 11 November and early March.[59] This was comparable to the sufferings of the worst-hit units, like Vivarais, on the Rhine that same winter and only slightly better than the experience of Schomberg's army in the winter of 1689. Moreover, 41

---

55 Dezon, *Lettres sur les Principles Maladies*, pp.5, 26; Paolo Valcarenghi, *Medicina rationalis ad recentiorum mentem observationibus adaucta* (Cremona: Peter Ricchini, 1737), pp.59-60, 239.

56 d'Espié, *Mémoires de la guerre d'Italie*, p.258.

57 Comte de Bueil, Cremona 14 March 1735, SHD A¹ 2812 no. 73.

58 Letter from Cremona, 21October 1734, *Daily Journal* (London), 29 October 1734; no. 4300; Pajol, *Les guerres sous Louis XV*, Vol.I, p.538; Milan, 5 December 1734, in *MR* (1735), p.68; Belhomme, *Histoire de l'infanterie en France*, Vol.III, pp.110-115; Monique Lucenet 'Les épidémies dans l'infanterie au cours de la première moitié du xviii siecle', in Centre d'histoire militaire et d'études de défense nationale, (eds.), *Forces Armées et Société*. (Montpelier: Centre d'histoire militaire et d'études de défense nationale, 1985), p.211; Comte de Bueil, Cremona 14 March 1735, SHD A¹ 2812 no. 73; Intendant de Fontanieu, Milan, 19 March 1735, Returns of soldiers in Hospital SHD A¹ 2812 no. 103.

59 Commissaire de Barjolles, Guastalla, 1 and 12 March 1735, SHD A¹ 2812 no. 8.

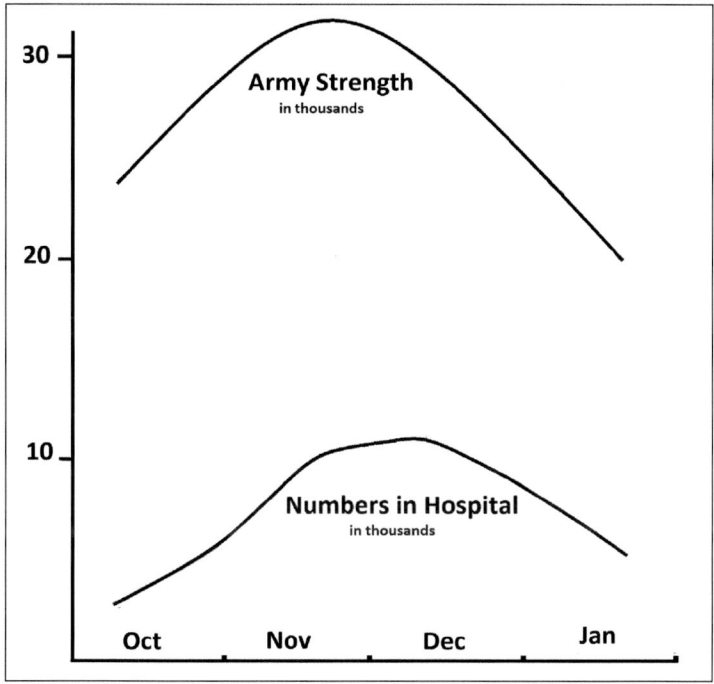

5.2 French army strength: Lombardy 1734-35.

percent is an average, and units in the Guastalla pocket, like the Swiss regiment of Bourqui or Bourquy, lost no fewer than 1,300 men, or 54 percent of paper strength, over those miserable winter months.[60] Only 5,000 of the 14,000 perished in the hospitals, the rest evidently died in their winter quarters.

De Broglie attributed the sickness to 'the constant marches, the unhealthy encampments, little and poor food'.[61] Matters were improving a little by March 1735 when *Lieutenant Général* Antoine-Pierre Comte de Beuil could write from Cremona that 'few' were dying and most hospitals were 'well run', but, he warned, the 40 battalions south of the Po were hard-pressed on account of the many garrisons and detachments 'which will totally destroy them', unless they were to be given a respite:

> Truly Monsieur, you would have to see this country in the present weather to understand the difficulties. It is nothing like it was in the last war. I have followed this trade for 59 years, I have served in every country but I have

---

60 Belhomme, *Histoire de l'infanterie en France*, Vol.III, p.120; Ordonnance pour augmenter de 40 hommes les anciennes compagnies des 8 régimens suisses et en lever 8 nouvelles, de 200 hommes chacune... (Paris, 1733), p.2. The regiment was shifted to Modena in January: Paris, 27 January 1735, MR (1735) No. 7.

61 Pajol, *Les guerres sous Louis XV,* Vol.I, pp.549-550.

never seen infantry so worn-out [*travaillée*] and bad as has been the case since winter began.[62]

Evidently, hospitals were but a part of the whole problem. Cremona was the main hospital accommodating about two-thirds of those hospitalized and was 'fairly well run', as were the eleven smaller hospitals except for Reggio, Parma and, worst of all, 'miserable' Guastalla, a disused church where the sick lay three to a palliasse. These palliasses were laid out on damp flagstones, while the straw had rotted and not been changed for eight days. The patients were prey to chest infections, which were 'in every case fatal'.

Instructions for *Commissaires de Guerre* stipulated that those struck down by a 'contagious' sickness should be isolated and certainly not share a bed, whereas soldiers suffering from the common fevers or stomach bugs [*cours de ventre*] could safely be laid two or three to a (four-foot wide) bed.[63] Such precautions were not observed at Guastalla and the *commissaire* complained that the militiamen of the Calvisson Regiment (from a district nestling in the Cevennes) were intermingled with the regulars. Because of the former's 'habitual dirtiness' they were crawling with 'vermin' which spread to the regular soldiers and so 'made sickness even worse'.[64] The *commissaire's* remarks do not imply that he had somehow intuited the link between lice and typhus but, rather, he was repeating the truism discussed in chapter two that 'nastiness' (that is, lice infestation) inhibited respiration from the skin and that the 'lice sickness' infects the soldier whose pores are clogged with dirt. Consequently, given the dirtiness of camps, this is was 'a truly common affliction of the army'.[65] The *commissaire* also blamed the officers of the Calvisson Regiment for the 'neglect' of their men in hospital and of doing nothing about living quarters 'infected with ordure'.

Records of the medical crises present a familiar bias. The records in the army archives capture the reports of officials, like the *commissaire de guerre*, who were answerable to the Secretary of State for War and who enjoyed that overriding authority that would be embodied in the 1747 hospital regulations. Whether by accident or design, *Commissaire* Barajolles came on the scene late in the day when the crisis had almost passed. He was thus able to present a problem to his masters, but not one so complex or insurmountable that he, the energetic official on the spot, could not resolve. Nowadays we prefer to attribute poor outcomes in health service delivery to systemic errors in which no one person can be held to account. However, Barajolles needed an identifiable culprit (other than one of his own protégés and subordinates of course) and duly found him in the major of the Calvisson Regiment. This is not to suggest that Barajolles was a mendacious drone. He doubtless believed

---

62   Comte de Bueil, Cremona 3 March 1735, SHD A¹ 2812 no. 8 no. 14.

63   *Ordonnance… portant règlement général concernant les hôpitaux militaires…* (Paris, 1747) p.12; François de Chennevières, *Détails militaires dont la connaissance est nécessaire* (Paris: Charles-Antoine Jombert, 1750), Vol.II, pp.170. 405, 425, 431.

64   Commissaire de Barjolles, Guastalla, 1 and 12 March 1735, SHD A¹ 2812 no. 8; Léon Clément Hennet, *Les milices et les troupes provinciales*, (Paris: L. Baudoin, 1884), p.73.

65   Baldinger, *Von den Krankheiten einer Armee*, p.91.

what he wrote and may even have worked himself to death, if he is the 'poor Barajoles' who is reported later that month to be 'in the last extremity'.[66]

However, the *commissaire*'s reports do not fully get across the scale of the problem and the fact that it extended well beyond the hospitals More than 5,000 men died in the hospitals but another 9,000 died elsewhere in their quarters between 11 November and mid-March: the latter figure can be inferred from marginalia in Barajolles's report.[67] In contrast to Perpignan in 1674, the typhus epidemic that swept through the army of Italy in 1734-5, was not incubated in the hospitals but was more general and was inseparable from morale. Troops who were cold, wet, (those in the Guastalla salient spent much of the winter in trenches) tired, hungry, and demoralized were sure to be lousy as well.

Germany 1743

In the War of the Austrian Succession, France, Prussia and other powers sought to exploit the Habsburg succession crisis by seizing Austria's far-flung territories. France's threat to the Austrian Netherlands was of greatest concern to Britain and over three years a British expeditionary force took part in a creakingly slow and desultory war punctuated by just two battles, Dettingen in Bavaria (27 June 1743) and Fontenoy in Flanders (11 May 1745).

The campaign proper may be said to have begun on 23 May 1743 when 16,000 British troops, marched over 270 miles all the way from their cantonments in Flanders, encamped near Frankfurt-am-Main and joined with Hanoverian and Austrian contingents.[68] From their base at Hanau in Hesse, the Pragmatic Army (so-called because the component states recognised the Pragmatic Sanction of 1713 whereby Maria Theresa was recognized as sovereign of the Habsburg Empire) marched south-west, up the narrow valley of the Main River, but were blocked by the French near Aschaffenburg and turned back for Hanau. Maréchal de Noailles tried to block their retreat but was pushed aside with 'considerable loss' in the Battle of Dettingen (27 June 1743). On the march to Aschaffenburg the troops had been on short rations: 'we are almost starved', complained one guardsman.[69] The reason for the food shortage was that Noailles controlled the river, and the British had but 30 wagons for their entire army which meant that the sick and wounded had to be abandoned when the British slunk back to Hanau the day after the Battle of Dettingen.[70]

The collapse of Broglie's position in Bavaria (a knock-on consequence of the Prague disaster discussed earlier) forced Noailles on to the defensive, leaving the

---

66   d'Agenvilliers to unk, nd. SHD A¹ 2812 no 163.

67   Comte de Bueil, Cremona 14 March 1735, SHD A¹ 2812 no. 73.

68   H.A.L. Howell, 'The Story of the Army Surgeon and the Care of the Sick … from 1715 to 1748' in *Journal of the Army Medical Corps* (1914) xxii. p.329.

69   Howell, 'The Story of the Army Surgeon' p.330

70   Chevalier de Malbez (ed.), *Campagne de M. le maréchal de Noailles en l'année MDCCXLIII, journal du chevalier de Malbez, commissaire d'artillerie* (Paris: A. Picard, 1892), p.21.

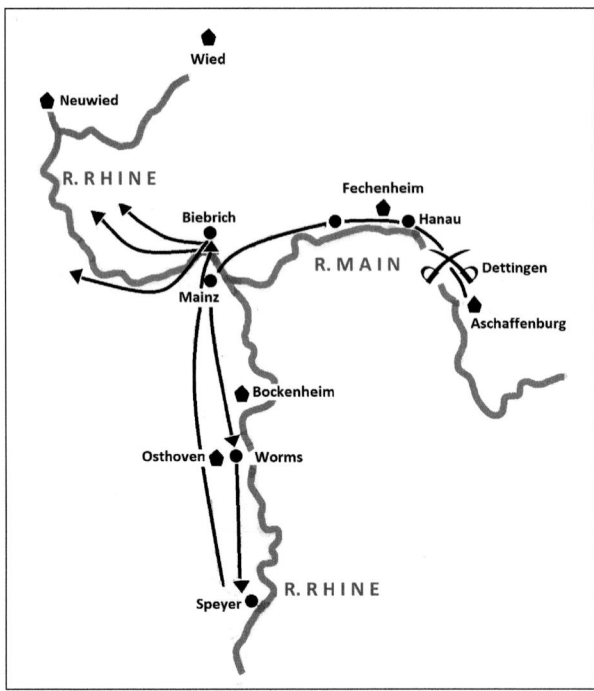

5.3 British hospitals in Germany, 1743.

Pragmatic Army of about 60,000 men free to strike out west on 16 August towards the Rhine where it camped for a month at Worms. On 25 September the allied army marched upriver to join Dutch troops at Speyer where they failed to force a passage across the Rhine and then retreated to Mainz on 11 October. Eight days later, the British troops broke up into divisions and marched to their assigned winter quarters in the Austrian Netherlands.[71]

Before Dettingen, the army had been reasonably healthy, with just 250 British troops admitted to a flying hospital at Wied and another 500 to a temporary hospital at Aschaffenburg. These 500 were left behind in the hasty retreat and fell into the hands of the French. The main hospital at Fechenheim now grew very busy as British troops encamped at nearby Hanau took sick, 'most of the Flux'. For Pringle the change came about because the summer heat promoted perspiration which was now interrupted by rain which blocked the pores. On the night after Dettingen the men slept on the field of battle without tents and exposed to heavy rain. In a 'few weeks' about half of them were struck down with dysentery, that 'constant and fatal epidemic of camps'.[72] About 1,500 of them were admitted to the hospital at Fechenheim and:

---

71   Pringle, *Diseases of the Army*, p.22.
72   Pringle, *Diseases of the Army*, pp.19-20.

By these men, the air became so much vitiated, that not only the rest of the patients, but the apothecaries, nurses, and others employed in the hospital, with most of the inhabitants of the place, were infected. To this was added a still more alarming distemper, the jail-or hospital-fever, the common effects of foul air from crowds and animal corruption. These two combined, occasioned a great mortality in the village, among the natives as well as the soldiers; while such of ours as were seized with the dysentery, and not removed from the camp, though wanting many conveniencies others had in hospitals, yet kept free from this fever, and commonly recovered of the flux.[73]

Flux was a camp disease, as Pringle noted: 'From the time of our leaving Hanau, the dysentery so sensibly abated, that the change could only be ascribed to leaving the infectious privies, the foul straw, and the filth of a long encampment'. John Buchanan, surgeon with the Blues, recorded that flux was well established by mid-July and by the middle of August he 'could not keep a list', a reminder of how record-keeping usually fails when an epidemic is at its worst. Those who remained in the camp infirmary recovered, except for a quartermaster and a trooper. From the outset the quartermaster was 'voiding pure foetid blood': he 'died of this distemper, nor was he in the least relieved by any medicine'. He complained that it all began when he had 'catched cold' while out foraging. Like Pringle, Buchanan rejected some common dietary explanations of dysentery such as fresh fruit or freshly killed meat in favour of the 'great fatigue & violent raine' that came after the Battle of Dettingen.[74] The fluxes 'decreased' towards the end of August to be succeeded by a slow fever' which was 'attended with violent headaches, watchfulness, faintness & universal weakness' and 'a constant drought' [thirst]. The pulse was so low that bleeding did not seem proper'.[75] This sounds like Pringle's 'bilious fever', that nebulous autumnal fever that came on between the peaks of dysentery and typhus.[76] By the middle of September, Buchanan was attending a dozen men struck down by this fever and lying in houses adjoining the camp. Others must have been sent to hospital like Private Rushworth who passed away with 'his voice sunk and broke'. He 'would eat & drink such things as were offered but never called for any'. Likewise, Private Muncke 'would neither eat nor drink, nor taste medicines, saying he was certain he must dye & did dye in his tent, our men had taken a dislike to the hospital would rather suffer the injuries of the weather in the field, or think themselves happy if they got into a Boners outhouse & lye on straw'.[77]

Pringle ascribed 'hospital fever' to foul air and, crucially, noticed that those patients lucky enough to avoid Fechenheim normally recovered. Buchanan confirmed Pringle's suspicions about the Fechenheim hospital. Those sent there might recover from the flux, but they 'fevered and died' in a place that was in 'great

---

73 Howell, 'The Story of the Army Surgeon' p.331; Pringle, *Diseases of the Army*, pp.19, 22.
74 Kopperman (ed.), *Regimental Practice*, pp.156, 159, 161.
75 Kopperman (ed.), *Regimental Practice*, pp.161, 164.
76 Pringle, *Diseases of the Army*, p.24.
77 Kopperman (ed.), *Regimental Practice*, p.165.

disorder': that word again. The sick lay 'on straw only in Barns, Stables, outhouses & c'. German princes did not let their allies set up hospitals in their main towns for fear of contagion and, evidently, the Landgrave of Hesse was no exception. This meant that larger public buildings were off-limits. The barns and stables that made up the hospital 'stinke abominably in warm weather, & great swarms of vermine are daily produced so fluxes and fevers were 'universal & very mortal'.[78] At first the sickness was 'moderate' and caused by the 'bad air & Season'. Later it grew contagious and infectious (Buchanan uses both terms interchangeably) and those tending the sick died 'so fast' that the sick were 'neglected and abandoned': of fourteen surgeon's mates, nearly all fell sick and five died. The hospital fever was doubtless typhus when one reads the symptoms listed by Pringle, *petechiae* and *vibices* (blueish-black streaks left by subcutaneous bleeding) gangrene-like 'mortifications', infectiousness (it 'almost surely' struck every patient), and lethality: almost half of patients admitted to Fechenheim died.[79]

Worse was to come. Three thousand patients were left behind when the British army broke up, most at Fechenheim and the rest at Bockenheim and Osthoven which were roomier and healthier hospitals. Patients from all three hospitals were next congregated in a new general hospital at Neuwied. The hitherto relatively healthy patients from Bockenheim and Osthoven 'caught the infection' when they were all embarked on 'bilanders' (small two-masted merchant ships) to Ghent to arrive in the middle of December. Half of the patients died on the long journey, 'the fever having acquired new force by the confinement of the air', and 'many' of the rest died soon after arriving in Ghent in mid-December.

Pringle remarked that the disease bore a 'resemblance to the plague' in that (somehow) it could be spread by clothes or bedding and in support of this theory he noted that the patients embarked on the bilanders had been given old tents for bedding. A merchant at Ghent later bought the tents to refit them and 17 of the 23 journeymen he employed to do the refitting died of 'the same distemper'.[80] Pringle came tantalisingly close to identifying the cause of typhus, but faltered at the final hurdle. James Lind is best known for his work on scurvy but he had a further insight into typhus or 'Jail distemper' which offered practicable and effective control measures. He doubted that the disease was generated and spread by bad air, citing disappointing experiments with ventilators in hospitals. Lind blamed a localised and 'envenomed' source of effluvia, poison seed, or 'corpuscle' which was to be found, he reasoned (correctly), in contaminated clothing. In support of this hypothesis Lind noted that 'poor negroes' shipped as slaves and kept almost naked were less prone to jail distemper than transported felons or soldiers in troop-ships clothed in dirty rags.[81]

The death toll in the hospitals was grave: 640 died in Fechenheim, 397 in Neuwied, 122 in the base hospital at Ghent, and at least 2,000 while being ferried down the Rhine or shortly after disembarking at Ghent. The toll does not include the hospitals

---

78   Kopperman (ed.), *Regimental Practice*, p.157.
79   Pringle, *Diseases of the Army*, p.25.
80   Pringle, *Diseases of the Army*, p.27.
81   Lind, *An essay on the most effectual means of preserving the health of seamen in the Royal Navy*, pp.309, 314, 317.

of Bechtheim, Octhoven, or Wied, the 500 men taken prisoner at Aschaffenburg, or the scattering of men who died in the camp infirmary at Hanau but, amounts, at the very least, to 19.8 percent of a total strength of 16,000.[82] Though grave, the death toll was, in relative terms, less than half that of the French in Lombardy in 1734-5 or in Roussillon in 1674. There are important circumstantial differences, not least that the French stretched the campaigning season by two months in 1734 into torrentially wet and cold weather. Or perhaps hospitals were getting better.

Portugal 1762-63

A large Franco-Spanish army set about invading central Portugal in 1762 in pursuit of the 'Family Compact', a Bourbon alliance to attack British colonial and merchant interests.[83] Delays in this offensive gave the British time to ship an expeditionary force.[84] The first wave comprised a detachment of Burgoyne's Dragoons and two regiments (Armstrong's and Blayney's) that had embarked at Cork.[85] The second echelon consisted of four infantry regiments under John Campbell, 4th Earl of Loudoun, which sailed from the occupied island of Belle-île-en-Mer. These four regiments arrived in Lisbon in the third week of July, making a total of over 5,000 men.

Table 5.2 British Expeditionary Force in Portugal 1762[86]

Unit	Officer Commanding	Strength
16th Light Dragoons	Colonel Burgoyne	200
3rd Foot	Colonel George Howard	825
9th Foot	Lord Blayney	1,000
67th Foot	Colonel Hamilton Lambert	824
75th Foot	Colonel Marescoe Frederick	800
83rd Foot	Colonel Bigoe Armstrong	1,000
85th Light Infantry	Colonel John Crawford	600
Total		5,249

Loudoun would be second-in-command to Wilhelm, Count of Schaumburg-Lippe, a German noble. On 25 August 1762 the Bourbons besieged and captured the key border fortress of Almeida. Meanwhile, Lippe sent a detachment along the Tagus which took the Spanish border city of Valencia de Alcántara by surprise

82   Pringle, *Diseases of the Army*, p.27.
83   Patrick J. Speelman, 'Strategic Illusions and the Iberian War of 1762' in Speelman and Danley eds, *The Seven Years' War: Global Views*, p.431.
84   Instructions for Lord Tyrawly as G.O.C. of the British forces in Portugal, 22 Feb. 1762 in SP 89/55/28, fol. 82.
85   *The London Chronicle for the Year 1762* (London, n.d.), xi, p.302.
86   Return of the 83rd Regiment, Cork, 10 April 1762 TNA WO 17/204; Richard Cannon, *Historical record of the Sixty-seventh, or the South Hampshire Regiment* (London: Parker, Furnivall and Parker, 1849), p.6.

on 27 September. Most of the British infantry regiments were kept initially near Abrantes, a central location, to act as a reserve.[87] Hearing that Almeida had fallen, Lippe hastened north on 2 September, taking five of the British regiments, leaving Burgoyne's Dragoons and Crawford's behind to cover the frontier between Portalegre and Villa Velha.[88] Lippe feared an attack from Almeida against Coimbra that might threaten communications between Lisbon and Oporto.[89] It was a punishing march over the distance of about 112 miles and of the four regiments or 3,500 British who set out, all but 737 had fallen by the wayside before they reached their destination, near Coimbra.[90] Quickly, however, Lippe realized that the real threat lay in a Bourbon march towards the Tagus and by 19 September he had raced back to Abrantes and thence westwards to block this thrust. Four of the British regiments (Lambert's had been left 50 miles north to guard the river Alva) raced north-east to Macao and Sobrira Formosa where they put on an 'admirable countenance'.[91] Lippe then pulled together a line of defence along the Zêzere River and held it until late-October when heavy rains swelled the Zêzere and a Bourbon crossing was no longer to be feared.[92] A month later, Lippe was told that an armistice had been agreed. The conflict is known in Portuguese historiography as the *Guerra Fantástica* or 'Fantastical War' and is so called because of the unreal or phoney quality of a war with so little fighting. However, there was marching, and dying, aplenty.

The distribution of the hospitals at any one time mirrors the general push of the army up the Tagus as far as the border with Spain as well as the thrusts north and south of that axis of advance. On 22 June, the first general hospital was opened for British troops at Lisbon under Dr William Young assisted by two physicians, three surgeons, and 18 assistant surgeons or surgeon's mates whose relative salaries of twenty, ten and five shillings a day respectively conveys the relative status of these medical practitioners. Young later removed to Santarem, which served as the general or fixed hospital from August onward. The hospital at Lisbon took in the sick from the camp near Coimbra who had been evacuated by sea from Oporto but otherwise it was a resort of 'malingerers', together with 'incurables and tedious cases'.[93] A snapshot of the distribution of hospitals and their relative size between 27 October and 5 November 1762 shows a half-dozen regimental or flying hospitals widely scattered where the army was, or had recently been, operating. These were to 'be set up in tents behind the regiment when towns are not nearby'.[94] The distances do not do justice

---

87   Friedrich Wilhelm Ernst von Schaumberg-Lippe (ed. James Ferrier), *Mémoire de la Campagne de Portugal de 1762* (Place of Publication Unknown: Publisher Unknown, 1770), p.11; A.D. Francis, 'The Campaign in Portugal, 1762', *JSAHR* 54, (1981), p.3.

88   Francis, 'The Campaign in Portugal, 1762', p.35; Lippe, *Mémoires*, p.11.

89   Richard Cannon, *Historical record of the British Army: The Third Regiment of Foot* (London: Adjutant General's Office, 1839), pp.186-187; Francis, 'Campaign in Portugal, 1762', pp.35-36.

90   Speelman, 'Strategic Illusions and the Iberian War of 1762', p.450.

91   Lippe to Earl of Egremont, Macao 10 October, *London magazine or Gentleman's monthly intelligencer*, Vol.31 (November 1762), p.597.

92   Lippe, *Mémoire*, pp.4, 52.

93   Young to Loudoun, Santarem, 13 September 1762 MS0192/2fos 91r and 91 v; Unk to Young, Miranda de Corva, 15 September 1762, Loudon MS0192/2 fo 94r.

94   Young to Loudon, Santarem 20 September, Loudon MS0192/2, fo., 99.

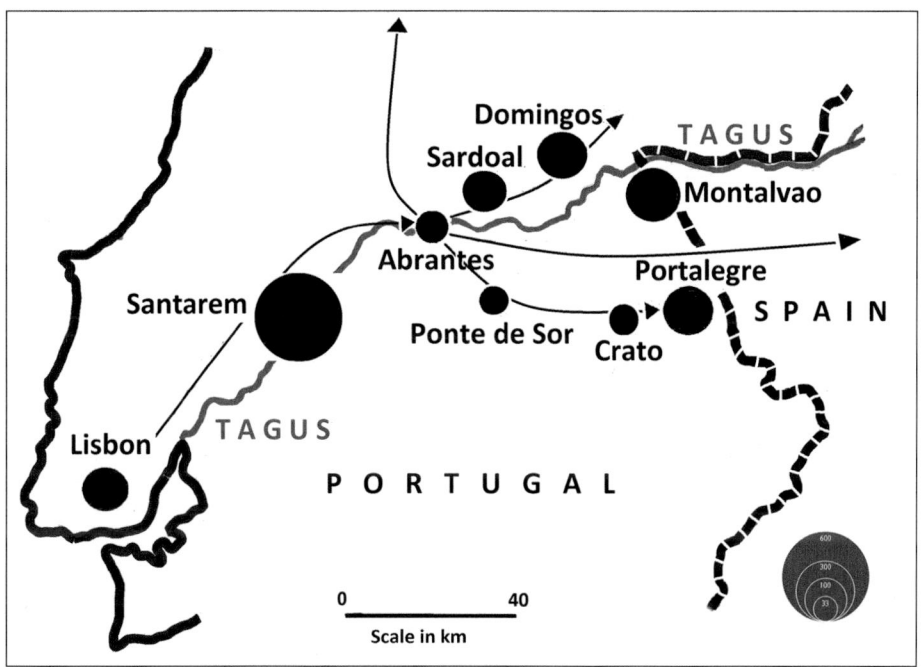

5.4 British hospitals in Portugal, 1762-63.

to just how widely dispersed the hospitals really were, given that overland transport was punishingly difficult and that Abrantes was the furthest upriver that the army could rely on water transport. The hospitals at 'St Domingo' (presumably Domingos da Vinha), Montalvão, and Portalegre were the main flying hospitals in late October and early November but their relative size waxed and waned (Montalvão's prominence was only temporary) as the army marched hither and thither. Sardoal, Ponte de Sor, and Crato were simply places on the advance or retreat where laggards were left behind under the care of a sergeant or a surgeon's mate. Abrantes was a transit camp or station and, intermittently, a 'temporary' hospital that lay 'half way and between' Santarem and the flying hospitals. Some form of triage, properly speaking, seems to have been envisioned where 'slight cases' could recuperate all the sooner without a further long journey while 'bad cases' would not 'run the risk of their lives' on the eight-hour journey by water from Abrantes back to Santarem.[95] Did all these various hospitals amount to an articulated system or to a fragmented hodgepodge? The answer lies in the sickness and mortality statistics and, for once, these are adequate.

95   Young to Loudon, Santarem, n.d., 'Proposals on establishing a Temporary Hospital', Loudon MS0192/2, fo 130.

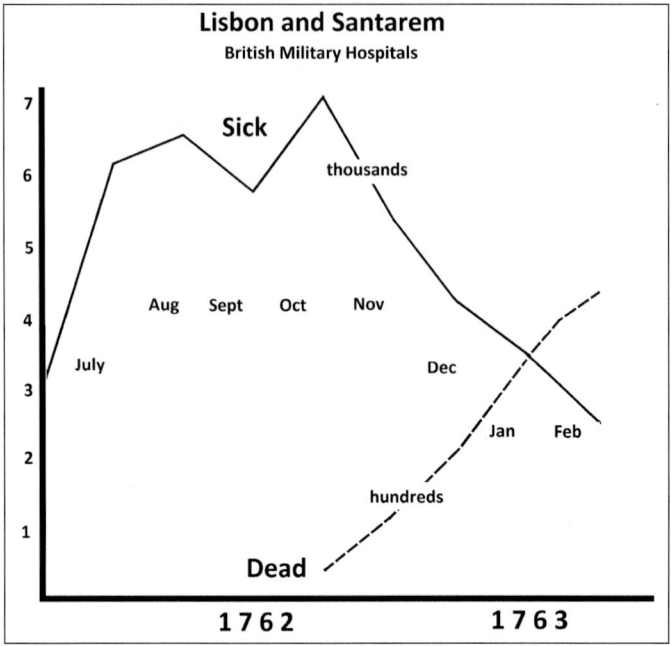

5.5 Lisbon and Santarem: patient numbers and mortality.

The graph of patient numbers in Lisbon and Santarem reveals two peaks.[96] The first spike captures the worst of the fevers and fluxes, some of the 'putrid kind'.[97] Sick returns from Abrantes show that of the 54 sick men in the 'Buffs', to take a typical example, 13 had been struck down with fever, another 13 were down with flux, and one poor fellow was afflicted with 'flux and fever'.[98] The 'flux' was of course dysentery and the 'fever' most likely malarial, since the Tagus basin comprised one of Portugal's four historic malarial hotspots.[99] The second morbidity spike followed the deterioration in the weather in mid-October and no doubt represented a continued, if declining incidence of dysentery and malaria topped-up by a third disease, a fever. This was 'malignant', 'very fast', and 'infecting'. It was also deadly: on 1 February, an officer left behind with the sick when the army evacuated Portalegre complained that he had recently lost 23 men to the disease and that many of the orderlies left

96 An Account of the Sick in the Hospital at Lisbon 17 July 1762 to 18 March 1763, Loudon MS 0/92/1, fos.,41, 44, 51r, 58r, 70r, 83r, 95r; Loudon MS0192/2fos. 113, 120,142, 157r, 193, 233, 276, 283, 294, 306, 308, 312: 'Account of the Sick in the hospital at Santarem' 20 September 1762 to 17 February 1763, Loudon MS0192/2, fos. 111, 129, 133, 149,165v, 178, 198, 217, 253, 257, 266, 286, 296.

97 Hugh Smyth to Loudoun, Santarem, 13 August 1762, Loudon MS0192/1, fo 61 v.

98 Sick Returns, Abrantes, 1 September, Loudon MS0192/2, fos 79-82.

99 Eduardo Gomes, et al., 'Mapping Risk of Malaria Transmission in Mainland Portugal Using a Mathematical Modelling Approach', *PLoS One*. 2016; 11:11, (2016): https://www.ncbi.nlm. nih.gov/ (accessed 05/04/2019).

behind had also succumbed.[100] William Cadogan, the physician in charge at Lisbon, left an account on 21 October of his own disabling illness.[101] In late August he had been 'seized with a violent flux' but was beginning to recover from 'extreme weakness' when at the beginning of October he was

> …seizd with the most malignant fever that ever was. It did not let me close my eyes for three weeks nor suffer me to remain either in bed or out of bed long enough to hope for a moment's sleep at last by the use of laudanum I have obtained a few deceitful intervals but I cannot recover having yet not the slightest appetite nor natural rest. I am daily & hourly sinking into more pain and weakness…[102]

Cadogan was granted permission to go home and recovered sufficiently to complain of rivals soliciting for his post and beseeched Loudon 'not to let the crows eat me before I am dead'.

'We have been very sickly here for some time past', reported Young from Abrantes on 2 December, 'and a very bad fever now prevails which carrys off a good many Men'.[103] Shortly after this report, however, Young opined that 'our sickness here [is] rather diminished' and the fevers 'not so malignant'.[104] He would be proved quite wrong. The graph shows the numbers of dead continued to rise more sharply than ever, even as the numbers in hospital tumbled. Mortality peaked in January, the coldest and wettest month of the year as it had with the typhus outbreak in Lombardy in 1734-35. Sixty-two patients passed away in Santarem hospital between 8 and 30 January and 21 died in Portalegre between 12 January and 3 February. From Abrantes came complaints of 'rather more than usual' sickness and, especially, 'malignant fevers' amongst the troops in the town.[105] Given the timing and level of case mortality, among other indices, one can be fairly sure that this second spike was largely caused by typhus.

The British were creditably successful in coping with a full three-phase epidemic beginning with dysentery and culminating in typhus. In all they lost about 800 men through sickness, just over half in the hospitals of Lisbon and Santarem and the rest in the flying hospitals or while jolted in carts over rutted tracks or packed like sardines into river boats.[106] That figure of 800 represents about 15 percent of the whole army, five percent less than the figure for the British army in Germany in 1743, which itself ran at less than half the mortality rate of the French army in

100 Francis Roper to unk., Portalegre 1 Feb 1763 Loudon MS0192/3, fo 285; Earl of Loudoun to Earl of Egremont, Portalegre 11 December 1762, The National Archives, SP 89/57/99 fol. 279
101 William Cadogan to Loudon, Lisbon 21 October 1762, Loudon MS0192/2, fo 137.
102 J. Rendle-Short, 'William Cadogan, Eighteenth Century Physician' Medical History,4:4 (1960), pp.288-309.
103 Young to Loudoun, Santarem 2 December, Loudon MS0192/2, fo 197r; Francis Tomkins to Young, Montalvão 16 December 1762, Loudon MS0192/2 fo 149fo 225.
104 W. Young to Colonel Cosnan, Adjutant General, Santarem, 11 Dec 1762, Loudon MS0192/2 fo 216.
105 Francis Tomkins to Young, Montalvão, 27 January 1763. Loudon MS0192/2, fo 280.
106 Speelman, 'Strategic Illusions and the Iberian War of 1762', p.450.

Lombardy during that wretched winter of 1734-5. Hospital mortality was, of course, higher (one fifth of those who left Santarem hospital did so in coffins) but not excessive for the time. How is this success to be explained?

Initially, the general hospital seemed likely to serve as the vector for a typhus epidemic. Successive hospital directors pressed the local *corregidor* to acquire the Jesuit College in Santarem. This building was large enough to accommodate 300 inmates, sat atop an airy hill and was abundantly supplied with water but Young had to make do with a smaller building capable of holding just 120 patients who were 'in want of necessaries of all sorts' with nearly half of them lying on the floor. The overspill was scattered in 'many old houses that are in bad repair and not water tight'.[107] One would expect a severe typhus epidemic in these conditions and a clue to understanding why the outbreak was not more severe can be glimpsed in the graph of morbidity and mortality in Lisbon/Santarem (see image 5.5). Counter-intuitively, the number of patients in the hospital and its outliers fell rapidly during the worst of the typhus epidemic.

The hospital director seems to have deliberately kept numbers low in the hospital, in defiance of standing orders that patients be moved to the general hospital as soon as possible. Young pleaded with Loudon to allow the surgeon's mate to judge if the journey might kill the patient, warned of the 'inconveniency' of sick men being moved from place to place, and pointed out that no fewer than fourteen patients had recently died on their way from Montalvão to Abrantes.[108] He also kept numbers low by discharging convalescents to recuperate in billets. By the end of December there were almost as many (390) convalescents billeted in Santarem as there were sick in the hospital itself and almost half of those convalescents were still sick enough to be 'unfit for duty'.[109]

To sum up, the British developed an articulated, flexible, and integrated system that comprised a base hospital at Lisbon, a general hospital at Santarem, a 'half-way' hospital at Abrantes, and, finally, the flying hospitals. Once cannot really include within the meaning of system the many places where small groups of sick men were left behind and, commonly, neglected. The success of the system can be inferred from the relatively low mortality during a strenuous campaign in rough countryside and an unfamiliar climate. Young's determination to keep numbers in the general hospital low must have been the key to heading off a full-scale typhus epidemic and the frightful mortality that brought.

In this respect he anticipates the advice of Donald Monro who was struck by the mortality pattern across the Brigade of Guards at Paderborn in the winter of 1760-61. The 1st and 3rd Regiments lost 'several' (by which he meant one third) of the men to 'malignant fever' because they were left in a 'particular' hospital by themselves. This happened even though the wards were 'as clean and well-aired as possible', the patients had clean bedding, each man had 'clean linen' and the patients were 'laid

107 Hugh Smyth to Loudoun, Santarem 13 August 1762, Loudon MS0192/2 fo 61 v; Young to Loudoun Santarem 15 October, Loudon MS0192/2, fo 125.
108 Young to Loudon, Santarem 8 January 1663, Loudon MS0192/3, fo 252.
109 Young, 'A Return of the Convalescents of different Regiments in billets at Santarem 1 January 1763', Loudon MS0192/3, fo.244.

thin'. The Coldstream, or 2nd Regiment, and the grenadiers happened to be scattered piecemeal in smaller overflow hospitals and they lost few by comparison.[110] More explicit was Jean Colombier who deplored packing the soldier off unnecessarily to the fixed hospital to be exposed to 'deadly contagion'. Would it not be much better, he pleaded, for a soldier to be treated by his own regimental surgeon 'a man he knows, and is known to, and whom he trusts'?[111]

Conclusion

There was a general tendency to prefer the general or fixed hospital over the field hospital at the outset of our period, but seventy years later physicians and, especially, surgeons were less convinced of the merits of the general hospital and worried that 'corruption of the air' made bigger hospital more dangerous than smaller ones.[112]

> Among the chief causes of sickness and mortality in an army, the reader will little expect that I should rank what was intended for its health and preservation, the hospitals themselves – and that on account of the bad air and other inconveniences attending them.[113]

Public sanitation, better diet, and medical breakthroughs, roughly in that order, drove death rates downwards from the closing decades of the nineteenth century in the West. As discussed in Chapter 1, the hospital was a necessary precondition for the medical innovations as a place where clinicians could practice, and prove, their cures. According to Pringle, who was 'the greatest single figure in eighteenth-century military medicine', sanitation presented a huge challenge in the hospital, where the core objective – isolation of the sick – intensified a disease outbreak within the isolated population.[114] A new technique or technology may well be better than that which it supplanted, in the long run. However, in the short run, the new will often be worse. One thinks, for example, of the arquebus that displaced the longbow which latter was more accurate and had a higher rate of fire. Persisting with a new technique or technology sometimes requires irrational optimism or an overriding conviction that the new way is, if not measurably better in terms of outcomes, somehow more appropriate. The preference for isolating the sick in hospitals reflected less a belief that it would yield better medical outcomes than a growing intolerance of 'disorder' and was of a piece with the top-down disciplinary impulse to contain and regulate, to dress soldiers in uniforms, drill them, count them, stop them marauding, and extrude their women from camp and train.[115]

---

110 Monro, *An Account of the Diseases,* p.3.
111 Colombier, *Préceptes sur la santé des gens de guerre*, pp.324, 355.
112 Baldinger, *Von den Krankheiten einer Armee*, p.114; Bessel, *Entwurf eines Militair-Feld-Reglement*, p.317.
113 Pringle, *Diseases of the Army*, cited in Graham A. J. Ayliffe, and Mary P. English, *Hospital Infection: From Miasmas to MRSA* (Cambridge: Cambridge University Press, 2003), p.89.
114 Kennett, *French Armies in the Seven Years' War*, p.134.
115 Schomberg to Louvois, Camp at Saint-Jean de Pages, 12 August 1674, *SHD* A¹ 415, no. 84.

Wartime hospitals could not actually cure the major diseases, which would not really be curable before antibiotics. The increasingly fashionable variant of Hippocratic medicine espoused by Pringle, Lind, and Colombier laid great emphasis on environment and, specifically, vitiated air. This miasmic model, which would persist until Pasteur and germ theory, would do some incidental good insofar as it promoted camp sanitation and cleanliness. On the other hand, the miasmic paradigm obscured the real cause of typhus and it was not until the end of the period under review that James Lind began to suspect that typhus was not spread through the air.[116] The continuing and intensifying use of venesection, purges, and emetics embodied, at least, a comforting ritual. However, the incarceration (and the military hospital was a lock-up policed by an armed guard) and isolation of a hospital represented a downright harmful innovation.

A bad hospital is worse than no hospital when it acts as an 'epidemic amplifier'. This happened in 1976, for example, at the fatally primitive Yambuku and Maridi Mission Hospitals in Zaire (as it was then called) where Ebola was transmitted by such mechanisms as dirty needles to nearly half of the patients who were admitted for other complaints.[117] However, sometimes even a good hospital was worse than no hospital when the air of that hospital, as it was commonly (mis)understood, generated typhus.

Given the prevalence of iatrogenic disease, did the military hospital mostly care and/or cure or did they mostly kill? Did the win/lose outcomes get better or worse over time?

The answer must be sought in mortality rates. It is true, but unhelpful, to simply note that 'hospitals differed'.[118] However fragmentary and inadequate the data, a statistical evaluation of how many died compared to how many were discharged cannot be postponed. Physician John Millar claimed that 'nearly one half of the sick' in the British army died in the War of the Austrian Succession. Monro cholerically accused Millar of producing 'counterfeited returns', but Monro's rebuttal is unsatisfactory. He obfuscates, claims that no deaths occurred for an improbably long period and, in a 'dog ate my homework' moment, pleaded that the relevant records that would support him had been burnt.[119] The equivalent proportion for the Seven Years War was one third, which is very close to Colombier's estimate of 30 percent for the French service in that same war.[120] That is as good as it got: mortality

---

116 Ayliffe and English, *Hospital Infection: From Miasmas to MRSA*, p.90.

117 Laurie Garret, *The Coming Plague: Newly Emerging Diseases in a World Out of Balance* (New York: Penguin, 1995), pp.128, 130, 145-146.

118 Mary Lindemann, *Medicine and Society in Early Modern Europe* (Cambridge: Cambridge University Press, 1999) pp.158, 176, 184-87.

119 J. Millar, *Observations on the practice of the medical department of the Westminster General Dispensary. London: by order of the Governors, 1777* (London: Publisher Unknown, 1777) p.75; Donald Monro, *Observations on the means of preserving the health of soldiers; and of conducting military hospitals* (London: J. Murray, 1780), pp.324-330; Ulrich Tröhler, M.D, 'Quantification in British Medicine and Surgery 1750-1830, with special Reference to its Introduction into Therapeutics', pp.54, 426; http://jameslindlibrary.org (accessed 05/04/2019).

120 The English Secretary-At-War of the day noted that by the 'usual computation' one third of the sick of the English corps in Germany in December 1760 would die before the next

rates in the British army during the early years of the Peninsular War (1808-14) ran as high as 60 percent, though they tumbled subsequently.[121] These estimates relate to *all* hospitals from the fixed hospital to the camp infirmary: hard data for fixed hospitals reveal a much lower number of patients who died of sickness as compared to the numbers discharged. There are a few points to note before attempting to discern general patterns of progress, or otherwise.

Table 5.3 Fixed Hospital Mortality Rates[122]

War	Theatre	Troops	Mortality
Nine Years War (1689-97)	Catalonia	Spanish	14.1
War of the Spanish Succession (1701-1714)	Catalonia 1706	British	38
War of the Spanish Succession (1701-1714)	Valencia 1706	British	14
War of the Polish Succession (1734-35)	Milanese	French	12.5
War of the Austrian Succession (1740-48)	Germany, Flanders	British	11.88
Seven Years War (1756-63)	Saxony 1756	Prussia	24.4
Seven Years War (1756-63)	Rhineland 1761-2	French	6
Seven Years War (1756-63)	Brittany 1758	French	30
Seven Years War (1756-63)	Hanover 1758	French	44

campaigning season Tony Hayter (ed.), *An Eighteenth-Century Secretary at War: The Papers of William Viscount Barrington* (London: Army Records Society, 1988), p.62; Colombier, *Code de médecine militaire pour le service de terre*, p.299.

121 Jack Edward McCallum, *Military Medicine: From Ancient Times to the 21st Century* (Santa Barbara CA: ABC-CLIO, 2008), p.219.

122 Hospital de Santa Cruz (Barcelona) in 1694; Christopher Storrs, 'Health, Sickness and Medical Services in Spain's Armed Forces c.1665–1700', *Med Hist.* 50:3 (Jul., 2006), pp.325–350; L'Arxiu General i Fotogràfic, Hospital General de València, Relació de malats ingressants HG.IV.2.1,1/155, pp.8-30; 'Llibres d'entrades de soldats anglesos. 1706-1707', fons historic de l'Hospital de la Santa Creu, Biblioteca de Catalunya AH136; Paul. E. Kopperman, 'Medical Services in the British Army, 1742–1783', *Journal of the History of Medicine and Allied Sciences*, 24:4 (1979), p.454; Luh, *Kriegskunst in Europa*, p.68. This figure relates to the first six months of the war; 'Etat general du movement journalier des soldats, cavaliers, entrés, sortis, morts, et journées en total dans chacun des hôpitaux sédentaires de l'armée du bas Rhin à commencer du 1er juin 1761 jusqu'au 1er juin 1762', SHD A¹ 3621 no. 288; B. Fonssagrives, 'Recherches historiques sur l'epidémie qui en 1758 ravagea l'escadre de l'amiral Dubois de la Motte et la ville de Brest', *Annales d'hygiene publique*, 2:12 (1859) p.243-4; Lind, *An Essay on Most Effectual Means Preserving the Health of Seamen*, pp.323-32; M. Poissonnier-Desperrières, *Traité des Maladies des Gens de Mer* (Paris: Imprimerie Royale, 1780), pp.297-301; Camille Rousset, *Le comte de Gisors, 1732-1758: étude historique* (Paris: Didier, 1868), pp.373-374; Loudon MS0192/3, fos., 129, 142, 149, 165, 178, 198,217, 237, 253, 266, 286, 294, 296; The Prussians massed troops in Silesia and in Saxony, on the borders of Bohemia, during the desultory operations. Of the total 50,983 patients admitted to the *Hauptfeldlazareth* at Neisse and the various six field hospitals, 9,607 [18.8 percent] of them died and the rest recovered. Johann Gottlieb Fritze, *Das königlich Preussische Feldlazareth. im Kriege von 1778 und 1779* (Leipzig: Weygand, 1780), pp.434-5, 453; Sir George Ballingall, 'Lectures on Military Surgery' in *The Medico-Chirurgical Review* (London, 1833), p.429; Sir James McGrigor, *Sketch of the Medical History of the British Armies in the Peninsula of Spain and Portugal* (London: Publisher Unknown, 1815), p.482.

Seven Years War (1756-63)	Portugal 1762	British	20.4
War of the Bavarian Succession (1778-79)	Saxony, Silesia	Prussian	18.8
Napoleonic Wars	Iberia	British	5.6-9.7

5.6 Register of L'Hopital de la Santa Creu 1706: British troops.

British hospitals seem to have grown 'more proficient' in time of war, only for the painfully accumulated know-how to be forgotten in peacetime. From the first large-scale land operations of the War of the Austrian Succession on the continent in 1742 until the close of 1743, 6,104 men were admitted to hospital of whom 20.3 percent died. However, from the start of 1744 to the end of the war in 1748, 24,612 British soldiers entered and only 9.8 percent died. The rate in the table is 11.88 overall, which is an average of the earlier and later figures.[123] Of course, it could

---

123 Kopperman, 'Medical Services in the British Army, 1742–1783', pp.453-454.

be that higher mortality at the beginning of each war reflects, not improvements in medical treatment, but the predominance of raw recruits in recently raised or expanded armies and what we saw to be the vulnerability of newcomers to demoralisation and to crowd diseases.

The second point is the sheer variability of hospitals. The Spanish and Dutch had been the pace-setters in medical provision for most of the 17th century, but from the latter decades of that century they were overtaken by France and Britain. The Prussians were furthest behind and Frederick the Great's medical services relied largely on the *feldsheerer* or barber-surgeon.[124] It would be hazardous to infer French pre-eminence from the low mortality in French hospitals on the Lower Rhine in 1761-62: when the dead (2,435) and the discharged (37,609) are added together the dead represent only six percent of the whole. The fact that directors were forbidden to admit soldiers struck with 'incurable sickness' doubtless helped to keep mortality rates down because the incurables obligingly died off the books.[125] Moreover, two other French hospital case studies from the Seven Years War show a very high mortality rate. The surviving ships of Comte Dubois de la Mothe's expedition to Cape Breton Island straggled into Brest on 3 November 1758 and disgorged their typhus-ridden sailors and soldiers into the local military and naval hospitals. The disease continued to rage for another three months until it abated quite suddenly in early February. The total number of sailors who had died by then in the overcrowded hospitals was 2,518 compared to 5,842 who had been discharged. The second emerged when the Comte de Clermont took over command of the French forces occupying Hanover in mid-February 1758. He vividly described the hospitals he inspected in terms that are wearisomely familiar.

> The dirt and stench alone would kill the healthiest man. Almost all the doctors, surgeons and attendants are sick and many have died. There are no beds, sheets, medicines and sometimes even no broth.[126]

During the War of Spanish Succession, Barcelona's general hospital recorded 545 admissions of English soldiers, mostly from the regiments of William Breton and Sir Charles Hara, between 26 May and 3 October 1706. Some 38 percent of the British entries were concluded with the notation 'died' [*obita*]. Yet only 14 percent of the troops, Aragonese, Catalan, and English, died among those admitted to the general hospital in Valencia in June of that same year.

Kopperman's verdict on British military hospitals, 'some advance, some retrogression, and in the end a nebulous legacy', holds true for all of the general hospitals.[127]

---

124 Kennett, *French Armies*, p.134.
125 M. Flobert, de, *Mémoires sur la guerre, tirés des originaux de M*** [de Turenne], avec plusieurs mémoires concernant les hôpitaux militaires* (Paris: Rolin,1739), pp.79-80, 192.
126 Rousset, *Le comte de Gisors*, pp.373-374.
127 Kopperman, 'Medical Services in the British Army, 1742–1783', pp.428, 453-454. Kennett, *French Armies*, p.134.

Conclusion

While accepting that each case study is singular and distinct, the time has come to generalize. In aggregate, the case studies do tell us something of what were the killer epidemics afflicting European armies in wartime, how many typically fell sick of these diseases, and how many died. They also point to the strategic, tactical, or logistical conditions most likely to generate an epidemic.

This study began with the preliminary expectation that differences in morbidity and mortality rates would largely be explicable by the distinct tactical scenarios and challenges presented by encampments, sieges, and marches. The last two, it was expected, would present the most severe challenges. In a siege, the immobility of besiegers and besieged let dirt accumulate and so multiplied the choices of food contamination by flies. The besiegers and besieged were also constricted, which multiplied the possibilities of contagion, in the modern sense of the term, namely the person-to-person transmission of morbid matter. A march, and especially a forced retreat from contact with the enemy, could ratchet an epidemic into a catastrophe, as the hopeless cases were left behind, and the walking sick straggled and fell out of the column, to lie down for ever.

Yet the graph in Chapter 4 plotting various mortality trajectories, shows that the second and third sharpest falls actually arose from encampments, at Saint-Jean and Dundalk respectively. Münnich's trek to, through, and from Crimea in 1736 exhibits the sharpest fall of all, but could also be categorized as a camp epidemic since sickness must have been at its worst during the six-week encampment near Perekop, following the gruelling retreat from Bakhchysarai. To these examples of encampments might be added the experience of French regiments quartered in the Rhineland and Lombardy during the winter of 1734-35 that lost between 30 and 60 percent of their strength. Long encampments were central to a typical campaign strategy of limited territorial ambition and subsistence on enemy territory embodied in the phrase, 'occupy, entrench, and wait', and could not but produce a heavy toll of sick soldiers.[1]

Nor, contrary to Pringle's expectation, was there a straightforward relationship between sickness rates and the point at which the commanders chose to end their campaign. Pringle recommended doing so no later than mid-October in northern Europe and this was precisely when the English did so in Ireland (1689) and the French and British did so in the Rhineland (1734 and 1743). Nonetheless, they would all go on to suffer heavily from epidemics.

---

1   Vauban, *A Manual of Siegecraft and Fortification*, p.3.

A more convincing case can be made that susceptibility might arise from the make-up of the army. Did the ranks contain many raw recruits, as tended to be the case at the beginning of wars? Schomberg's army at Saint-Jean, for example, contained thousands of young militiamen who proved especially susceptible to that *maladie du pays*, which is not to be confused with the 'country disease' that afflicted Schomberg's army at Dundalk. The latter army lacked cohesion not just because it was a multinational force, or because an unsettling number of politically unreliable officers and men lurked in the ranks, but because a half-dozen regiments (which proved to be the sickliest) were commanded by colonels who enjoyed no connection to the localities where their troops were recruited.

Can the prevalent or dominant diseases explain morbidity and mortality rates? Imposing a modern diagnostic category on typhoid or any other disease is complicated by the tendency of *ancien regime* physicians to perceive a single shape-shifting sickness that mutated according to season, treatment and circumstances. We saw that the *Morbus Hungaricus*, for example, passed under different names if it reached the head or the throat.[2] Diarrhoeas subtly mutated into fevers and the latter assumed progressively darker gradations from 'bilious' to 'putrid' to 'malignant', according as the qualities of the air grew worse. There is something to be said for the generalized way in which contemporary physicians conceived of camp diseases potentially forming a single seasonal continuum with 'bloody flux' marking the beginning (from mid-August) and 'malignant fever' marking the end (in January or February) of the morbidity and mortality bulge. Flux and malignant fever can be made correspond to modern diagnostic categories but between them in time fell a nebulous sickness which can sometimes be equated with malaria or with typhoid. The Sommerlatte Regiment's experience after embarking at Wischniz for Orsova presents an unambiguous example of a malaria epidemic. It proved harder to recognize typhoid, since the symptoms that distinguish it from flux, namely, continued fever and petechiae, are so similar to those of typhus. It proved necessary to infer typhoid from, among other things, the presence of a likely mechanism, such as the Tech and its tributary streams tainted by run-off from Saint-Jean camp in 1674.

Enough caveats. Table 6.1 ranks most of the case studies in ascending order of gravity and assigns each of them one or, at most, two principal diseases. Table 6.1 confirms that plague was the most lethal disease of all. In almost 60 percent of cases death followed just a few days after the buboes erupted, while the pneumonic variant was almost always fatal. However, bubonic plague was slowly retreating and our only case study concerns the outbreak at Riga in 1709-10, which was almost the last in the Baltic region. By the time of the outbreaks that wiped out two-thirds of the Russian troops garrisoned at Ochakov and Kinburn on the Black Sea coast in 1737-38, the plague had retreated to its original reservoir on the Pontic steppes. Table 6.1 also shows that dysentery alone caused monthly mortality rates of 6-10 percent, with the exception of British troops despatched to Portugal in 1762. This exception reflects real progress in medical care. Table-6-1 further shows that typhus doubled monthly mortality rates to between 10-20 percent, with the exception of the

---

2   Günther Christoph Schelhammer, *De Genuina Febres Curanda Methodo* (Jena: Johann Bielck, 1693), p.207.

British troops in Germany in 1743 which exception probably demonstrates, again, the emerging superiority of British army medical care compared to that of its allies and enemies.[3]

Table 6.1 Monthly Mortality Rates (Rounded)

Place	Time	Troops	Disease(s)	Percent
Ukraine	Jan. 1738	Russian	Plague	22
Hungary	1691	Bavarian	Dysentery & Typhus	18
Ireland (Dundalk)	1689	British	Dysentery & Typhus	14
Rhineland	1734-35	French	Dysentery & Typhus	11
Lombardy	1734-35	French	Dysentery, Typhoid & Typhus	10
Roussillon	1674	French	Dysentery & Typhus	10
Serbia	1717	Bavarian	Dysentery	10
Crimea	1736	Russian	Dysentery	9
Bohemia	1742-43	French	Dysentery	9
Serbia	1737	Brunswicker	Dysentery & Malaria	8
Ireland (Derry)	1689	British	Dysentery & Typhoid	8
Rhineland	1743	British	Dysentery & Typhus	2
Portugal	1762-63	British	Dysentery	2

The absence of smallpox from Table 6.1 is unexpected, given that it was lethal (for adults as well as children, its primary victims) and was on the increase during the period under review. Chapter 3 noted how Salzmann and Baumler, among other physicians, closely observed the symptoms of the epidemic that afflicted the French and Imperial armies in the Rhineland in the summer and autumn of 1734. Smallpox produces a distinctive rash that progresses to pus-filled blisters. These physicians could tell the difference between varioles and petechiae and were clear that the smallpox epidemic had largely spluttered out just before the 1734 campaign began. In short, if smallpox was the main component of this and other outbreaks of camp diseases one would expect physicians and surgeons to have noted that fact. They did not.

Smallpox should have found optimum conditions in wartime camps with the attendant 'chaos, connections, and a steady supply of susceptible victims'.[4] And in fact half the manpower of the Continental expedition that invaded Canada in 1776 was 'destroyed' by smallpox: 'Our Misfortunes in Canada, are enough to melt an Heart of Stone', lamented John Adams, adding that 'Small Pox is ten times more terrible than Britons, Canadians and Indians together'.[5] Most British soldiers were,

---

3   Luh, *Kriegskunst in Europa*, p.65.
4   Elizabeth A. Fenn, *Pox Americana: The Great Smallpox Epidemic of 1775-82* (New York: Hill and Wang, 2001), p.107.
5   Joshua S. Loomis, *Epidemics: The Impact of Germs and Their Power Over Humanity* (Santa Barbara, CA: ABC-CLIO, 2018), p.44; John Adams to Abigail Adams, 26 June 1776, https://

in contrast, more immune to smallpox since it had long been an endemic child-hood disease to which they had been exposed. Acquired immunity may explain why smallpox was not, apparently, a prime camp disease of European armies.

To sum up, the higher mortality band in Table 6.1 confirms that this was 'an age of typhus'.[6] The key to explaining mortality rates is to understand the conditions that gave rise to this, the deadliest fever.

Of all the non-natural conditions, diet as an explanation for disease predominated at the beginning of the period under review but receded, albeit slowly amongst laymen. Colonel Gustav Ernst Albedyll's reports from Riga of 30 May and 6 June 1710 complains of inflated food prices and soldiers eating carcasses, cats, and dogs. Münnich initially blamed the epidemics at Ochakov and Kinburn on hunger. There was some basis to such claims. Land scurvy resulted from a diet heavily reliant on salted meat and biscuit and lacking fruit and greens and was most prevalent at peninsular or island outposts like Gibraltar and Belle-île-en-Mer or in Baltic garrisons. Moreover, hunger can influence the length and severity of dysenteric diseases, though it is less clear if a hungry person is more susceptible to the sickness in the first place. However, the shift to perceiving air, not diet, as a non-natural cause put in place a more useful theory that could inspire good practice. Foul smells were the olfactory manifestation of miasma and 'a camp could commonly be detected by its smell long before it came into view'.[7] Disgust at such noisome vapours drove important changes in camp sanitation, as discussed in the context of Saint-Jean (Chapter 2) and Belgrade (Chapter 3). The end point was a code like that of the Hanoverians which stipulated that it was best to decamp if or when dysentery broke out, but if this were not possible 'the latrines should be dug very deep and earth shovelled over the ordure every day'.[8] As it happened, regulations that soldiers should defecate designated long trench latrines would, if enforced, have reduced the chances of contaminating groundwater, streams, or rivers, and have cut down the transfer of pathogens by flies onto food.

The prevalence of flux would tell us if such rules were actually enforced or if their repetition and elaboration was a symptom of ongoing failure. Nine examples of camp dysentery outbreaks arranged in chronological order in Table 6.2 present a general trend of decreasing morbidity. The fourth example on the list is a fairly typical early example, with peak morbidity hitting 30 percent. In his 1702 Italian campaign, Louis Joseph de Bourbon, duc de Vendôme, left about half his army encamped north of Mantua, and formed the other half into a field army. On 15 August the Austrians attacked him in his fortified camp at Luzzara on the southern bank of the Po. Vendôme beat off repeated attacks and remained camped, in effect, on the battlefield for 54 days until 4 November. A 'great number' succumbed to bloody flux and by October a 'shocking' number of men were being buried every

www.masshist.org/digitaladams/archive/doc?id=L17760626ja (accessed 07/04/2019).

6   J. R. Bruijn, 'Dutch Men of War-Those on Board c. 1700-1750' *Acta Historiae Neerlandicae*: *Studies on the History of The Netherlands* VII (The Hague: Martinus Nijhoff, 1974), p.111.

7   John Childs, *Warfare in the Seventeenth-Century* (London: Cassell, 2001), pp.36-37.

8   Von Bessel, *Entwurf eines Militair-Feld-Reglements*, pp.309, 313.

day at Luzzara.[9] Sickness was worst among the cavalry and by the end of September three-quarters of the troopers in four regiments were out of action.[10] The disproportionately heavy sickness amongst the cavalrymen suggests that the problem really was fly-borne dysentery, because, as noted, flies had a special affinity for horse manure which piled up around cavalry lines.

Table 6.2 Peak Prevalence of Flux[11]

Place	Date	Troops	Percent
Elne	20 September 1674	French	37.5
Dundalk	18 October 1689	British	39
San Pedro Pescador	2 July 1693	French	25
Luzzara	31 October 1702	French	30.8
Belgrade	2 October 1717	Imperial	24.7
Kuppenheim	24 August 1736	French	c.25
Hanau	28 September 1743	British	23
Warburg	11 December1760	British	c.50
Santarem	23 October 1762	British	19.6

The second-last example contradicts the trend of decreasing morbidity. Three battalions of Foot Guards arrived at Warburg camp, in Westphalia, on 25 August 1760 and remained there in a large camp of German and British troops until 11 December. It rained incessantly for several months and 'great sickness' (diarrhoea, dysentery, and 'malignant fever') broke out so that by the time the camp broke up, half the men in the Brigade of Guards were 'unfit for duty'.[12] Warburg, then, was a

9   d'Esgrigny to Chamillart, Camp at Luzzara, 10 October 1702, SHD A[1] 1595, no. 110.
10   Louis XIV to Vendôme, 30 September 1702, SHD A[1] 1591, no. 320.
11   Ayats, *Armées et Santé*, p.130.; A muster on 18 October returned 206 Huguenot *incorporés* effective, 134 sick and 16 dead; Dalton, *English Army Lists*, Vol.III, pp.118-120; Noailles to Barbézieux, Pescador Camp, 2 July 1693, *SHD* A[1] 1237, no. 48; There were 6,766 sick in an army of 21,900: *Mercure Historique et Politique…Mois d'Août 1702* (The Hague, 1702), p.144; Bouchu to Chamillart, Camp at Luzzara, 31 October 1702 *SHD* A[1] 1595, no. 180; Pelet, *Mémoires militaires* ii, pp.743, 752-55; Schuster, *Militärsanitätswesens*, p.21; de Chabannes to Intendant de Brou, Kuppenheim Camp, 24 August 1734, Pajol, *Les guerres sous Louis XV*, Vol.I, pp.255, 270. Chabannes confessed that the number of sick in the hospitals 'scared' him since they amounted to at least a quarter of the whole; Pringle, *Diseases of the Army*, pp.26, 120; half the men in the Brigade of Guards were 'unfit for duty' when the camp broke up in December. Pringle, *Diseases of the Army*, p.278; Walter Evelyn Manners, *Some account of the military, political, and social life of … John Manners, marquis of Granby* (London & New York: Macmillan, 1899), pp.144, 180; Of 5,500 troops, 1,078 were sick. Howill to Loudoun, 23 September 1762, fo. 102: Sick returns from; Santarem, 23 October, fo. 715; Lisbon, 23 October, fo. 117; Abrantes, 23 October, fo. 121; St Domingo 25 October, fo. 125; Sardoal, 9 November, fo. 105; 'An Account of the Sick in the hospital at Santarem between the 19th and 23rd of October 1762' fos. 129 and 133 Loudon MS0192/2; 'An Account of the Sick in the Hospital at Lisbon between the 16th and 23rd of October 1762' Loudon MS0192/3 fo 142.
12   John Pringle, *Observations on the Diseases of the Army* (London: A. Millar,1764), p.278; Manners, *Granby*, pp.144, 180; Heinrich Haeser, *Historisch-pathologische untersuchungen als*

truly exceptional camp both in duration and weather conditions. The commander of the British expedition to Portugal two years later considered his troops 'very sickly', when one in five of them was disabled.[13] Planning for the expedition assumed that the proposed army of 6,000 men (the actual number would be around 5,500) should allow for 800 sick, or just over or 13 percent of the whole. The proportion 'seldom' exceeded that, advised William Young the senior physician with the expedition, unless the army encamped before May, after September, or for a 'long' time.[14] How long was 'long'? Pringle urged armies to move camp twice or more in late summer when the 'flux' begins to spread and so leave behind the 'filth of the camp' and the putrid 'effluvia' or 'vapours' of befouled water, privies and dirty straw.[15]

The unmistakable overall trend revealed by Table 6.2 was towards the decreasing prevalence of flux. It must be recalled that this impressive improvement came about in an epoch when field armies more than doubled in strength, an increase associated with the more rational and efficient administration of the state-commission army. Moreover, armies were in the field for longer: they seldom enjoyed the dog-days respite of yesteryear and more often prolonged their marches and manoeuvres into November. The peak prevalence of bloody flux was a crucial variable since it was not one disease, even one as deadly as typhus, that pushed up mortality rates but, rather, the interaction of dysentery and typhus causing the wartime morbidity and mortality peak of late summer and autumn to spike rather than subside in winter. When deaths in the Vivarais Regiment during the War of the Polish Succession are plotted, a pronounced peak emerges in December 1734.[16] This winter wartime spike, while not regular or predictable, is simply too frequent to be dismissed as an anomaly. If dysentery outbreaks were growing rarer, the state-commission army responded to the 'disorder' of epidemics and to revivified notions of contagion by congregating and incarcerating the sick in large hospitals and so creating the conditions for a typhus epidemic. One innovation, hospitalization, worked against another innovation, sanitation, to keep morbidity and mortality stubbornly high. There was not much progress to celebrate or regress to deplore.

beiträge zur Geschichte der Volkskrankheiten (Dresden and Leipzig: Gerhard Fleischer, 1839), p 309.

13   Earl of Loudoun to Earl of Egremont, Venda Nova 10 Sept 1762 SP 89/57/59 fos. 159-160.
14   Loudon MS 0/92/1, fos. 1 r, 1v.
15   Pringle, Diseases of the Army, pp.102, 174.
16   Corvisier, 'La Mort du Soldat', p.14.

Bibliography

Manuscript Sources

Archives Départementales Bas-Rhin, Registres Paroissiaux, Bischheim: sépultures (1725-1792), Fort-Louis, Hôpital Militaire, sépultures (1716-1734), Hoenheim: sépultures (1685-1758), Illkirch-Graffenstaden: sépultures (1715-1774), Lampertheim: sépultures (1712-1744), Lauterbourg: baptêmes, marriages, sépultures (1720-1738), Mittelhausbergen: sépultures (1686-1742), Ostwald: sépultures (1685-1741), Salmbach: baptêmes, marriages, sépultures (1727-1757), Schiltigheim: sépultures (1637-1738), Wolfisheim: marriages, sépultures (1724-1787).

Archives Départementales de Meurthe-et-Moselle, Registres Paroissiaux, http://www.archives.meurthe-et-moselle.fr/fr/archives-en-ligne.html:Bourscheid: baptêmes, mariages, sépultures (1714-1746), Danne-et-Quatre-Vents: sépultures (1701-1741), Hommarting: baptêmes, mariages, sépultures (1701-1741), Vescheim: sépultures (1725-1783). Nancy: Registres de l'état civil, HôpitalMilitaire Nancy (1713-1714, 1733-1792).

Archives Départementales des Pyrénées-Orientales,'Estat de la despance fait…pour la subsistence des malades', C134; Memorial delssoldats son eixits del ospital general de Perpignan en la mois de Decembre 1674', C131.

Bayerisches Hauptstaatsarchiv, Kasten Schwartz. 1308. (1717).

Bibliothèque nationale de France, Département Cartes et plans, *Cartes des Marches & Campemens de l'Armée du Roy pendant la Campagne 1674*, Marches & Campemens 1675; Marches & Campemens 1676; Marches & Campemens 1677(1680), http://catalogue.bnf.fr/ark:/12148/cb33281721x; GE D-26051.*BNF*, department Cartes et plans, Lager vor Belgrad'. CPL GE DD-2987 (5903).*BNF*, department Cartes et plans, 'Chartederer von der Russisch-Keyser, armee, GE DD-2987 (3055 B). *BNF*, department Cartes et plans, Briffaut, Étienne, 'Théâtre de la guerre sur la Timock, 1737' (Vienna: Unknown Publisher, 1738), GE D-16599. Marsili, Luigi Ferdinando, *La Hongrie et le Danube* (The Hague, 1726-1741), *BNF*, department Cartes et plans, GE BB 565 (13, 15-42), Sectio, XV. Tab. 17. Ordonnance… portant règlement general concernant les hôpitaux militaires… (Paris, 1747). La Hongrie Et Le Danube en XXXI. Cartestrès fidelément gravées d'après les Desseins originaux & les Plans levez sur les lieux par l'Auteurmême. Sectio XV., Tab. 17 *Orsawa – Widdni*http://www.oldmapsonline.org (accessed 18 January 2018).

Hessisches Staatsarchiv Marburg, Russisch-Türkischer Krieg: *Karte der Kriegsoperationen der russischen Armeenan Don und Dnjepr, 1736*. Archivaliensignatur: HStAM\WHK\WHK 20/03.

National Archives of the UK, State Papers, 'Proposal concerning the next year's prosecution of the war in Ireland 1690'. 8/11 f.65; 'Instructions for Lord Tyrawly as G.O.C. of the British forces in Portugal, 22 Feb. 1762'. 89/55/28, fol. 82; 'Return of the 83rd Regiment, Cork, 10 April 1762'. WO 17/204; 'Earl of Loudoun to Earl of Egremont, Portalegre 11 December 1762' 89/57/99 fol. 279.

Österreichisches Staatsarchiv, Kriegsarchiv A, Turkenkrieg 1717, 13: 25. Anon, 'Remarques et Observations dans la campagne 1717'.

Royal College of Surgeons of England, Loudon MS 0192/1; MS0192/2 fos 91r and 91 v; MS0192/2 fo 94r; MS0192/2, fo., 99; MS0192/2, fo 130; MS0192/1, fos. 41, 44, 51r, 58r, 70r, 83r, 95r; MS0192/2 fos. 113, 120, 142, 157r, 193, 233, 276, 283, 294, 306, 308, 312; MS0192/2, fos. 111, 129, 133, 149, 165v, 178, 198, 217, 253, 257, 266, 286, 296; MS0192/1, fo 61 v; MS0192/2, fos. 79-82; MS0192/3, fo 285; MS0192/2, fo 137; MS0192/2, fo 197r; MS0192/2 fos. 149, 225; MS0192/2 fo 216; MS0192/2, fo 280; MS0192/2 fo 61 v, MS0192/2, fo 125; MS0192/3, fo 252; MS0192/3, fo.244; MS0192/3, fos., 129, 142, 149, 165, 178, 198, 217, 237, 253, 266, 286, 294, 296.

Sächsisches Hauptstaatarchiv Dresden 'Letter from Major General VonJasmund to Count Sulkowski, Belgrade, 22 October 1737, SächsischesHauptstaatarchiv, Saxon State Archive, Dresden, Loc. 3281 [unpag.].'General Tabella', Neustadt 15 June 173; 'Tabella', Gradovica 8 October 1737, 'Monaths Tabella', 31 August, 31 October, 30 November, 30 December; 'Tabella' 8 October 1737, Loc. 3281/6 unpag. Monats-Listen und Tabellen vom Rochauischen Infanterie Regiment, 11237, Loc. 10863/1.

StadStarchiv Braunschweig 'NotizenzurGeschichte des Braunschweiger Infantcric Rcgimcnts von Sommcrlattc, nachhcr von Both währcnd dcs FeldzugsnachUngarn 1737-38', H VI 6: 4., fos., 2-4.

Service historique de la défense à Vincennes, Archives Guerre, A12810, A^l 415, A^{l}1322, A^{l}1591, A^{l}2383, A^{l}3006, A^l 3621, GR 1 Yc 602, A^{l}2812, A^{l}3621

Printed Primary Sources

Angeli, Moriz, Edler von, *Feldzüge Des Prinzen Eugen Von Savoyen* (Vienna: KK Generalstabes, 1876).

Anon., *A relation of what most remarkably happened during the last Campaign in Irela*nd (Dublin: James Malone, 1689).

Anon., *A Full and True Account of all the Remarkable Actions and Things that have happen'd in the North of Ireland since 15th of November to the 17th instant…* (London: Richard Baldwin, 1689).

Anon., *Account from Colonel Kirk of the relieving of London-Derry* (Edinburgh: Unknown Publisher, 1689).

Anon, *An Exact account of the raising the siege of Londonderry and the deplorable condition the town was in, till happily reliev'd by Major-General Kirk* (London R. Wood, 1689).

Anon, *An Account of the most remarkable occurrences relating to London-Derry with a relation of the signal defeat given to the French and Irish papists* (London: Richard Baldwin, 1689).

Anon, *An impartial account of the late famous siege of Gibraltar: To which are Added, Most Accurate Plans of the Town, and of the Approaches and Camp.* (London: Warner, 1728).

Anon, *Ausführliche Relation des Herrlichen Sigs* (Munich: Matthias Riedl, 1717).

Anon, *Campagnes de Monsieur le prince Eugène en Hongrie* (Lyon: Thomas Armaulry, 1718).

Anon, *Commercium litterarium ad rei medicae et scientiae naturalis incrementum institutum quo quicquid novissime observatum agitatum scriptum vel per actum est succinted ilucideque exponitur* (Nuremberg: Sumptibus Societatis, 1735).

Anon., *CSPD: William III February 1689-April 1690* (London: H.M. Stationery Office, 1895).

Anon. *Der orientalische Mercurius* (Frankfurt and Leipzig: Unknown Publiher, 1737).

Anon, *Die grossen Thaten...in dem Königreich Ungarn.* (Nuremberg: Unknown Publisher, 1717).

Anon., *Extract-Schreibenaußdem Feld-Lager vor Belgradvom 2. Augusti 1717* (Vienna, 1717).

Anon., *Geschichte und Thaten des jüngstverstorbenen grossen Kriegs-Helden, Ludwig Andreas Grafen Khevenhüller* (Breslau and Leipzig: Unknown Publisher, 1744).

Anon, *Glücks- und Unglücksfälle der Haupt-Vestung Belgradoder Griechisch-Weissenburg* (Augsburg: Unknown Publisher, 1717).

Anon. *La Conduite de Mars* (Rouen: Unknown Publisher, 1711).

Anon., *Lettres historiques, contenant ce qui se passe de plus important...'* (Amsterdam: Adrian Moetjens, 1717).

Anon. 'Memoirs of the Lord Viscount Dundee' in *Miscellanea Scotica* (Glasgow: R. Chapman, 1820).

Anon., *Relation Von der Belagerung Prag* (Unknown Publisher, 1742).

Anon, *The Life and Military Actions of Prince Eugene* (London: T. Read, 1739).

Anon., *The Political State of Great Britain* (London: J. Baker, 1717).

Anon., 'Zapiska o tom, skol'ko ia pamiatuiu o krymskich i turetskikh pokhodakh' http://www.runivers.ru/doc/d2. (accessed 11 December 2017).

Abercromby, David, *A moral discourse of the power of interest* (London: Thomas Hodgkin, 1690).

Allmacher, Johanne Friderico, *De morbis castrensibus defendente,* (Leyden: Rijksuniversiteitte Leiden, 1672).

Andler, R., 'Die württembergischen Regimenter in Griechenland 1687–89', *Württembergische Vierteljahrshelfte für Landesgeschichte,* 31 (1922/4).

Anselm, Heinrich, *Historisches Labyrinth der Zeit: darinnen die Denckwürdigsten Welt...* (Leipzig: Gleditsch, 1718).

Armand Bourgeois, M. (ed.) *Lettres inédites de Jean Devillers d'Epernay* (Reims, Impr. de l'Académie, 1898).

Baldinger, Ernst Gottfried, *Von den Krankheiten einer Armee: auseignen Wahrnehmungen in demletztern preußischen Feldzuge* (Langensalza: Johann Christian Martini, 1765).

Basnage, Jacques *Annales des Provinces-Unies* (The Hague: C. Le Vier, 1726).

Bauermüller, Johann Simon, *Dissertatio. Medica inaugralis de fibre castrensi.* (Würzburg: Unknown Publisher, 1735).

Baumler, G. S., *Kurze Beschreibung des im Wintermonat 1734 zu Germersheim und anderen Orten am Rheinstrom herumgegangenen hitzigen und bösartigen Fiebers.* (Strasbourg: Dulßecker, 1743).

Belle-Isle, Charles Louis Auguste Fouquet duc de, *Campagne de messieurs les maréchaux De Broglie et De Belle-Isle, en Boheme...* (Amsterdam: Marc Michel Rey, 1772).

Bellerive, Jules-Alexis-Bernard, Chevalier de, *Histoire des Campagnes de Monsieur le Duc De Vendosme* (Paris: Saugrain l'aîné, 1715).

Benkotzi, Stephan, *De Febre Hungarica seu Castrensi* (Erlangen: Unknown Publisher, 1759).

Bennet, Joseph, *A true and impartial account of the most material passages in Ireland since December, 1688 with a particular relation of the forces of Londonderry* (London: John Amery, 1689).

Bernard, Jacques, *Lettres Historiques contenant ce qui se passe de plus important en Europe* (Amsterdam: Jacques Desbordes, July 1717).

Berwick, James Fitzjames Duke of, *Mémoires du Maréchal de Berwick* (Paris: Moutard, 1780).

Bessel, Friedrich Wilhelm von, *Entwurfeines Militair-Feld-Reglements*, (Hanover: H. E. C. Schlüter, 1778).

Black, William, *Observations Medical and Political on the Small-pox* (London: J. Johnson, 1781).

Blond, Guillaume Le, *Essai sur la castrametation* (Paris: C.A.Jombert, 1748)

Boate, Gerard, *Irelands naturall history* (London: Samuel Hartlib, 1652).

Boisvillette, Guérineau de (ed.), 'Lettre inédite sur le siège de Prague en 1742, par le fils du comte d'Entraignes, seigneur de Saint-Prest', *Procès-verbaux de la Société archéologique d'Eure-et-Loir, 1861-1863*, (Chartres: Petrot-Garnier, 1864).

Boyer, Abel, *The Political State of Great Britain*, (London: J. Baker, 1717).

Boyle, Robert, *Of the reconcileableness of specifick medicines...* (London: Sam. Smith, 1685).

Boyle, Robert, *An experimental discourse of some little observed causes of the insalubrity and salubrity of the air and its effects* (London: Sam. Smith, 1685).

Brambilla, G. A., *Discours sur la Prééminence et l'utilitité de la Chirurgie* (Brussells: Emmanuel Flon, 1786).

Brocklesby, Richard, *Oeconomical and Medical Observations* (London: T. Becket, and P. A. De Hondt, 1764).

Cabié, Edmond, *Notices communales, Saint-Sulpice-de-la-Pointe* (Toulouse: A. Chauvin, 1876).

Caissel, Sauvé de, *Relation de Ce Qui s'Est Passé En Catalogne* (Paris: G. Quinet, 1678).

Carlyle, Thomas, *Oliver Cromwell's Letters and Speeches: With Elucidations* (London: Chapman and Hall, 1846).

Cazals, Rémy (ed.), *Poilu: The World War I Notebooks of Corporal Louis Barthas, Barrelmaker, 1914-1918* (New Haven CT: Yale, 2015).

Clarke, Rev. J.S., *The Life of James the Second* (London: Smith, Elder & Co., 1816).

Cocula, Anne-Marie (ed.) La Colonie, Jean Marie de, *Mémoires De Monsieur De La Colonie*. (Paris: Mercure de France, 1992).

Colombier, Jean, *Code de medicine militaire pour le service de terre* (Paris: Costard, 1772.

Colombier, Jean, *Préceptes sur la santé des gens de guerre ou hygiene militaire* (Paris: Lacombe, 1775).

Cullen, William, *Nosology: Or, a Systematic Arrangement of Diseases, by Classes, Orders, Genera and Species* (Edinburgh: William Creech, 1800).

Dalrymple, James, *Memoirs of Great Britain and Ireland* (London: W. Strahan and T. Cadell, 1773).

Delaye, A.J., *Formules de médicamens rédigées par ordre du roi, à l'usage des hôpitaux* (Paris: Marseilles: Jean Mossy, 1781).

Diderot, Denis, et al. *Encyclopédie, ou Dictionnaire raisonné des science, des arts et des métiers* (Berne and Lausanne: Société typographique, 1780).

D'Espié, Félix François, *Mémoires de la guerre d'Italie* (Paris: Veuve Duchesne, 1777).

D'Exile, Antoine Francois Prevost, *Histoire generale des voyages* (The Hague: Pierre de Hondt, 1753).

De Beaurain, Jean, *Histoire militaire de Flandres, depuis l'année 1690 jusqu'en 1694* (Paris: Antoine Jombert, 1755).

De Chennevières, François, *Détails militaries dont la connaissance est nécessaire* (Paris: Charles-Antoine Jombert, 1750).

De Homann, Héritiers, 'Kriegs-Expeditions-Carte von Bohmen: Carte des expéditions de la guerre en Boheme' (Nuremberg: Unknown Publisher, 1743).

De Larrey, Issac, *Histoire de France sous le regne de Louis XIV* (Rotterdam: Unknown Publisher, 1718).

De Schmettau, Comte, *Mémoires secrets de la guerre d'Hongrie durant les campagnes de 1737, 1738 et 1739* (Frankfurt: Unknown Publisher, 1771).

Dezon, M., *Lettres sur les Principales Maladies qui ontregné dans les Hospitaux d'Italie en 1734-5-6*, (Paris: Lambert & Durand, 1741).

Drinkwater, John, *History of the Late Siege of Gibraltar: With a Description and Account of that Garrison, from the Earliest Periods* (Dublin: Colles et al., 1786).

Dumont, Jean, *The Military History of the late Prince Eugene of Savoy* (London: W. Rayner, 1737).

Dumoulin, Pierre François, *Campagnes de Messieurs les maréchaux de Maillebois, de Broglie, de Belle-Isle, de Noailles, et de Coigny: l'an 1741-1744*, (Amsterdam: M.M. Rey, 1760).

Duvivier, Fracia des Fleurus, *Observations Sur la Guerre de la Succession* (Paris: J. Corréard jeune, 1830).

Espagnac, Jean-Baptiste Joseph Damarzit de Sahuguet d', *Histoire de Maurice, comte de Saxe* (Paris: Saillant and Nyon, 1775).

Ettmüller, Michael, *Etmullerus abridg'd: or, A compleat system of the theory and practice of physic* (London: E. Harris 1699).

Fallois, Joseph de, *Traité de la castrametation et de la défense des places fortes* (Berlin: J.Decker, 1771).

Faure, Hippolyte, *Hospices de Narbonne. Classement des archives antérieures à l'année 1790 …* (Narbonne: Collard, 1855)

Favier, Pierre, *Quaestio medica proposita … seu anxio patriam repetendi desiderio vulgo maladie du pays* (Avignon: F. Mallard, 1713).

Ferrier, James, (ed.), Friedrich Wilhelm Ernst von Schaumberg-Lippe, *Mémoire de la Campagne de Portugal de 1762* (Unknown Publisher, 1770).

Feuquières, Marquis de, *Mémoires* (Amsterdam: François L'Honore & Zacharie Chatelain, 1741).

Flemming, Hans Friedrich von, *Der Vollkommene teutsche Soldat* (Leipzig: Johann Christian Martini, 1726).

Flobert, M., de, *Mémoires sur la guerre, tirés des originaux de M*** [de Turenne], avec plusieurs mémoires concernant les hôpitaux militaries* (Paris: Rolin, 1739).

Floderus, Gustaf F.,'Jaurnalöfver Staden Rijgas Belägringh' in *Handlingarhörande till Konung Carl XII:s historia* (Stockholm: Unknown Publisher, 1819-26).

Fontenelle, Bernard Le Bovier de *Œuvres* (Paris: Chez Brunet, 1752).

Fontenelle, Bernard Le Bovierde, 'Eloge de Monsieur Chirac', *Œuvres de Monsieur Bernard Le Bovier de Fontenelle* (London: Unknown Publisher, 1785).

Foster, T., (ed.), *Frederick II (King of Prussia), Military Instruction from the Late King of Prussia to His Generals* (London: Cruttwell, 1818).

Fritze, Johann Gottlieb, *Das königlich Preussische Feldlazareth.im Kriege von 1778 und 1779* (Leipzig: Weygand, 1780).

Gaya, Louis de, *L'Art de la Guerre* (The Hague: Adrian Moetjens, 1689).

Gaydon, Richard, (ed. L. Ó Briain) 'The Chevalier Gaydon's Memoir of the Regiment of Dillon, 1738' in *Irish Sword*. no 22, Summer & Winter, 1963.

Gardiner, John, *Observations on the animal oeconomy, and on the causes and cure of diseases* (Edinburgh: Royal Society, 1789).

Gilbert, John Thomas (ed.), *A Jacobite Narrative of the War in Ireland, 1688-1691* (Dublin: J. Dollard, 1892).

Glisson, Francis, *A treatise of the rickets being a disease common to children* (London: P. Cole, 1651).

Grey, Anchitell, (ed.), *Debates of the House of Commons from 1667 to 1694* (London: D. Henry, R. Cave, J. Emonson, 1763).

Griffet, Henri (ed.), *Recueil de lettres, pour servir d'éclaircissement à l'histoire militaire du regne de Louis XIV* (Paris: Antoine Boudet, 1760).

Grimoard, Philippe-Henri de (ed.) René de Froulay de Tessé, *Mémoires et lettres du maréchal de Tessé* (Paris: Treuttel and Würtz, 1806)

Harris, Walter, *The History of the Life and Reign of William-Henry, Prince of Nassau and Orange...* (Dublin: Edward Bate, 1749).

Hautesierck, Richard, de, *Recueil d'Observations de Médecine des Hôpitaux Militaires* (Paris: Imprimerie Royale, 1772).

Helvetius, Jean Claude Adrien, *Lettre de M. Helvetius, Conseiller d'état, premier médecin de la reine* (Paris: Quillau, 1748).

Helvetius, Jean Claude Adrien, *Memoires instructifs sur l'usage de different remèdes specifiques pour les armées du roy, & les malades de la champagne* (Paris: Pierre Le Mercier, 1705).

Hempel, Christian Friedrich, *Leben, Thaten, Und Betrübter Fall, Des Weltberufenen, Russischen, Grafens, Burchards Christophs von Münnich...* (Bremen: Nathaniel Saurmann, 1742).

Hennet, Léon Clément, *Les milices et les troupes provinciales*, (Paris: L. Baudoin, 1884).

Hoelder, Christoph Ferdinand, *De Morbo Castrensi Epidemico* (Württemberg and Stuttgart: Müller, 1736).

Hoffman, Frederick, *Dissertation on Endemial Diseases* (London: Thomas Osborne, 1746).

Hogan, J. (ed.), *Négociations de M. le Comte D'Avaux en Irlande 1689-90.* (Dublin: Government Publications Office, 1934).

Hume, David, (ed.), C.H. von Manstein, *Memoirs of Russia, Historical, Political, and Military* (London: T. Becket and P. A. Hondt, 1770).

Huxham, John, *Observations on the Air and Epidemic Diseases* (London: J. Hinton and Henry Whitfeld, 1759).

'Impartial Hand', An, *A system of camp-discipline, military honours garrison-duty, adjutants-duty, and other regulations for the land forces* (London: J. Millan, 1760).

Inselin, Charles, 'Le Roussillon: Le comté de Roussillon', (Paris: Mr de Beaurin, 1710-1746).

Jackson Lawlor, Hugh (ed.), 'The diary of William King, D.D.: Dean of St. Patrick's, afterwards Archbishop of Dublin kept during his imprisonment in Dublin Castle, 1689' *JRSAI* (1903).

Kane, Richard, *Campaigns of King William and Queen Anne 1689-1712 and A New System of Military Discipline for a Battalion of Foot in Action* (London: Unknown Publisher, 1745).

Keralio, Louis-Félix Guynement de, *Histoire de la guerre des Russes et des impériaux, contre les Turcs* (Paris: Debure 1780).

Khevenhüller, Ludwig Andreas Graf, *Observations Puncten* (Vienna: P. Kraus, 1748).

Kober, Tobias, *Observationum Medicarum Castrensivm Hungaricarvm Decades Tres* (Helmstad: Friedrich Lüderwald, 1685).

Kramer, Johann Georg Heinrich, *Medicina Castrensis* (Nuremberg: Peter Conrad Monath, 1735).

Lecestre, Léon, (ed.), *Mémoires de Saint-Hilaire* (Paris: la Société de l'histoire de France, 1903-16).

Lenihan, Pádraig, and Sidwell, Keith, (eds.), *Poema de Hibernia* (Dublin: IMC, 2018).

Lidl, Johann Jacob, Plan von der Attaque deren Türcken unter den 28. Septembris 1737, alwo das unter commando des Herrn Feld-Marschallen Grafen von Khevenhüller Excellenz stehende Corpo... (Vienna: Unknown Publisher, 1737)

Lind, James, *An Essay on the Most Effectual Means of Preserving the Health of Seamen* (London: G. Wilson and D. Nicoll, 1774).

Mackenzie, John, *A narrative of the siege of London-Derry* (London: Richard Baldwin, 1690).

Malbez, Chevalier de, (ed.) *Campagne de M. le maréchal de Noailles en l'année MDCCXLIII, journal du chevalier de Malbez, commissaire d'artillerie* (Paris: A. Picard 1892).

Manesson-Mallet A., *Les travaux de Mars, ou l'Art de la Guerre* (Paris: Unknown Publisher, 1691).

Manstein, Christoph Hermann von, *Mémoires historiques, politiques et militaires sur la Russie* (Lyon: Jean-Marie Bruyset, 1772).

Marconnay, Thiers de, *Nouvelles découvertes en médecine, ou Ancienne medicine développée* (The Hague: P. Gosse & J. Neulme, 1731).

Marsili, Luigi Ferdinando, *Stato militare dell' Impèrio Ottomanno, incremento e decremento* (The Hague: Pierre Gosse, 1732).

Massuet, Pierre, *Histoire de la Derniere Guerre* (Amsterdam: François L'Honore, 1737).

Massuet, Pierre, *Histoire de la guerre présente, contenant tout ce qui s'est passé de plus important en Italie, sur le Rhin, enPologne et dans la plupart des cours de l'Europe* (The Hague: François l'Honoré, 1735).

Mauvillon, Eleazar, *Histoire de la derniére guerre de Boheme* (Amsterdam: D.Mortier, 1750).

Mauvillon, Eléazar, *Histoire du Prince François Eugene de Savoie…* (Amsterdam: D'Arkstee & Merkus, 1740).

Miall, Bernard, (ed.), *Master Johann Dietz* (London: George Allen & Unwin, 1923).

Millar, J., *Observations on the practice of the medical department of the Westminster General Dispensary. London: by order of the Governors, 1777* (London: Unknown Publisher, 1777).

Molitor, *Dissertatio Inauguralis Medica De Febre Continua Maligna Et Intermittente Tertiana* (Heildeberg: Zinenau, 1736).

Monro, Donald, *An account of the diseases which were most frequent in the British military hospitals in Germany: from January 1761 to the return of the troops to England in March 1763* (London: A. Millar et al., 1764).

Monro, Donald, *Observations on the means of preserving the health of soldiers; and of conducting military hospitals* (London: J. Murray, 1780).

Mottley, John, *The Life of Peter the Great, Emperor of All Russia*, (London, 1755), ii.

Nedham, Marchamont, *Medela medicinae, a plea for the free profession and renovation of the art of physic* (London: R. Lownds, 1665).

Nihell, James, *A Journal of the Most Remarkable Occurrences that happened between His Majesties Army and the Forces under the command of Maréshal de Schomberg* (Dublin: James Malone, 1689).

Norton, Lucy, (ed.), *Memoirs of Duc de Saint-Simon 1691-1709* (Warwick NY: Carelton Books, 2007).

Oldmixon, John, *History of England* (London: Thomas Cox, 1735).

Orrery, Roger Boyle Earl of, *A treatise of the art of war* (London: Henry Herringman, 1677).

Parker, Robert, *Memoirs of the most Remarkable Military Transactions* (London: S. Austen, 1747).

Pelzel, F.M. *Geschichte der Böhmen* (Prague and Vienna: Hagen, 1782).

Peña y Farrel, Feliu de la, *Annales de Cataluña* (Barcelona: Jayme Sur, 1709).

Poissonnier-Desperrières, M., *Traité des Maladies des Gens de Mer* (Paris: Unknown Publisher, 1780).

Porterie, M. De La, *Institutions militaires pour la cavalerie et les dragons* (Paris, Guillyn, 1754 and Paris: Imprimerie Royale, 1780).

Porzio, Luca, *The soldier's Vade Mecum: or, the method of curing the diseases and preserving the health of soldiers* (London: R. Dodsley, 1747).

Pringle, John, *Observations on the diseases of the army, in camp and garrison* (London: Millar and Wilson, 1752).

Pringle, John, *Observations on the Diseases of the Army* (London: A. Millar, 1764)

Puységur, J.F. De Chastenet, Marquis de, *Art de la Guerre par Principes at par Régles* (Paris: C.-A. Jombert, 1748).

Quincy, Charles Sévin, marquis de, *Histoire militaire de Louis le Grand roi de France* (Paris: Jean Baptiste Coignard et. al., 1726).

Quincy, Charles Sévin, marquis de, *L'Art de La Guerre* (The Hague: Scheurleer, 1741).

Ramazzini, Bernardino, *Demorbis artificum diatribe* (Utrecht: William Van De Water, 1703) and (Venice: Joseph Corona: 1743).

Ravaton, Hugues, *Chirurgie D'Armee* (Paris: Didot le Jeune, 1768).

Roscoe, Thomas (ed.), *The Miscellaneous Works of Tobias Smollett ... With Memoir of the Author* (London: Henry Washbourne, 1841).

Rouge Georges-Louis, Le, 'Retraite de Monsieur le Marechal Duc de Belleisle de Prag a Egra' in *Recueil contenant des cartes nouvelles dressees sur des morceaux leves sur les lieux et les memoires les plus nouveaux.* (Paris: Le Rouge, 1742).

Salzmann, G., *Historiam Purpurae Miliaris Albae* (Strasbourg: Unknown Publisher, 1736).

Sandras, Gatien de Courtilz de, *Histoire de la guerre de Hollande* (The Hague: H. van Bulderen, 1689).

Schelhammer, Günther Christoph, *De Genuina Febres Curanda Methodo* (Jena: Johann Bielck, 1693).

Schneider, Daniel and Schweder, Gabriel, *Theatrum Europeum* (Frankfurt-am-Main: Merian, 1738).

Schmidts, M. I., *Geschichte der Deutschen...Kaiser Karl VI. VomJahr 1715 bis 1740* (Vienna and Ulm: August Lebrecht Stettins, 1803).

Scott, Sir Walter (ed.), *A Collection of Scarce and Valuable Tracts...* (London: T. Cadell, W. Davies, 1809-15).

Scrinci, Johann and William Bache, *Diss. De febri maligna castrensi Gallorum* (Prague: Unknown Publisher, 1743).

Simpson, Robert, *The Annals of Derry: Showing the Rise and Progress of the Town* (Derry: Hempton, 1847).

Sorbait, Paul de, *Praxios medicæ, auctæ* (Vienna: Unknown Publisher, 1701).

Storchens, Johann, *Theoretisch und practische Abhandlung von ... Kranckheiten* (Eisenach and Nuremberg: Grießbach, 1735).

Story, George, *A True and Impartial History of the Most Material Occurrences in the Kingdom of Ireland* (London: Richard Chiswell, 1691).

Story, George Warter, *A continuation of the impartial history of the wars of Ireland* (London, Richard Chiswell, 1693).

Tennetar, Michel. Du, *Lettre à M. P***, doct. méd., sur les flux dyssentériques, épidémiques en Lorraine* (Nancy: P. Barbier, 1777).

Turner, Sir James, *Pallas armata, Military essayes of the ancient Grecian, Roman, and modern art of war* (London: Richard Chiswell, 1683).

Ulmann, Isaiah, *Dissertatio medica inauguralis De fibre maligna Hungarica vulgo Castrensi* (Heidelberg: J.C.L. Hornung, 1731).

Valcarenghi, Paolo, *Medicina rationalis ad recentiorum mentem observationibus adaucta* (Cremona: Peter Ricchini, 1737).

Villette, Marquis de … (ed. Honoré Bonhomme), *Madame de Maintenon et sa famille, lettres et documents inédits* (Paris: Didier et Cie., 1863).

Voltaire, *Histoire de la guerre de mil sept cent quarante & un. Parties 1 et 2* (London: Unknown Publisher, 1756).

Walker, Rev. George, *A true account of the siege of Londonderry* (London: Robert Clavel and Ralph Simpson, 1689).

Wille, Johannes Valentinus, *Tractatus Medicus De morbis castrensibus internis* (Copenhagen: John Christopher Rieger, 1674 and The Hague: Matthew Godicchen, 1676).

Wirz, Heinrich, *Einrichtung und Disziplinein es eidg. Regiments zu Fuß und zu Pferd* (Zürich: Heidegger, 1758).

Zwinger, Theodor, *Epitome totius medicinae* (Lyon: Boudet, 1712).

Newspapers and Newsbooks

Ausführliche Beschreibung des Ungarischen Feld-Zugs Anno 1717 (Nuremberg, 1717).

Courier, XC, (9 November 1736).

Daily Journal. August 16, 1734, no. 4237.

Daily Courant, 23 August 1717, 24 December 1717, 6, 7, 9 August and 4 September 1734; no. 5747.

Gazette de France (Lyon, 1710).

General Evening Post (London, December 1734-January 1735).

Gentleman's Magazine, (London, 1736).

Lettres Historique et politique (Amsterdam, July 1734).

Lettres Historiques, July 1717. (Paris, 1717).

London Chronicle for the Year 1762 (London, nd).

London magazine of Gentleman's monthly intelligence, vol. 31 (November 1762).

London Evening Post. 15 – 17 October, 1734. (London, 1734) no. 1078.

Mercure de France, October, 1734; September, October 1736; December 1742; January 1743. (Paris, 1734-43).

Mercure Galant, June 1695; July 1702. (Paris, 1695-1702).

Mercure Historique et Politique, July –August 1695 (The Hague, 1695)

Mercurii Relation, oder wochentliche Ordinari Zeitungen von underschidlichen Orthen (Munich, December 1734-January 1735; 1735 [8/9, No. 1]; Milan, 5 December 1734; Parma, 13 December, 1735 [8/9, No. 1]).

Nouveau Mercure, September, 1717. (Paris, 1717).

Ordinarii Post-Zeitungen. 2 January, 1735. (Bremen, 1735).

Ordinari Post-Zeitungen (Bremen, December 1734; Cremona, 25 October, 23, 29 November, 13, 23 December 1734; Mantua, 16 November 1734; Milan, 20 November; Modena, 24 October 1734; Parma, 8, 13 December 1734; Savoy, 22 November).

Extra Ordinari Zeitungen (Munich, December 1734-January 1735).
Post und Ordinari Mittwochs-Zeitung (Augsburg, December 1734).

Ordinances and Parliamentary Papers

Ordonnance...sur les décomptes (Paris, 26 March 1735).
Ordonnance pour augmenter de 40 hommes les anciennes compagnies des 8 régimens suisses et en lever 8 nouvelles, de 200 hommes chacune...(Paris, 1733).
Parliamentary Papers, 'Report on the Londonderry Borough Improvement Bill' vol. xxxi (London, 1847-48).

Secondary Sources

Aberth, John, *An Environmental History of the Middle Ages: The Crucible of Nature* (London and New York: Routledge, 2013).
Adler, Richard and Mara, Elise, *Typhoid Fever: A History* (Jefferson, NC: McFarland & Co., 2016).
Alexander, John T., *Bubonic Plague in Early Modern Russia: Public Health and Urban Disaster* (Oxford: Oxford University Press, 2003).
Aksan, Virginia, *Ottoman Wars, 1700-1870: An Empire Besieged* (Harlow: Longman, 2014).
Aksulu, NurdanMelek, *Die Hohe Pforte, Türkenkriege, Konflikte und Beziehungen zwischen Abendland* (Norderstedt: Wolf & Sohn, 2009).
Anderson, Martin Smith, *War and Society in Europe of the Old Regime* (London: Fontana Press, 1988).
André, Louis, *Michel Le Tellier et Louvois* (Paris: Armand Colin, 1942).
Applebaum, Anne, *Gulag: A History of the Soviet Camps* (London: Allen Lane, 2003).
Arfwidsson, F., *Försvaretav Östersjö provinserna 1708-1710* (Celle: Gefleborgs Tryckeri Aktiebolag, 1936).
Arni, E. Gruber von, *Hospital Care and the British Standing Army, 1660–1714* (Aldershot: Ashgate, 2006).
Ayats, Alain, 'Les Premieres Années de l'Intendance du Roussillon, *Histoire, économie et société* 15:1 (1996).
Ayliffe, Graham A. J. and English, Mary P., *Hospital Infection: From Miasmas to MRSA* (Cambridge: Cambridge University Press, 2003).
Backer, Augustin et Alois de, Bibliothèque des écrivains de la Compagnie de Jésus (Liege & Paris: C. Sommervogel, 1861).
Baldinger, Ernst Gottfried, *Von den Krankheit eneiner Armee: auseignen Wahrnehmungen* (Langensalza: Johann Christian Martini, 1765).
Ballingall, Sir George, 'Lectures on Military Surgery', *The Medico-Chirurgical Review* (London, 1833).
Bamford, Andrew, *Sickness, Suffering, and the Sword: The British Regiment on Campaign, 1805-1815* (Norman: University of Oklahoma Press, 2013).

Barre, Jean de la, *Continuation de l'histoire universelle* (Amsterdam: Etienne Roger, 1738).

Barbier, Edmond-Jean-François, *Chronique de la régence et du règne de Louis XV (1718-1763), ou Journal de Barbier.* (Paris: Charpentier, 1857-1866).

Bartlett, Thomas, and Jeffery, Keith, (eds.), *A Military History of Ireland* (Cambridge: Cambridge University Press, 1997).

Bäumler, Georg, 'Medizinalstatistische Untersuchungen über Weiden/Opf: Von 1551 bis 1800', *Archiv fur Hygiene und Bakteriologie.* no.120 (1938).

Becker, Ann M, 'Smallpox in Washington's Army: Strategic Implications of the Disease during the American Revolutionary War', *The Journal of Military History*, 68:2 (Apr., 2004).

Bekh, W. J., *Alexander von Maffei. Der bayerische Prinz Eugen* (Pfaffenhofen: Ludwig, 1982).

Belhomme, Victor, *Histoire de l'infanterie en France* (Paris: Lavauzelle, 1893-1902).

Biggs, William. *The Military History Of Europe, From The Commencement Of The War With Spain In 1739, To The Treaty Of Aix-La-Chapelle In 1748* (London: R. Baldwin, 1755).

Black, Jeremy, *European Warfare in a Global Context, 1660–1815* (New York: Taylor & Francis, 2007).

Bodart, Gaston, *Losses of life in modern wars, Austria-Hungary and France* (Oxford: Clarendon Press, 1916)

Bonser W. and MacArthur, W., 'Epidemics during the Anglo-Saxon period, with appendix: Famine fevers in England and Ireland' in *Journal of the British Archaeological Association*, 3:9 (1944).

Borges, Augusto, *Reais Hospitais Militares em Portugal 1640-1834* (Coimbra: Universidade de Coimbra, 2009).

Borreguero Beltrán, Cristina, 'The Spanish Army in Italy, 1734', *War in History* (October 1998), 5.

Bourgoing, Jean-François de (transl. Gerhard Anton von Halem), *Vie du comte de Munnich...* (Paris: Nicolle, 1807).

Broglie, Duc de, (ed.), *Frédéric II et Louis XV: d'après des documents nouveaux; 1742-1744* (Paris: Calmann-Lévy, 1887).

Browning, Reed, *The War of the Austrian Succession* (New York: Macmillan, 1995).

Bruijn, J. R., 'Dutch Men of War-Those on Board c. 1700-1750' in *Acta Historiae Neerlandicae: Studies on the History of The Netherlands* VII ('Ihe Hague: Martinus Nijhoff, 1974).

Bufalini, Robert, 'The Czarina's Russia through Mediterranean Eyes: Francesco Algarotti's Journey to Saint Petersburg' in *Modern Language Notes*, 121:1, (2006).

Bulmerincq, A. V. (ed.), *Aktenstücke und Urkundenzur Geschichte der Stadt Riga 1710-1740* (Riga: J. Deubner, 1902-06).

Burke, Sir Bernard, *A Genealogical and Heraldic History of the Extinct and Dormant Baronetcies of England* (London: Scott, Webster, and Geary, 1838).

Busvine, James Ronald, *Insects, Hygiene and History* (London: Athlone Press, 2015).

Butler, Rohan, *Choiseul. Vol. 1: Father and Son 1719-1754* (Oxford: Oxford University Press, 1981).

Campbell, Peter, *Power and Politics in Old Regime France, 1720-1745* (London: Routledge, 1996).

Candler, Stephen Curtis, *A Theory of the Causation and Suggestions for the Prevention of Dysentery* (London: Henry Renshaw, 1873).

Cannon, Richard, *Historical record of the British Army: The Third regiment of Foot* (London: Adjutant General's Office, 1839).

Cannon, Richard, *Historical record of the Sixty-seventh, or the South Hampshire Regiment* (London: Parker, Furnivall and Parker, 1849).

Cárat, Jean Philippe, 'Les Fonctions de Général Maréchal Des Logis à L'Epoque de Louis XIV', *Revue Historique Des Armées*, 257 (April, 2009).

Carlton, Charles, *Going to the Wars: The Experience of the British Civil Wars 1638-1651* (London: Routledge, 2002).

Carlyle, Thomas, *History of Friedrich II of Prussia: Called Frederick the Great* (London: Chapman and Hall, 1871).

Carmichael, Ann G., '1 Universal and Particular: The Language of Plague, 1348–1500' in *Medical History.* Supplement 27 (2008).

Cassels, Lavender, *The Struggle for the Ottoman Empire 1717-1740* (London: John Murray, 1966).

Castellví, Francesc, *Narraciones Históricas* (Madrid: Erásmo Percopo, 1999).

Caulaincourt, Armand-Augustin-Louis (ed. Jean Hanoteau), *With Napoleon in Russia* (New York: Mineola, 2005).

Cérino, Christophe, 'L'hôpital militaire de Belle-île-en-Mer au siècle de Louis XV: les conditions sanitaires d'une garnisonen milieu insulaire', in *Annales de Bretagne et des pays de l'Ouest*, 104:4 (1997).

Chagniot, Jean, *Guerre et société à l'époque modern* (Paris: Presses Universitaires de France, 2001)

Chandler, D., *The Art of Warfare in the Age of Marlborough* (Tunbridge Wells: Spellmount Books, 1990).

Charters, Erica, 'Colonial Disease, Translation, and Enlightenment: Franco-British Medicine and the Seven Years', in De Bruyn, Frans, and Regan, Shaun, (eds.) *The Culture of the Seven Years' War: Empire, Identity, and the Arts in the Eighteenth-Century Atlantic World* (Toronto: University of Toronto Press, 2014).

Charters, Erica, *Disease, War and the Imperial State: The Welfare of the British Armed Forces during the Seven Years' War* (Chicago, IL: University of Chicago Press, 2014).

Childs, John, *Armies and Warfare in Europe, 1648-1789* (New York: Holmes and Meier 1982).

Childs John, *The Army of Charles II* (London: Routledge and Kegan Paul, 1976).

Childs, John, *The Williamite Wars in Ireland 1688-91* (London: Hambledon Continuum, 2007).

Cirillo, Vincent J., '"Winged Sponges": Houseflies as Carriers of Typhoid Fever in 19th- and Early 20th-Century Military Camps' in *Perspectives in Biology and Medicine no.* 49 (1).

Clausewitz, Carl von (ed. Anatol Rapaport), *On War* (London: Penguin, 1982).

Cockayne, Emily, *Hubbub, Filth, Noise, & Stench in England 1600-1770* (New Haven, Conn: Yale University Press, 2007).

Colletta, Pietro (trans. S. Horner), *History of the kingdom of Naples, 1734-1825* (Edinburgh & London: Constable & Hamilton, 1858).

Comité d'histoire du service de santé, *Histoire de la médecine aux armées*, (Paris-Limoges: Charles Lavauzelle, 1982).

Cornet, Henry (ed.), *Siége de Prague: Journal Critique d'un Lieutenant-Ingénieur dans l'armée Autrichienne devant Prague* (Vienna: Tendler, 1867).

Corvisier, André, *L'armée française de la fin du XVIIe siècle au ministère de Choiseul. Le soldat* (Paris: Presses Universitaires de France, 1964).

Corvisier, André, 'La Mort du Soldat' in *Revue historique* (1975) no.254.

Corvisier, André, *Les Contrôles de Troupes de l'Ancien Régime* (Paris: Service historique de la défense à Vincennes, 1968).

Coxe, William, *History of the House of Austria* (London: Unknown Publisher, 1807).

Cunningham, Andrew and Grell, Ole Peter, *The Four Horsemen of the Apocalypse: Religion, War, Famine and Death in Reformation Europe* (Cambridge: Cambridge University Press, 2001).

Datour, Olivier and Buzhilova, Alexandra, 'Palaeological Study of Napoleonic Mass Graves Discovered in Russia' in Christopher Knüsel and Martin Smith (eds.), *The Routledge Handbook of the Bioarchaeology of Human Conflict* (London: Routledge, 2013).

Davenport, R., Schwartz, L. and Boulton, J., 'The decline of adult smallpox in eighteenth-century London', *Econ. Hist. Rev.* Nov, 2011; 64:4.

Davies, Brian, *Empire and Military Revolution in Eastern Europe Russia's Turkish Wars in the Eighteenth Century* (London: Continuum, 2011).

Davies, Brian, *Warfare, State and Society on the Black Sea Steppe, 1500–1700* (Oxford: Routledge, 2007).

Debrett, John, *Debrett's Peerage of England, Scotland, and Ireland* (London: G. Woodfall, 1831).

De Paoli, Oscar, *Les regiments d'autrefois: Le regiment de la Couronne...* (Paris: Conseil Héraldique de France, 1891).

Doherty, Richard, *The Siege of Derry 1689: The Military History* (Stroud: Spellmount Publishers, 2010).

Duffy, Christopher, *Fire and Stone: The Science of Fortress Warfare, 1660-1860* (New York: Hippocrene, 1975).

Du Plessis Richelieu, Louis-François-Armand de Vignerot, *Mémoires du Maréchal duc de Richelieu* (Paris: Librarie de Fermi Didot, 1858)

Elster, Otto, *Geschichte der stehenden Truppenim Herzogtum Braunschweig-Wolfenbüttel von 1600-1714* (Leipzig: Heinsius, 1899-1901).

Englund, Peter, *The Battle that Shook Europe: Poltava and the Birth of the Russian Empire* (London & New York: I.B. Tauris, 2003).

Finger, Simon, *The Contagious City: the politics of public health in early Philadelphia* (Ithaca: Cornell University Press, 2012).

Finlay, George, *A History of Greece* (Oxford: Clarendon Press, 1877).

Fonssagrives, B., 'Recherches historiques sur l'epidémie qui en 1758 ravagea l'escadre de l'amiral Dubois de la Motte et la ville de Brest', *Annales d'hygiene publique*, 2:12 (1859).

Francis, A. D., 'The Campaign in Portugal, 1762', *Journal of the Society for Army Historical Research*, 54, (1981).

Frandsen, Karl-Erik, *The Last Plague in the Baltic Region, 1709-1713* (Copenhagen: Museum Tusculanum Press, 2010).

Fraser, C. (ed.), *History of the War in Bosnia During the Years 1737-1739* (London: Oriental Translation Fund, 1830).

French, Roger, *Medicine before Science: The Business of Medicine from the Middle Ages to the Enlightenment* (Cambridge: Cambridge University Press, 2003).

Frost, Robert, *The Northern Wars: War, State and Society in Northeastern Europe, 1558-1721* (Harlow: Longman, 2000).

Fuster, Joseph Jean Nicolas, *Des changements dans le climat de la France: histoire de sesrévolutions* (Paris: Capelle, 1845).

Garrett, Laurie, *The Coming Plague: Newly Emerging Diseases in a World Out of Balance* (New York: Penguin, 1995).

Gavin, J. and O'Sullivan, H., *Dundalk: A Military History* (Dundalk: Dundalgan Press, 1987).

Gébelin, Jacques, *Histoire des milices provinciales (1688–1791)* (Paris: Hachette, 1882).

Gebler, Carlo, *The Siege of Derry* (London: Little Brown, 2005).

Gillespie, Joshua, *A Narrative of the Most Remarkable Events in the Life of William the Third* (Derry: M. Hempton, 1823).

Glozier, Matthew, *Marshal Schomberg, 1615-1690: 'The Ablest Soldier of His Age'* (Brighton: Sussex Academic Press, 2008).

Glynn, I. and J, *The Life and Death of Smallpox* (London: Profile Books, 2004).

Goelicke, Andreas, *Disputatio Medica Inauguralis De Febre Catarrhali Maligna Petechizante* (Frankfurt: Philip Schwartz, 1741).

Goger, J. M., and Marty, N. (eds), *Cadre de vie, équipement, santé dans les societies mediterranées* (Perpignan: Presses Universitaires de Perpignan, 2006).

Gomes, Eduardo et al. 'Mapping Risk of Malaria Transmission in Mainland Portugal Using a Mathematical Modelling Approach', *PLoS One*. 2016; 11:11, (2016)

Haeser, Heinrich, *Historisch-pathologische untersuchungen als beiträge zur Geschichte der Volkskrankheiten* (Dresden and Leipzig: Gerhard Fleischer, 1839).

Hamilton, David, *A Treatise of a Miliary Fever; with a collection of histories* (London: A. Bettesworth and C. Hitch, 1737).

Hanlon, Gregory, *The Hero of Italy: Odoardo Farnese, duke of Parma, his soldiers and his subjects in the Thirty Years War* (Oxford: Oxford University Press, 2014).

Hanlon, Gregory, *Italy 1636 Cemetery of Armies* (Oxford: Oxford University Press, 2016).

Harrison, Mark, 'The Armies of British India, 1750-1830: The Treatment of Fevers and the Emergence of Tropical Therapeutics', in Hudson, Geoffrey., (ed.), *British Military and Naval Medicine, 1600-1830* (Amsterdam and New York: Rodopi, 2015).

Harrison, Mark, 'Disease and Medicine in the Armies of British India, 1750-1830' in G. Hudson (ed.), *British Military and Naval Medicine, 1600-1830* (Amsterdam and New York: Rodopi, 2007).

Hammer, J. (transl. J. Hellert), *Histoire de l'Empire ottoman, depuis son origine jusqu'à nos jours* (Paris: Bellizard, 1835-43).

Hays, J. N., *The Burdens of Disease: Epidemics and Human Response in Western History* (New Brunswick: Rutgers University Press, 2009).

Hayter, Tony (ed.), *An Eighteenth-Century Secretary at War: The Papers of William Viscount Barrington* (London: Army Records Society, 1988).

Hempton, J. (ed.), *The Siege and History of Londonderry* (Derry: Hempton, 1861).

Henderson, Nicholas, *Prince Eugen of Savoy* (London: Weidenfeld & Nicolson, 1966).

Henry, D.M.J., *Histoire de Roussillon comprenant l'histoire du Royaume de Majorque* (Paris: Imp. Royale, 1835).

Herrmann, Ernst, *Beiträgezur Geschichte des Russischen Reiches* (Leipzig: J.C. Hinrichsen, 1843).

Hertz, A. Z., 'The Ottoman Conquest of Ada Kale 1738', *AO*, 6 (1980).

Hochedlinger, Michael, *Austria's Wars of Emergence: War, State and Society in the Habsburg Monarchy* (New York and London: Longman, 2003).

Howell, H.A.L. 'The Story of the Army Surgeon and the Care of the Sick ... from 1715 to 1748', *Journal of the Army Medical Corps* (1914), xxii.

Howard, Martin R., *Napoleon's Doctors: The Medical Services of the Grande Armée* (Staplehurst: Spellmount, 2006).

Hudson, Geoffrey L. (ed.), *British Military and Naval Medicine 1600-1830* (Amsterdam: Rodopi, 2007).

Hume, John, *Derry Beyond the Walls: Social and Economic Aspects of the Growth of Derry* (Belfast: Ulster Historical Foundation, 2002).

Humphreys, Margaret, 'A Stranger to Our Camps. Typhus in American History', *Bulletin of the History of Medicine*, 80:2 (Summer, 2006).

Humphreys, Margaret, *Marrow of Tragedy: The Health Crisis of the American Civil War* (Baltimore: The Johns Hopkins University Press, 2013).

Ingrao, Charles W., Nikola Samardžić and Jovan Pesaljeds, *The Peace of Passarowitz, 1718* (Bloomington IN: Purdue University Press, 2011).

Johnson, James, *Medico-Chirurgical Review* (London: S. Highley, 1833).

Jordan, Claude (ed.), *Journal Historique* (Paris, 1734) vol. xxxvi.

Kazner, J.F.A. *Leben Friederichs von Schomberg, oder Schoenburg* (Mannheim: Schwan & Götz, 1789).

Kelly, Catherine, *War and the Militarization of British Army Medicine, 1793–1830: Studies for the Society for the Social History of Medicine* (Abingdon-on-Thames: Routledge, 2011).

Kennett, Lee, *The French Armies in the Seven Years' War* (Durham NC: Duke University Press, 1967).

Kettering, Sharon, *Patrons, Brokers, and Clients in Seventeenth-Century France* (New York: Oxford University Press, 1986).

Khodarkovsky, Michael, *Russia's Steppe Frontier: The Making of a Colonial Empire, 1500–1800* (Bloomington, IN: Indiana University Press, 2002).

Knight, Joe, "Napoleon Wasn't Defeated By The Russians" in *Slate*. December 11, 2012. http://www.slate.com/articles/health_and_science/pandemics/2012/12/napoleon_march_to_russia_in_1812_typhus_spread_by_lice_was_more_powerful.html. Accessed 21 Aug 2018.

Kohn, George C, *Encyclopedia of Plague and Pestilence: From Ancient Times to the Present* (New York: Infobase Publishing, 2008).

Kopperman, Paul E., 'Medical Services in the British Army, 1742–1783,' *Journal of the History of Medicine and Allied Sciences*, 24:4 (1979).

Kopperman, Paul (ed.), *'Regimental Practice' by John Buchanan MD* (Farnham: Ashgate, 2012).

Kroll, Stefan, "Die 'Pest' im Ostseeraum zu Beginn des 18 Jahrhunderts. Stand und Perspektiven der Forschung" in Stefan Kroll and Kersten Krüger (eds.) *Städtesystem und Urbanisierung im Ostseeraum in der frühen Neuzeit* (Münster: LIT Verlag, 2006).

Kroll, Stefan, *Soldaten im 18. Jahrhundertz wischen Friedensalltag und Kriegserfahrung Lebenswelten und Kultur in der kursächsischen Armee* (Paderborn: Ferdinand Schöningh. 2006).

Laidre, Margus,'Förluster och sjukvårdisvensk aarmén i Estland och Livland under senarehälftenav 1600-talet' in *Karolinska förbundetsårsbokv* (Stockholm: Karolinska förbundet, 1989).

Laidre, Margus, *The Great Northern War and Estonia: the trials of Dorpat, 1700-1708* (Tallinn: Argo, 2010).

Laiffe, F.X., 'Die Seuchen während der Belagerung von Wien und während des letzten Türkenkrieges 1683–1699' in *Archivfür Hygiene und Bakteriologie* 119: 1937.

Landersdorfer, Melchior, 'Das Schicksal der bayerischen Soldatenim Türkenkrieg' (Dissertation: Technische Universität München, 1984).

Lane, Joan, *A Social History of Medicine: Health, Healing and Disease* in England, 1750–1950 (London: Routledge, 2001).

Le Roy Ladurie, Emmanuel *Histoire du Climat Depuis l'An Mil* (Paris: Flammarion, 1983).

Lersch, B. M., *Geschichte der Volksseuchen. nach und mit den Berichten der Zeitgenossen, mit Berücksichtigung der Thierseuchen* (Berlin: Karger, 1896).

Ligne, Charles Joseph, Prince de, *The Life Of Prince Eugene, Of Savoy* (London: J. Davis, 1812).

Limelette, Renaud. 'La Gouvernance du Service de Santé des hôpitaux: La gouvernance du service de santé des hôpitaux militaires de la réforme de 1747 à 1789' (2017). https://hal.archives-ouvertes.fr.

Lindemann, Mary, *Medicine and Society in Early Modern Europe* (Cambridge: Cambridge University Press, 1999)

López, Antonio Espino, 'Los Tercios Catalanes durante el reinado de Carlos II, 1665-1697', *Brocar. Cuadernos de Investigación Histórica, 22,* (1998).

López, Antonio Espino, *Las Guerras de Cataluña* (Madrid: EDAF, 2014).

Lozembrune, François C. Le Roy de, *Histoire de la guerre de Hongrie pendant les campagnes de 1716, 1717 et 1718* (Vienna: Graeffer, 1788).

Lucenet, Monique,'Les épidémies dans l'infanterie au cours de la première moitié du XVIIIe siècle' in *Forces armées et sociétés, Actes du Colloque du 1er au 5 avril 1985* (Paris: Centre d'histoire militaire et d'études de défense nationale, 1987).

Lucenet, Monique, *Médecine, chirurgie et armée en France au siècle des Lumières* (Paris: Editions I&D, 2006).

Luh, Jürgen, *Kriegskunst in Europa (1650 – 1800)* (Köln: Böhlau Verlag, 2004).

Lund, Erik, *War for the Every Day: Generals, Knowledge, and Warfare in Early Modern Europe, 1680-1740* (Westport CT, Praeger, 1999).

Lynn, John A., 'The Evolution of Army Style in the Modern West, 800-2000' in *The International History Review*, 18:3 (Aug., 1996).

Lynn, John A., *The Wars of Louis XIV, 1667–1714* (London: Longman, 1999).

Lynn, John A., *Women, Armies, and Warfare in Early Modern Europe* (Cambridge: Cambridge University Press, 2008).

McCallum, Jack Edward, *Military Medicine: From Ancient Times to the 21st Century* (Santa Barbara CA: ABC-CLIO, 2008).

Macfarlane, Alan, *The Savage Wars of Peace: England, Japan and the Malthusian Trap* (Basingstoke: Palgrave Macmillan, 2003).

McGrigor, Sir James, *Sketch of the Medical History of the British Armies in the Peninsula of Spain and Portugal* (London: Unknown Publisher, 1815).

McNeill, J. R., *Mosquito Empires: Ecology and War in the Greater Caribbean, 1620-1914* (Cambridge: Cambridge University Press, 2010).

McNeill, William H., *Plagues and Peoples* (London: Penguin, 1979).

Mäkinen, Martti, 'Efficacy phrases in Early Modern English medical recipes'; in Taavitsainen, Irma and Pahta, Päivi (eds.) *Medical Writing in Early Modern English* (Cambridge University Press, 2013).

Manchip White, Jon, *Marshal of France: The Life and times of Maurice, Comte de Saxe* (London: Hamish Hamilton, 1962).

Mann, Charles C., *1493: Uncovering the New World Columbus Created* (New York: Random House, 2012).

Markov, Konstantin, 'L'Etude du Paludisme en Bulgarie' (1923) in 'Hostilities Against Malaria', http://berberian11.tripod.com/markov_malaria.htm.

Marston, Daniel, *The Seven Years' War* (Oxford: Osprey, 2013).

Martines, Lauro, *Furies: War in Europe, 1450-1700* (New York: Bloomsbury Press, 2013).

Matuschka, Ludwig (ed.), *Feldzüge Des Prinzen Eugen von Savoyen* (Vienna: Gerold, 1891).

May, Wallas, *Luc de Clapiers, marquis de Vauvenargues* (Cambridge: Cambridge University Press, 1928).

Mège, Alexandre Du, (ed.), De Vic, Claude and Vaisette, Joseph, *Histoire générale de Languedoc...* (Toulouse: J.B.Paya, 1846).

Menning, Bruce W., 'The Imperial Russian Army, 1725-96' in Kagan, F., and Higham, R., (eds.,) *The Military History of Tsarist Russia* (Basingstoke: Palgrave, 2008).

Messenger, Charles, *For Love of Regiment: A History of British Infantry 1660-1914* (Barnsley: Leo Cooper, 1994).

Mettig, C., *Geschichte der Stadt Riga* (Riga: Jonk & Poliewsky, 1897).

Mitchelburne, John and Graham, John (eds.), *Ireland Preserved; or the Siege of Londonderry* (Dublin: Hardy and Walker, 1841).

Kausler, Franz Georg Friedrich von, *et al., Das Leben des Prinzen Eugen von Savoyen, hauptsächlich ausdem Militärischen* (Freiburg im Breisgau: Herder, 1838).

Molo, Ph. J. von, *Über Epidemienim Allgemeinen und Wechselfiebe repidemien insbesondere* (Regensburg: J. Manx, 1841).

Mortimer, Geoff, *Wallenstein: The Enigma of the Thirty Years War* (New York: Palgrave Macmillan, 2010).

Mowery Andrews, Richard, *Law, Magistracy, and Crime in Old Regime Paris, 1735-1789* (Cambridge: Cambridge University Press, 1994)

Nouzille, Jean, *Le Prince Eugene de Savoie et le Sud-Est Europeen 1683-1736* (Paris: Honoré Champion, 2012).

Odenthal, J., *Oesterreichs Turkenkrieg 1716-1718* (Düsseldorf: G.H. Nolte, 1938).

Olier, F., 'Les Hopitaux Sedentaires francais aux Arméesd'Allegmagne durant la guerre de Sept Ans (1757-1763)', 'Service De Santé' at http://vial.jean.free.fr/new_npi/revues_npi/22_2001/npi_2201/22_fra_sante4.htm (accessed 04/04/2019).

Outram, Quentin, 'The socio-economic relations of warfare and the military mortality crises of the Thirty Years' War' in *Medical History*, 45: 2, (2001).

Page, Logan Walleretal, *How to prevent typhoid fever* (Washington: Office of the Surgeon General, 1911).

Pajol, Charles Pierre Victor comte de, *Les guerres sous Louis XV* (Paris: Firmin-Didot, 1881).

Parker, Geoffrey. *Global Crisis: War, Climate Change and Catastrophe in the Seventeenth Century* (New Haven, Conn: Yale University Press, 2013).

Pickstone, J.V., 'Dearth, dirt and fever epidemics: rewriting the history of British public health, 1780-1850' in Ranger T. and Slack, P. (eds.), *Epidemics and Ideas* (Cambridge: Cambridge University Press, 1992).

Porter, Roy, *Blood and Guts: A Short History of Medicine* (London: Penguin Books, 2003).

Porter, Roy, *Flesh in the Age of Reason* (London: Allen Lane, 2001).

Post, J.D., *Food Shortage, Climatic Variability, and Epidemic Disease in Preindustrial Europe* (Ithaca: Cornell University Press, 1985).

Raoult, D., et.al., 'Evidence for louse-transmitted diseases in soldiers of Napoleon's Grand Army in Vilnius', *Journal of Infectious Diseases*, 193:1 (Oxford University Press, 2006).

Rembe, Heinrich, *Lambsheim. Die Familien von 1547 bis 1800* (Kaiserlutern: Verlag Franz Arbogast, 1971).

Rey, H., 'Les Medecins navigateurs' in *Archives de medicine navale* (Paris: J.B. Ballière, 1871).

Rocco, Fiammetta, *The Miraculous Fever-Tree* (New York: HarperCollins, 2016)

Rosenberg, Charles E., *Explaining Epidemics* (Cambridge: Cambridge University Press, 1992).

Rousset, Camille *Histoire de Louvois* (Paris: Didier, 1864).

Rousset, Camille, *Le comte de Gisors, 1732-1758: étude historique* (Paris: Unknown Publisher, 1868).

Rowlands, Guy, *The Dynastic State and the Army Under Louis XIV: Royal Service and Private Interest 1661–1701* (Cambridge: Cambridge University Press, 2002).

Sabbatani, Sergio, 'Il tifo petecchiale. Storie di uomini, eserciti e pidocchi', *Le infezioni in medicina*, 14:3 (2006).

Schuster, Joseph, *Studien zur Geschichte des Militärsanitätswesens im 17. und 18. Jahrhundert, mit besonderer Berücksichtigung der kurbaye* (Munich: J. Lindauersche Buchhandlung, 1908).

Schwenke, Alexander, *Geschichte der Hannoverschentruppen in Griechenland 1685–89* (Hanover: Hahnsch Buchhandlung, 1854).

Scott, B. G., Brown, R. R., Leacock, A. G., and Salter, C. J., *The Great Guns Like Thunder: The Cannon From The City Of Derry* (Derry: Guildhall Press, 2008).

Scott, B. G., 'Plans and economies: defending the Plantation city of Londonderry', *The Journal of Irish Archaeology* Volume XX, (2011).

Short, Rendle, J., 'William Cadogan, Eighteenth Century Physician', *Medical History*, 4:4 (1960).

Short, Thomas, *A General Chronological History of the Air, Weather, Seasons...* (London: T. Longman, 1749).

Signoli, M., *et al.*, 'Discovery of a mass grave of Napoleonic period in Lithuania (1812, Vilnius)'. *Comptes Rendus Palevol*, 3:3 (May 2004).

Smallman-Raynor, M., and Cliff, A.D., *War Epidemics: An Historical Geography of Infectious Diseases in Military Conflict and Civil Strife, 1850–2000* (Oxford: Oxford University Press, 2004).

Soubbotitch, V., 'A Pandemic of Typhus in Serbia in 1914 and 1915' in *Proceedings of the Royal Society of Medicine.* 1918: 11.

Speelman, Patrick J, 'Strategic Illusions and the Iberian War of 1762' in ibid and Danley, Mark H. (eds.,) *The Seven Years' War: Global Views* (Leiden: Brill Academic Publishers, 2012).

Stevens, Carol B., *Russia's wars of emergence, 1460-1730* (Harlow: Pearson Longman, 2007).

Stevens, Carol B, 'Food and Supply: Logistics and the Early Modern Russian Army' in Davies, Brian L., (ed.), *Warfare in Eastern Europe, 1500-1800* (Leiden: Brill Academic Publishers, 2012).

Stone, David R, *A Military History of Russia: From Ivan the Terrible to the War in Chechnya* (Westport, CT: Praeger, 2006).

Storrs, Christopher, 'Health, Sickness and Medical Services in Spain's Armed Forces c.1665–1700', *Medical History,* 50:3 (July 2006).

Stoye, John, *Marsigli's Europe 1680-1730* (New Haven, CT: Yale University Press, 1994).

Stoye, John, *The Siege of Vienna: The Last Great Trial Between Cross & Crescent* (Reading: Birlinn, 2000).

Stoyanov, A., 'Russia marches South: army reform and battlefield performance in Russia's Southern campaigns, 1695-1739' (Ph.D Leiden University, 2017), http://hdl.handle.net/1887/48241 (accessed 20 February 2018).

Sunderland, Willard, *Taming the Wild Field: Colonization and Empire on the Russian Steppe* (Ithaca, N.Y.: Cornell University Press, 2004).

Sutton, John, The *King's Honor* and the *King's Cardinal: The War of the Polish Succession* (Lexington: The University Press of Kentucky, 1980).

Sydenham, Thomas, *The Whole Works* (London: W. Feales, 1734).

Tallett, Frank, *War and Society in Early Modern Europe* (London: Routledge, 1992).

Toole, M., 'Complex Emergencies: Refugee and other Populations' in Eric K. Noji (ed.) *The Public Health Consequences of Disasters* (Oxford: Oxford University Press, 1997).

Tröhler, Ulrich, M.D, 'Quantification in British Medicine and Surgery 1750-1830, with special Reference to its Introduction into Therapeutics'. (Bern, 1978), http://jameslindlibrary.org.

Trompeo, Pietro Paolo (ed.), *Franceso Algarotti, Viaggi di Russia* (Turin: G. Einaudi, 1961).

Urlanis, Boris Z., *Bilanz der Kriege: Die Menschen verluste Europas vom 17. Jahrhundert bis zur Gegenwart* (Berlin: Dt. Verlag der Wiss, 1965).

Vigarello, Georges. *Histoire des pratiques de santé* (Paris: Seuil, 1993).

Vogüé, Melchior, *Une famille vivaroise, histoires d'autrefois racontées à ses enfants, par le Mis de Vogüé,...* (Paris: H. Champion, 1912).

Webb, Penny and Bain, Chris, *Essential Epidemiology: An Introduction for Students and Health Professionals* (Cambridge: Cambridge University Press, 2016).

Westergaard, Harald, and Prinzing, Friedrich, *Epidemics Resulting from Wars* (Oxford: Clarendon Press, 1916).

Wheatcroft, Andrew, *The Enemy at the Gate* (New York: Perseus, 2008).

White, Lorraine, 'Strategic Geography and the Spanish Habsburg Monarchy's Failure to Recover Portugal, 1640-1668', *The Journal of Military History*, 71:2, (2007)

Winkle, Stefan, *Geisseln der Menschheit: Kulturgeschichte der Seuchen* (Munich: Artemis & Winkler, 2005).

Witherow, Thomas, *Derry and Enniskillen in the Year 1689* (Belfast: William Mullen, 1873).

Woods, Robert, *The Demography of Victorian England and Wales* (Cambridge: Cambridge University Press, 2007).

Young, Robert M. (ed.), *The Town Book of the Corporation of Belfast, 1613-1816* (Belfast: Marcus Ward, 1892).

Zamoyski, Adam, *1812: Napoleon's Fatal March on Moscow* (London: Harper Perennial, 2005).

Zimmerman, John George (Trans. C.R. Hopson), *A Treatise on the Dysentery...* (London: John and Francis Rivington, 1771).

Zinsser, Hans, *Rats, Lice and History* (New York: Leventhal & Black Dog Publishers, 1935).

Index

From Reason to Revolution series – Warfare 1721-1815

http://www.helion.co.uk/published-by-helion/reason-to-revolution-1721-1815.html

The 'From Reason to Revolution' series covers the period of military history 1721–1815, an era in which fortress-based strategy and linear battles gave way to the nation-in-arms and the beginnings of total war.

This era saw the evolution and growth of light troops of all arms, and of increasingly flexible command systems to cope with the growing armies fielded by nations able to mobilise far greater proportions of their manpower than ever before. Many of these developments were fired by the great political upheavals of the era, with revolutions in America and France bringing about social change which in turn fed back into the military sphere as whole nations readied themselves for war. Only in the closing years of the period, as the reactionary powers began to regain the upper hand, did a military synthesis of the best of the old and the new become possible.

The series will examine the military and naval history of the period in a greater degree of detail than has hitherto been attempted, and has a very wide brief, with the intention of covering all aspects from the battles, campaigns, logistics, and tactics, to the personalities, armies, uniforms, and equipment.

Submissions

The publishers would be pleased to receive submissions for this series. Please contact series editor Andrew Bamford via email (andrewbamford18@gmail.com), or in writing to Helion & Company Limited, Unit 8 Amherst Business Centre, Budbrooke Road, Warwick, CV34 5WE

Titles

No 1 *Lobositz to Leuthen. Horace St Paul and the Campaigns of the Austrian Army in the Seven Years War 1756-57* Translated with additional materials by Neil Cogswell (ISBN 978-1-911096-67-2)

No 2 *Glories to Useless Heroism. The Seven Years War in North America from the French journals of Comte Maurés de Malartic, 1755-1760* William Raffle (ISBN 978-1-1911512-19-6) (paperback)

No 3 *Reminiscences 1808-1815 Under Wellington. The Peninsular and Waterloo Memoirs of William Hay* William Hay, with notes and commentary by Andrew Bamford (ISBN 978-1-1911512-32-5)

No 4 *Far Distant Ships. The Royal Navy and the Blockade of Brest 1793-1815* Quintin Barry (ISBN 978-1-1911512-14-1)

No 5 *Godoy's Army. Spanish Regiments and Uniforms from the Estado Militar of 1800* Charles Esdaile and Alan Perry (ISBN 978-1-911512-65-3) (paperback)

No 6 *On Gladsmuir Shall the Battle Be! The Battle of Prestonpans 1745* Arran Johnston (ISBN 978-1-911512-83-7)

No 7 *The French Army of the Orient 1798-1801. Napoleon's Beloved 'Egyptians'* Yves Martin (ISBN 978-1-911512-71-4)*

No 8 *The Autobiography, or Narrative of a Soldier. The Peninsular War Memoirs of William Brown of the 45th Foot* William Brown, with notes and commentary by Steve Brown (ISBN 978-1-911512-94-3) (paperback)

No 9 *Recollections from the Ranks. Three Russian Soldiers' Autobiographies from the Napoleonic Wars* Translated and annotated by Darrin Boland (ISBN 978-1-912174-18-8) (paperback)

No 10 *By Fire and Bayonet. Grey's West Indies Campaign of 1794* Steve Brown (ISBN 978-1-911512-60-8)

* indicates 'Falconet' format paperbacks, page size 248mm x 180 mm, with high visual content including colour plates; other titles are hardback monographs unless otherwise noted.